1994

An Ethical Education

State, Law and Society

Series Editor: **A. Altman**

The series presents major authors in the continental, and particularly the German, tradition of legal and political theory. It is concerned with recent comparative work in the field of legal and political history, but it also makes available in translation some of the classics of this tradition.

Ernst-Wolfgang Bockenforde, *State, Society and Liberty: Studies in Political Theory and Constitutional Law*

Franz Neumann, *The Rule Law: Political Theory and the Legal System in Modern Society*

Anthony Woodiwiss, *Rights v. Conspiracy: A Sociological Essay on the History of Labour Law in the United States*

Petra T. Shattuck and Jill Norgren, *Partial Justice: Federal Indian Law in a Liberal Constitutional System*

An Ethical Education

Community and Morality in the Multicultural
University

Edited by
M. N. S. Sellers

BERG
Oxford/Providence, USA

First published in 1994 by

Berg Publishers

Editorial offices:
221 Waterman Road, Providence, RI 02906, USA
150 Cowley Road, Oxford, OX4 1JJ, UK

Library of Congress Cataloging-in-Publication Data
A catalogue record for this book is available from the Library of Congress.

British Library Cataloging in Publication Data
A catalogue record for this book is available from the British Library.

ISBN: 1 85973 056 6 (Cloth)
      1 85973 061 2 (Paper)

Printed in the United Kingdom by WBC Book Manufacturers,
Bridgend, Mid Glamorgan.

To Lucy Bell Newlin Sellers
my first and best teacher

Contents

Preface

The Hoffberger Center for Professional Ethics was established in 1987 with a grant from the Hoffberger Foundation and is affiliated with the University of Baltimore and the University of Maryland System. The Center promotes reflection, discussion, and academic research about the values and ethical responsibilities facing practitioners in the fields of academia, law, business, and public administration. The Center's work includes research, publication, and the provision of a public forum for the discussion of the ethics of particular professions and public issues.

This volume grew out of a Public Forum on Ethics in the University held in Baltimore during March of 1992. The Forum was supported by a grant from the Maryland Humanities Council, without which this project would not have been possible, and for which the editor is very grateful. Lively and protracted discussions in Baltimore were followed by further thought and correspondence that ultimately resulted in the essays published here. Fred Guy, Jane Schukoske, Thomas Simon, Jean Tullius, William Weston, and Susan Zacur all greatly contributed to the proceedings and the success of the conference.

Thanks are also due to Barbara Jones, Kay Martel, and Janet Pagotto for assistance in editing this volume and administering the programs that produced it. Andrew Altman took the lead in suggesting publication. As with all Hoffberger Center events and accomplishments, this book would not exist without the inspiration and encouragement of Catherine Gira and Sheldon Caplis, who have now moved on to new responsibilities at Frostburg State University and the University of Maryland Baltimore County.

Above all, the Directors, and Senior Fellows of the Hoffberger Center would like to express their gratitude for the vision and support of the Hoffberger family.

Notes on Contributors

Andrew Altman is Associate Professor of Philosophy at The George Washington University.

K. Anthony Appiah is Professor of Afro-American Studies and Philosophy at Harvard University.

Randy E. Barnett is Professor of Law at the Boston University School of Law.

Arthur Brown is Director of the Center for Academic Ethics at Wayne State University.

Robert K. Fullinwider is Senior Research Scholar at the Institute for Philosophy and Public Policy at the University of Maryland, College Park.

J.L.A. Garcia is Professor of Philosophy at Rutgers University.

Robert Justin Lipkin is Professor of Law at the Widener University School of Law.

Kathryn Mohrman is the President of The Colorado College. She wrote her contribution to this volume while Dean for Undergraduate Studies at the University of Maryland College Park.

Sharon E. Rush is Professor of Law at the University of Florida College of Law.

Mortimer Sellers is Co-Director of the Hoffberger Center for Professional Ethics and Associate Professor of Law at the University of Baltimore School of Law.

Robert L. Simon is Professor of Philosophy at Hamilton College.

Thomas W. Simon is Professor of Philosophy at Illinois State University and at Miyazaki International College, Japan.

Nicholas H. Steneck is Director of the Historical Center for Health Sciences and Professor of History at the University of Michigan.

Mark Tushnet is Associate Dean and Professor of Law at the Georgetown University Law Center.

1
Introduction

Mortimer Sellers

Higher education in the United States has long provided the prototype of a self-governing profession. Lawyers, doctors, civil servants, and even business managers must earn academic and other outside approval or licensing before they can practice their trades. But the academic profession itself has remained a self-regulated guild.

This is not to say that university ethicists have not occasionally drafted codes and standards for their colleagues, just as they do for the other professions. But their focus has been on the details of individual behavior, rather than the basic purpose and assumptions of the academic enterprise. The shared premise of these essays and the exchanges that produced them is that universities will benefit from examining the ethical basis of their own fundamental policies. This requires a broader perspective than can be found in philosophy departments alone. Administrators and members of other learned professions gave the discussions leading to this volume a liberating diversity that helped participants to examine their ideas from new and unexpected perspectives.

Questions of community and diversity pervade all the essays collected here and determined the topics they address. American universities have increasingly diverse students and faculties, yet they still seek to maintain a sense of community and common purpose. This raises the four central questions in this volume: What should the aims of the universities be given their changed demography? How should the curriculum reflect these changes? Does the new environment require special treatment of campus speech? And what role should affirmative action play in promoting diversity or community in the American academy?

I. The Aims of the University

The underlying problem is set out in Nicholas Steneck's essay in Chapter 2. Steneck argues that the failure of universities to undertake serious moral and ethical self-evaluation is not accidental but the consequence of the historical evolution of the modern research university. This reflects two related historical developments: first, the redirection of faculty time and effort from the affairs of the particular university to the affairs of international research communities; and second, the gradual transfer of decision-making authority from faculty to administrators. Both contribute to lower faculty commitment to their own institutions. Thus even the many new university ethics programs tend to ignore ethical problems that arise within academic institutions as a consequence of the actions of and decisions made by universities. Steneck proposes a concerted effort to redirect teachers' attention to the campuses on which they work, to weigh institutional values, and to raise questions about right and wrong.

J.L.A. Garcia (Chapter 3) agrees that in considering the aims of the university one must look to the mission and circumstances of the particular campus in question. But any university's chief objectives should include providing "sentimental education," to foster the formation, development, and maturation of the sensibilities and desires necessary for ethical thought. Students need opportunities to develop their commitment to truth and goodness, to discover intellectual and moral virtues, and to cultivate habits of mind that blend the two. This does not mean that the university has any special mission to attack or defend the status quo. Rather it should be open to excellence, including non-traditional forms of excellence to which we may have been blind due to prejudice or self-satisfaction. Diversification of the curriculum and faculty is important, but only insofar as it aids the quest for truth. Unkind speech should be discouraged because it hampers the development of virtues such as civility, respect, and sensitivity.

Robert Lipkin (Chapter 4) sees a fundamental conflict in universities, as in society, between traditionalists and progressives. While defenders of tradition value orthodoxy and hierarchy, their opponents prefer to test received values against the best available objections. Lipkin questions Garcia's emphasis on truth. The better test of a society's health is whether it can survive criticism. This "pragmatic" test furnishes the universities with their distinctive role, which should be to challenge the dominant culture, whatever it happens to be. When radical critique of the dominant culture prevails, the dominant culture will be reformed; when it fails, the dominant culture is maintained. Universities alone have the stability, independence, and resources to provide systematic, persistent, and progressive criticism of the dominant culture. This should not mean attempts at "value-free" inquiry in pursuit of truth, which tend to support the status quo, but rather seeking out and defending unpopular proposals for revolutionary change as well as people who would be likely to have unconventional ideas and perspectives. Multiculturalism strengthens the university's pragmatic role by introducing new voices into the discussion and testing orthodoxy with criticisms that might otherwise have been overlooked.

II. Creating the Curriculum

Inevitably, the curriculum will embody (perhaps unwittingly) the aims of the university that promulgates it. Robert Simon (Chapter 5) echoes Garcia in suggesting that this process should not be allowed to become too political. By this he does not mean that the curriculum should be "value-free," or entirely abstracted from the cultural context in which it operates, but rather that conversations about the curriculum should seek common criteria of evaluation to resolve disputes. Rationality and objectivity provide powerful tools for challenging a biased or unrepresentative curriculum. It is counterproductive for revisionists to embrace relativism and skepticism as this precludes presenting their claims for reform as justified. Reformers need criteria for evaluating claims without simply asserting values accepted by a particular group at a particular time. Reasons other than pure interest and power must be given, to move the curriculum out of the political realm into an academic ethic of inquiry. The non-political curriculum will be decided on educational rather than ideological grounds. It will be normative, but non-partisan.

Administrators play a greater role than they used to in setting university policy, and this has a direct influence on the nature of classroom education. Arthur Brown (Chapter 6) discusses the need managers have felt for measurable manifestations of academic achievement in order to make teaching more assessable and teachers more accountable. But this move to objective standards threatens professional autonomy, pluralism, and academic freedom. Nor do academic grades and tests correlate very well with future accomplishments. Brown proposes program evaluation as a substitute for the academic assessment of individual students, when administrators seek to measure the effectiveness of university departments and programs.

Kathryn Mohrman (Chapter 7) discusses the curriculum in context of American society's increasing cultural diversity. The curriculum is the practical manifestation of our ideals about the university. These require increased inclusiveness, not as a matter of compensatory justice but simply as a means of protecting the self-interest of faculty and administrators. Diversity increasingly contributes to academic excellence in research and teaching, as the interests of scholarship become broader. Diverse faculties facilitate collaborative studies, and help students develop the flexibility necessary for their future careers. While acknowledging differences, universities should also focus on what we all have in common – the intellectual process of the search for truth. This does not imply either a fixed definition of truth or a consensus about how to go about the search, but it does involve a commitment to participating in the process as openly and honestly as possible.

III. Campus Speech

The search for truth also informs Andrew Altman's evaluation of the universities' recent restrictions on hate speech (Chapter 8). Altman defends such restrictions, so long as they conform to certain widely accepted ethical principles. Some forms of hate speech involve treating persons as morally inferior or subordinate. Such "speech acts" work to subordinate others, whether or not they accompany other nonverbal acts. Demeaning epithets, by denigrating the victim's standing in the moral universe, are the verbal instruments of subordination, marking others as inferior. This violates a widely accepted moral principle positing the moral equality of persons. Which is not to say that enforcing moral equality always justifies violating individual liberty: restricting speech may silence true or useful opinions. But demeaning epithets do not advance the search for truth. Argument and eloquence are powerless to counteract them because they cannot repair or erase the fact that someone has been treated as a moral subordinate.

Anthony Appiah (Chapter 9) also links the role of the university in teaching, researching, and disseminating the truth to its standing as a moral community. Universities depend upon rational discourse and the shared assessment of evidence and reasons with a minimum or partiality and prejudice. They find the truth by testing it against contrary views. Libertarian concerns also favor free speech when it does not harm others and takes place in the public sphere. This consideration also extends to expressive action. Like speech, action should not be limited simply because it will cause outrage. Policing the outraged is preferable to banning expressions that are outrageous.

Randy Barnett (Chapter 10) compares free speech in American Universities to principles developed in the public sphere through judicial interpretation of the First Amendment. One line of reasoning considers the value of free speech in promoting public understanding of truth. Another stresses the harm institutionalized coercion can do, leading at times to error and abuse. Like the state, universities are bureaucratic, hierarchical, and large enough to be subject to frequent error and abuse. But they also stand *in loco parentis*, and have a legitimate interest in guiding the ideas of their members. Barnett suggests that university communities may limit improper speech, without coercion, by acting collectively to express disapproval of expressions that violate civility and accepted canons of discourse.

Thomas Simon (Chapter 11) sees a positive value in outrageous speech when it serves to counter the effects of racism, sexism, ethnocentrism, and homophobia. Attempts to curb hate speech may privilege sophisticated racists at the expense of subordinated minorities. Simon challenges opponents of social oppression to attack it directly, not allowing themselves to be distracted by deplorable but less fundamental incidents of hate speech. Thus hate speech regulation should be evaluated only in the context of the broader battle against group subjugation. Fine distinctions between crude epithets and reasoned discourse, as advanced by Altman and Appiah, may disadvantage the very groups they were meant to protect. Simon suggests that universities concentrate less on regulating hate speech and more on removing structural supports for racism such as employment practices, investment decisions, and the prejudices of the wider community.

IV. Affirmative Action

Many institutions of higher education have embraced affirmative action as a weapon against racism and a means of protecting multicultural diversity. Mark Tushnet (Chapter 12) suggests that this raises important questions about classroom teaching. Teachers run two risks: they may not change their pedagogy enough, in the face of changed demographics, or they may change it in the wrong way. Tushnet calls these two reactions the pathology of resistance and the pathology of intellectual collapse. Affirmative action leads to student bodies with widely varied backgrounds and teachers should take this into account in structuring their courses. Different cultural references will be necessary to make points in class. Different sorts of intellectual abilities will have to be recognized and cultivated. Teachers should rework their classes in order to better serve their new students.

Sharon Rush (Chapter 13) sees affirmative action as creating tensions between women and men, people of color and whites, and insiders and outsiders. Nonetheless, she considers affirmative action to be justified by the inroads it makes into the hegemonic power of traditionally privileged groups. Affirmative action remedies past discrimination, promotes diversity, and provides services to underrepresented minorities by giving their leaders access to the academy. To worry, as some do, about the "innocent white victims" of affirmative action obscures the real harm done to people of color and women by past discrimination as well as its continuing effects. Moreover, rejected white male applicants retain their many other privileges. Rush advocates a positive definition of affirmative action that would recognize the importance of "investing" in women and people of color, who will soon make up a majority of workers in our society. Affirmative action can advance equal citizenship and participation only if we remove the stigma associated with affirmative action policies and their beneficiaries. Diversity must be taken into account, and protected. "Colorblindness" hurts people of color and is socially defeating.

Robert Fullinwider (Chapter 14) also supports affirmative action and proposes techniques for changing the attitudes of the displaced majority. Nonetheless, Fullinwider suggests that some public defenses of affirmative action may be counterproductive. Nothing is gained, he argues, by denying that those harmed by affirmative action are "innocent victims." Rather than let the costs of undoing our national history of discrimination fall on the backs of a few more or less randomly-placed individuals, proponents of affirmative action should promote policies that spread costs equally across society. Nor should affirmative action be presented as a matter of "desert." Affirmative action serves social goals, and those who fail to benefit are not "undeserving," simply poorly placed. Making it a question of personal merit creates unnecessary conflicts. When community-wide cost-sharing is not possible, those who do bear the cost will do so more cheerfully if they are not told that they deserve their fate. To see oneself as sacrificing as a citizen for the common good is much more palatable than to suffer as a white male for the corporate sins of a displaced elite.

Examining the ethical basis of university policies brings to light some of the unexamined assumptions that drive academic decision-making. Many of these seem inappropriate in an era of increased cultural pluralism, and student and faculty diversity. But despite their diverse perspectives, the contributors to this volume found consensus on several fundamental questions of academic ethics. All valued discourse and the search, if not always for "truth," at least for a shared understanding to serve as the basis for a sense of academic community and common purpose.

Diversity may be valuable and inevitable as part of our common search for truth and social justice, but the common goal remains to give diversity meaning and maintain the community and good will that make rational discourse possible.

2
Ethics and the Aims of Universities in Historical Perspective

Nicholas H. Steneck

Over the past two decades there has been an encouraging increase in the number of programs and centers on university campuses devoted to applied and practical ethics. And yet as encouraging as the increase in "ethics" centers may appear, they have so far failed in any serious way to confront the most crucial ethical and moral issues universities face today – those that grow out of their own actions and policies. The paper that follows argues that the failure of universities to undertake serious moral and ethical self-evaluation is not an accident but the consequence of the historical evolution of the modern research university, an evolution that if allowed to continue might result in the disappearance of research universities as vital, independent social critics.

The historical part of my argument, which is based primarily on events at the University of Michigan, focuses on two crucial and inter-related historical developments: *first*, the gradual redirection of faculty time and effort from the affairs of one particular university to the affairs of international research communities and professional organizations; and *second*, the gradual transfer of decision-making authority on university campuses away from faculty and governing boards to administrators and executive bodies. The consequence of these two developments is that the single most important component of any university community, the faculty, no longer has a significant or prevailing interest in that community. The loss of faculty commitment to their own institutions has turned universities into loosely knit multiversities that lack the will, individuals, and mechanisms to consider problems of common interest, especially when these problems bring into focus the very difficult issues of morality, ethics, and values.

I. Campus- and Teaching-Centered Faculty

One hundred and fifty years ago, faculty members at the University of Michigan spent most of their time on university affairs.[1] They admitted, registered, taught, examined, advised, disciplined, and graduated students personally. They staffed the library, organized the museum, supervised the construction of buildings, and even planted trees. They also planned courses of study, organized departments, and pursued their own research, as time and personal interests dictated. Academic life in the mid-nineteenth century centered around and was focused on a faculty member's university. It also was preoccupied with one overarching activity – teaching.[2]

The importance of teaching on the nineteenth-century university campus can be illustrated in a number of ways. Victor Vaughan reported as a junior faculty member to President James B. Angell in 1880 that during the previous academic year he had lectured three hours each week to a class of 200 medical students and two hours each week to 30 pharmacy students, as well as directed laboratory instruction two hours each day, five days a week. In addition, he gave a special course on "microscopy" Thursday evenings and Saturday afternoons, without receiving any extra pay. When asked how much time it took him to prepare for these classes, Vaughan replied, obviously with some displeasure intended:

all the time not spent as above [i.e. in class] and in attending to the necessities of life as eating, sleeping, etc.[3]

---

1. The University of Michigan traces its origins to the territorial "Cathelopistemiad" or "University of Michigania," which was founded in 1817 in Michigan Territory as part of a total "state" system of education. Trustees were appointed, a building erected, and a president hired, but the institution never functioned as an institution of higher learning. Within a few years it failed, but the trustees continued to exist as a corporate body and passed control for higher education to the State Board of Regents in 1837, thus establishing the continuity of the University of Michigan to 1817. The University was reorganized shortly after Michigan achieved statehood, and the first students enrolled in 1841. For a brief history of the University, see Howard Peckham, *The Making of the University of Michigan* (Ann Arbor, MI: The University of Michigan Press, 1967; revised and reprinted, 1994).

2. Faculty at Michigan were very early granted considerable autonomy in performing their duties as faculty, i.e., in teaching. The regents of the university agreed in 1838, a year after the university was founded, that "whatever the number [of professors] be, their respective duties should be independently performed. This is believed to be the principle of excellence in literary labors. It appeals at once to the highest motives, to intellectual exertion, and secures to its fullest extend individual accountability." University of Michigan, *Regents' Proceedings*, 1837-1864 (Ann Arbor, MI: University of Michigan, 1915): 42.

3. Victor Vaughan, Papers, 1876-79 and 1904, ms. Michigan Historical Collections, Bentley Historical Library; hereafter referred to as MHC.

Vaughan remained a dedicated teacher throughout his career, notwith-standing the fact that he went on to become Dean of the Medical School and an important national figure in medicine and public health.[4]

Another indication of the importance of teaching in the nineteenth-century university is the prominence of teaching-oriented organizations, such as the Michigan School Masters' Club, which was founded in 1886 by twenty of the State's and University's leading educators to provide a forum for the discussion of educational issues. It met regularly on the Ann Arbor campus "to secure an opportunity to discuss matters that per-tain to our common work, with particular reference to high school and collegiate training."[5] Over the years, Club members heard papers on and discussed the major educational problems faced at the secondary and col-legiate levels. The participants in these discussions included many of the University's leading faculty, from John Dewey, one of the founders of the Club, to the geologist/biologist Alexander Winchell and Burke Hinsdale, a pioneer in the development of courses on education in the university setting.[6]

The deep commitments to and personal nature of teaching in the nineteenth-century university is vividly captured in the unpublished autobiography of a Michigan faculty member who suffered the effects of the decline of teaching-oriented departments in the 1920s and 1930s. Looking back on his early days of teaching in the Speech Department during the first decade of the twentieth century, Richard Hollister wrote:

> In those early days, the machinery of education was simple and easy to get along with. The relationship between teacher and student was direct, friend-ly, and as a whole free from academic pressures and artificial stimulation or control. Unnecessary regulations and restraints had not yet accumulated. The faculty was relatively free from its own inhibiting regulations. Education was still more important than educational methods and machinery. Teaching and learning were still more vital than educational statistics, marking systems, and

4. Victor Vaughan, *A Doctor's Memories* (Indianapolis, IN: Bobbs-Merrill, 1926) pro-vides not only autobiographical material on Vaughan's life but rich, if not always accurate, insights into the crucial transition from teaching- to research-oriented universities.

5. Leslie A. Butler, *The Michigan Schoolmaster's Club: A Story of the First Seven Decades, 1886-1957* (Ann Arbor, MI: University of Michigan, [1957]): 14. In 1924, the club resoundingly defeated a motion to consolidate with the Michigan State Teachers' Association, preferring instead to preserve "the inspiration and help from a yearly visit to the University...." Ibid., p. 69.

6. For information on Dewey's early years at Michigan, see George Dykhuizen, *The Life and Mind of John Dewey* (Carbondale, IL: Southern Illinois University Press, 1978): 44-75.

futile struggles over core courses. The luscious fruit of the apple was still more life-giving than the polish of its skin and the preservation of its core. Honest teaching and learning was more common and more needed than public relations.[7]

This was the spirit that animated the early Michigan Schoolmasters' Club and faculty such as Richard Hollister; a spirit that made education the focal point of university life. It was not, however, a spirit that was shared by all faculty at the turn of the century. For some turn-of-the-century faculty, not only at Michigan but also on campuses across the country, advancing knowledge was becoming equally important to disseminating knowledge or teaching.

II. Research- and Professionally-Oriented Faculty

Keeping abreast of and helping to advance knowledge has always been an objective of some of Michigan's faculty. When the University reorganized itself as part of the formation of the State of Michigan in 1837, the first two faculty hired by the newly appointed Board of Regents were practicing scientists: the botanist, Asa Gray, and the geologist, Douglas Houghton.[8] Neither ever taught at the University. Asa Gray was hired away to Harvard before Michigan opened its doors for classes in 1841, while Douglas Houghton was fully occupied as the State Geologist up to his untimely and accidental death in 1845. However, their successors in both the sciences and humanities carried on the tradition of scholar-teacher that was so vital to the growth not only of the University of Michigan but to the other schools and colleges that have become the research universities of the twentieth century.[9]

With rare exceptions, however, such as Michigan's German-born

7. Richard Dennis Tiel Hollister, *My Yesterday*, unpublished ms., still held in family hands and kindly provided to this author by Marian Hollister Diechman, p. 187.

8. The hiring of Michigan's early science faculty is discussed in Nicholas H. Steneck, "The Origins of the Earliest Health Science Programs at the University of Michigan," in *The Origins of Michigan Leadership in the Health Sciences* (Ann Arbor, MI: Historical Center for the Health Sciences, 1994): 27-54.

9. Examples of early scholar-teachers at Michigan would include: Silas Douglas (1816-1890), who was responsible for establishing Michigan's strong commitment to chemistry in both the literary and medical programs; Alexander Winchell (1824-1891), a polymath who was hired to teach engineering but ended his career as a geologist-biologist writing on evolution; Franz Brünnow (1821-1891), Michigan's German born and trained astronomer; and Andrew Dickson White (1832-1918), who studied history in Europe before teaching at Michigan and becoming the first president of Cornell University.

and trained astronomer, Franz Brünnow, research did not define academic careers in the nineteenth-century university. Instead, research had
to be fit around the activity that did define academic life – teaching.
Research trips were taken during summer vacations or special leaves of
absence, something not surprising if Victor Vaughan's estimates of the
demands of teaching are correct. Research was undertaken in buildings
that were designed first and foremost for teaching, such as the new
chemistry laboratory built on the Michigan campus in 1856.[10]
Nonetheless, a great deal of research was undertaken, as it had been for
centuries, in the course of teaching. There was no other choice, since
teaching was the activity that defined and played the major role in the
lives of most of the faculty.

To make more room for research, in 1875 some of the University's
leading faculty joined with men *and* women in Ann Arbor to found the
Ann Arbor Research Club. The members of this new Club were "associated for *work* – for *research*.[11] At their meetings they listened to reports
on new research, some from the scientific literature and some the work
of Club members, and had occasional demonstrations of new scientific
apparatus, such as the "new Magneto-Electric Machine" demonstrated in
May of 1875 by Silas Douglas and reported to be "the only one of its size
in this Country."[12]

The Ann Arbor Research Club was not specialized enough for some
of the more serious-minded faculty researchers at the University who
conspired to replace it with a more professional research club. The new
club, which was formed in the 1880s, limited its members to professors at
the University, which excluded women and scientific amateurs, and to
persons actively engaged in research. This club would later grow into the
Research Club, formed in 1900 to, among other things, lobby for greater
attention to research at the University. The first paper presented to the
Club at its fortnightly meetings was by co-founder and then Dean of the

---

10. Michigan's observatory, the Detroit Observatory, which was completed in 1854,
was built primarily for research not teaching. It is indicative of Michigan's early commit-
ment to research, based on the German model, as articulated by its "first" president, Henry
Philip Tappan. Henry Philip Tappan, *University Education* (New York: G.P. Putnam,
1851), and James Turner and Paul Bernard, "The Prussian Road to University? German
Models and the University of Michigan, 1837-c.1895," in *Intellectual History and Academic
Culture at the University of Michigan: Fresh Explorations*, ed. by Margaret A. Lourie (Ann
Arbor, MI: The University of Michigan, 1989): 9-37.

11. "Record book of the Ann Arbor Scientific Club," 17 April 1875, from the opening
presidential address given by the philosopher, Benjamin Cocker, MHC.

12. Ibid.

Medical Department, Victor Vaughan, on "The Promotion of Research at the University of Michigan."[13]

The growing influence of research on university campuses slowly changed the focus of faculty life. For the new research-oriented faculty, teaching became a burden rather than the primary *raison d'etre* of academic life. The shift was far enough advanced by the end of World War I that James Rowland Angell, President of the National Research Council and son of Michigan's great nineteenth-century president, James Burill Angell, could assume:

> It is a matter of common knowledge that the most serious limitation of the research productivity of these [universities] is occasioned by the overwhelming burden of classroom instruction which many of the men are obliged to carry. Such classroom work is not only destructive to research because of the sheer intellectual and physical fatigue which it occasions, but also, and perhaps more significantly, because of the interruption to attention and the close observation of critical phenomena which it compels.[14]

Faculty were turning their attention from the classroom to the laboratory and, in the process, from the local work of their campus and students to the larger world of scholarship and professional life. They were, in a sense, abandoning their own university for an international world of scholarship and research.

The transition from campus-oriented teaching faculty to nationally and professionally oriented research faculty came in different decades in different fields, but the resulting imbalance before World War II was not extreme. It was not extreme because the resources for research were limited. Private funding was still the most important source of research support and a great deal was accomplished with spare parts, local shops, and ingenuity. Moreover, change in academia takes time, in part to allow for the gradual transition from one generation to the next. A few faculty recruited to Michigan at the end of the "golden era" of President Angell (1872-1909) were still teaching at the end of World War II.

However, the pace of change to a research-oriented university quickened considerably following World War II with the large-scale entry of government into research funding. Research budgets grew quickly, and

---

13. The history of Michigan's several research clubs can be found in John W. Langley, Mortimer Cooley, Warren Lombard, and Gardner S. Williams, "History of the Scientific Club of Ann Arbor, 1883-1932," May 7, 1932, in "University of Michigan, Scientific Club," MHC; and also Victor Vaughan, *A Doctor's Memories*, pp. 434-36.

14. James Rowland Angell, *The Development of Research in the United States* (Washington, D.C.: National Research Council, 1915): 6-7.

faculty could now buy their way out of their "burdensome" teaching duties. Other faculty (increasingly teaching assistants and non-tenure track instructors or lecturers) were hired to take their places. These changes, coupled with declining public support for pure educational activities, placed research in the central position of academic life at the University of Michigan and the nation's other major universities – a position previously occupied by teaching.

The growing importance of research in the modern university has distanced faculty from their colleagues on campus and joined them to international communities off campus. In the extreme, the modern university is simply a place where a faculty member happens to have her or his laboratory or office and may do some teaching. Laboratories and faculty easily move from place to place, commonly in response to offers of increased support and increased freedom from teaching. The ideal faculty position, it seems, is one that demands very little in terms of on-campus commitments and maximizes the opportunities to work with colleagues in specialized fields of research.

The new focus of academic life obviously makes the faculty member of the late twentieth century very different from the faculty member of the late nineteenth century. And this, I believe, has had a significant influence on the discussions that are possible or impossible on university campuses today.

III. The Growth of Administration

As universities grew in size and complexity during the last half of the nineteenth century, faculty could no longer be personally involved in all aspects of university affairs. At Michigan and most other large institutions of higher education, the administrative duties faculty had formerly assumed slowly passed first to faculty committees, then to executive bodies, and finally, over the first half of the twentieth century, to administrators. By the mid-twentieth century the modern research university was fully formed in the image of large corporations, with boards of directors, executive officers, large administrative staffs, and a shrinking cadre (proportionally) of teacher-researchers who were soon to become researcher-teachers.[15]

15. For a description of these changes, see Nicholas H. Steneck, *Faculty Governance at the University of Michigan: Principles, History, and Practice* (Ann Arbor, MI: University of Michigan Senate Advisory Committee on University Affairs, 1991).

The growth of administration has changed the daily life and experiences of faculty. Most faculty now have no contact with undergraduate students until they appear one day enrolled in a class; many may not ever see these students again once the class is over. Students have become names, numbers, and faces, not personalities or, as was once the case in the earliest days of the University, friends and colleagues.[16] Instead, students are known by admissions officers, residents in dormitories, counselors, and other non-academic staff. Most faculty also have very few contacts with the day-to-day running of the university as a whole. Fewer than one in ten faculty in the large academic units at the University of Michigan attend faculty meetings.[17] They do not participate in governance beyond the department or program level and do not understand, and perhaps do not care to, how most decisions about academic life are made. Campus life, in the sense of the intellectual atmosphere and academic decisions that affect the community of scholars on one university campus, have ceased to be a major concern in the lives of many faculty.

Some faculty have lamented the changes that have accompanied the growth of administration, but many more have welcomed them. One of the main attractions of academic life has always been the freedom to study, learn, and advance knowledge. By the late nineteenth century, research was seen by many as the key to progress in the coming century. Decreased administrative and teaching duties left more time for research. As research became not only intellectually but also personally and financially rewarding, faculty readily handed over the control of local administration to committees, executive bodies, and administrators. The modern corporate research university is not the result of a conspiracy but of a convenient arrangement worked out over time between faculty and administrators, always, of course, with some objections.

The new arrangements served administrators as well as faculty. As corporations, the success of the modern research university is measured in bottom-line terms – the volume of research, the number of National Academy or Nobel Prize scientists, the amount of giving, the size of endowments, and so on. From an administrative perspective, the more time faculty spend building national reputations the better, as this adds to the prestige of the university and in turn translates into rewards for the administrators who have skillfully built this prestige by encouraging and even in some cases demanding that faculty do more research. From some

16. In individual cases there are, of course, exceptions. These comments are intended to apply on average, to the several hundred students in large courses who cannot be known personally, rather than the few who can, if there is an effort to do so.

17. Steneck, *Faculty Governance*, p. 11.

perspectives, it makes a great deal of sense to have institutions of higher education run by administrators, leaving the faculty free to advance knowledge for the benefit of society.

From other perspectives the current organization of the modern research university makes less sense. There is, of course, the obvious problem of the quality of teaching on many research campuses and the impact that this is likely to have on society in the future. This is a problem that is currently being addressed nationwide. How successful efforts to improve teaching will prove to be remains in doubt, particularly if resources are not forthcoming to back up commitments. My primary concern, however, is not with teaching, the erosion of faculty governance, or the other problems that are currently being addressed in higher education, but with the consequences of the loss of community for ethics and values discussions.

IV. The Consequences of the Loss of Community

As suggested above, the proliferation of professional ethics programs on university campuses today is encouraging and, if it continues, promises to make the 1990s a decade of renewed ethical awareness. However, if one looks closely at the programs that are being developed it becomes apparent that, like the new focus of faculty life, they are specialized and outwardly focused on the ethical problems of particular professions and on professional life outside the academic community. Far less frequently do they focus on what one new center has called "academic ethics" or on ethical problems that arise within academic institutions as a consequence of the actions of and decisions made by universities.[18] There is also a growing tendency to "professionalize" professional ethics, through the founding of specialized journals and professional societies, thereby once more isolating ethical and values concerns from the general academic milieu of any one campus.[19]

18. Wayne State University in Michigan has recently organized a Center for Academic Ethics. This center is, to the best of my knowledge, the only one that focuses specifically on ethical issues that are first and foremost of interest to universities as academic institutions. Some "ethics" centers, such as Harvard's Program in Ethics and the Professions and The Poynter Center at Indiana University, do focus a great deal of their attention on raising ethical awareness and promoting discussion on campus.

19. The recently founded Association for Professional and Practical Ethics is a first attempt to professionalize the "professional ethics" community. The association is currently committed both to broad participation and to maintaining high scholarly standards. Continued professionalization will, however, eventually limit participation, when academics in other fields find that they can no longer keep abreast of the growing body of professional ethics scholarship.

17

These trends, in my view, leave some serious gaps to be addressed when ethics, values, and morality are raised within the context of academic life – gaps such as the following:

A concerted effort is currently underway to revitalize or rebuild the government-university compact for research funding worked out in the decade following World War II. There can be little doubt that the original compact drastically affected academic life on the nation's colleges and universities as well as life in the nation as a whole. However the current negotiations are concluded, there will be consequences for academic life. Will the consequences be acceptable? to whom? and under what assumptions? Will compromises be called for? of what principles? If the government decides to stress applied over basic research, will universities that depend on research funds for a significant percentage of their basic support be tempted to adjust? by strengthening some programs to the neglect of others? What principles will be used to evaluate possible adjustments? Who will or should have input into decision-making? How can and should actions and policies be judged as "right" or "wrong?"

A university's posture and actions relating to research raise questions about right or wrong, for universities, through their governing boards and administrators, take stands on these and other matters. Their actions are based on conclusions, usually unarticulated, about ethics, values, and morality. The stands they take can be as complicated and controversial as whether it is ethical to give liver transplants to alcoholics, or to displace American workers by moving basic manufacturing facilities to developing countries, or to violate client confidentiality for particular social goods. Academic professional ethics centers eagerly engage in discussions of all these issues, yet seldom do university scholars, either as professionals or communities, look inward and discuss in detail the ethics of their own actions.

Universities also take stands (make decisions about right or wrong) when they make appointments and distribute resources. For the most part, both processes take place in a wide variety of settings, with little common or community involvement. Most faculty appointments are made at the departmental level and reflect primarily departmental, i.e., disciplinary needs. This usually makes it difficult to hire faculty with interdisciplinary interests or who fill general needs, such as medical anthropologists, sociologists of science, and applied ethicists. Whether such hiring practices are in the best interests of society or meet the long-range needs of universities is certainly an issue worth debating.

At other levels, such as hiring key administrators – deans, provosts, and presidents – community involvement can also be limited and takes place on an ad hoc basis. And yet these decisions can have a major impact. The type of service a university provides to society will vary depending on whether the new dean of a medical school is clinically or basic-science oriented, whether the dean of a law school is more inclined to legal scholarship or legal service. Universities serve society through their scholarship, and the overall scope of their scholarly programs is deeply influenced by decisions about key administrative personnel and the distribution of resources.

In principle, university campuses provide an ideal setting for taking up, discussing, and weighing the most intractable issues relating to academic life – those that raise questions about right and wrong, about values, about what universities *should* do rather than what they *can* do. The diverse faculty on our campuses have vast expertise; they are capable of reasoning in many different ways; and they represent different genders, ethnic groups, political views, socio-economic backgrounds, and so on. If their collective attention were focused on problems of common interest, the benefits in terms of reasoned understanding could be enormous.

Unfortunately, I would argue, the organization of the modern research university does not encourage broad, campuswide discussion of common issues, excepting when there are immediate needs or problems.[20] Spending time with colleagues does not generate research grants and seldom results in publications. Nor does it advance disciplinary knowledge. The incentives to generate and participate in an intellectual life on a university campus are small in comparison to the incentives to engage in an intellectual life off campus. Moreover, many faculty are themselves the products of specialized educations and lack the intellectual skills needed to engage in discussions about the ethics of actions that may cut across many fields and involve a number of disciplines. It is even argued, all too frequently, that discussions about ethics, values, and morality are value-laden and therefore do not belong on university campuses.

If the alienation of faculty from the affairs of their own universities continues and if universities are increasingly run by administrators who are understandably concerned with numbers and prestige, all that will be left of universities as we enter the twenty-first century will be diverse corporations that will vie with one another for federally and privately funded research money, prestigious scholars, the most able post-docs and

20. The issues that have provoked some discussion are military and recombinant DNA research during the 1970s, and misconduct in research, free speech, and diversity/multiculturalism in the 1980s.

graduate students, and affluent undergraduates. Their one goal will be, as it already is for so many universities today, the advancement and dissemination of knowledge, without much general discussion or any concern about who benefits from that knowledge or how it is being employed. The way this goal will be achieved will be determined primarily by administrators seeking to improve the bottom line of their own institutions, for faculty will be largely concerned with advancing their own particular field of knowledge in order to attain the recognition and funding needed to do more research.

If this is to be the aim of the university of the future, sketched out admittedly in rather harsh and simplified tones, where will we look for and who will be responsible for ethics? Who will evaluate our knowledge mills to assess whether the products of their labors are indeed serving the best interests of society? My own belief is that if we are not ourselves willing to engage in discussions about the consequences of our actions (about the impact of our research, for example), then society at large will step in and assume the responsibility for ethics.

To some extent this is already happening. Government is increasingly regulating academic life. In Michigan, the constitutional autonomy given to the University in 1837 and upheld in the courts ever since is increasingly coming under attack. The need to increase private funding is also having an impact on academic life. If these trends continue, public universities could become simply the research and teaching arms of government and private industry, depending on who is willing to pick up the bill. When this happens, "universities," in my view, will cease to exist.

How can these trends be reversed and the vitality of the university maintained? The key to success lies in redirecting some of the attention of what is the main asset of any university, its faculty, back to the campuses on which it works. This does not mean that research agendas need to be abandoned or that the nineteenth-century preoccupation with teaching should be restored. It does mean, however, that faculty would need to share more of the responsibilities for the day-to-day operation of their university and have a voice in the most important decisions that are made. This kind of reinvestment of faculty resources in campus life and decision-making would, in my view, enrich campus life and improve the quality of academic decision-making.

3

The Aims of the University and the Challenge of Diversity: Bridging the Traditionalist/Multiculturalist Divide

J.L.A. Garcia

I. The Aims of the University

Our questions here concern the university, its aims and its ethics. Of course, we cannot answer them in the abstract. We must first identify which type of university we are considering: women's colleges, "historically Black colleges" (as they are nowadays called), denominational institutions (soon to be designated "historically religious"?), and privately-owned secular schools may, after all, have quite different missions. Here I focus on American-style, state-run public institutions of higher education and research.[1] To this I bring a newcomer's point of view: of my quarter century in the academy as student and teacher, I have so far spent only a few months in such an institution. With that caveat, then, I will say my piece in hopes that such a perspective may prove helpful.

We cannot be clear about ethics in the university without first attaining some clarity about ethics itself, and I fear that recent philosophical developments may retard this process more than help it. The recent philosophical trends are, first, to reduce ethics to politics, and second, to restrict politics to issues of power and distribution. Such an emphasis on the crude notion of power, however, ignores much that is most important politically, such as the distinctions between the

---

1. For an illuminating discussion of the process whereby American universities, especially state institutions, came to reconceive their mission in response to various nineteenth- and twentieth-century pressures toward secularization, see George Marsden, "The Soul of the American University," *First Things*, January, 1991, pp. 143-47. For a comparable treatment of how the process worked in private institutions with denominational origins, see a two-part article by James Burtchaell, "The Decline and Fall of the Christian College (I, II)," *First Things*, April, 1991, pp. 16-29, and *First Things*, May, 1991, pp. 30-38.

authorized and the unauthorized, the licit and the illicit, rational suasion and coercion, for example, as well as the significance for the polity of what is *decided* even when the decision is neither followed nor enforced. Such as emphasis on distribution is also misleading, I think, because it both misdirects our attention to results – and thus away from such matters as motive, plan, and process, which, arguably, are more important for moral assessment – and shrinks our moral field of vision to matters that can be straightforwardly quantified. Moreover, still further distortion can result when the theorist, in striving to evaluate the little that remains for her consideration, proceeds upon the presupposition that the crucial moral principles are those of egalitarianism and impartiality.

A richer notion of politics takes as its subject the life of the group (the *polis*) and its members' joint endeavor to secure for themselves a good common life. A society's members achieve this, in part, through exercising public power and through producing and distributing goods, to be sure, but also, and more significantly, they achieve it by cultivating certain traits of character that, among other things, motivate them to head in certain directions and guide their behavior. Politics, we might say, primarily concerns itself with what we do and how we live, not what we produce.

But even if I am wrong in thinking about politics this way, these issues nonetheless remain the proper concerns of ethics. Recent academic philosophy has acknowledged that ethics concerns much more than Kant's famous question, "What ought I to do?" Indeed, it is doubtful that one could even begin to answer Kant's question without first having a good idea of how in general one ought to feel about things, what one ought to like about the world and thus strive to realize or preserve, and what one ought to abhor and thus strive to eradicate or prevent. I want to suggest that it is this formation, development, maturation, and tutoring of our sensibilities and desires, this "sentimental education," that should constitute one of the university's chief objectives. A university education, then, by its nature is a *liberal* education, a *humane* education. This is not to say it must be a liberal *arts* education, nor something centered on those academic disciplines traditionally classified as "the humanities."[2] My point is rather that it should be an education befitting free human beings precisely because they are free and human. A humane education has a certain breadth and generality that helps distinguish it from one that is narrowly

2. On this distinction, see Ian Ker's "Editor's Introduction," in John H. Newman, *The Idea of the University*, (Oxford: Oxford University Press, 1976), pp. lviii-lx.

"technical" or "vocational."[3] Its primary concern is neither to convey a certain body of information, nor to train students in ratiocinative techniques. We can thus reject both sides of the old controversy over whether the chief goal of a university education should be to teach students "what to think" or to teach them "how to think" (in the sense of knowing which techniques to use).[4] The educated person should have learned both, but above all, should be characterized by a certain appreciation for, and even commitment to, truth and goodness.

If the university's aims thus extend to the formation of character, it follows that the university must provide students with a certain kind of environment: for, as Aristotle noted, virtuous character develops by habituation. The students, faculty, and others may still enjoy broad freedom, in the sense that there is no rigid enforcement of a restrictive code, but it should still be necessary to make clear that some available choices are better than others, some are highly objectionable, and some intolerable. Of course, if, as some contemporary political theorists contend, the state, and by extension the state university, are to maintain an unyielding neutrality across competing conceptions of what constitutes an admirable human life, it will then be simply impossible for a state university to achieve this sort of self-definition.[5] However, this merely shows that either the state should abdicate education, or political thinkers should abandon their fascination with neutrality.[6]

This idea of the university's mission also enables us to reject both sides of the more recent argument between certain traditionalists who maintain that the university should "transmit" a cultural tradition from one

3. Thus, it cannot be the primary task of a university to address itself to solving various transient social or technological problems, however pressing. Of course, the quest for such solutions was a major impetus behind the formation of America's land grant colleges, and there are political pressures currently building to re-direct the attention and resources of state universities from humanities, arts, and social sciences to technology. My point is that while public (and private) financial sources can direct their funds as they wish, the university should resist such direction when it threatens to pervert the institution's pursuit of its more central mission of providing a humane education. This is a point more fully addressed in Nicholas Steneck's contribution to this volume. I am not in a position to say whether his pessimism is warranted.

4. John Dewey was notable for his insistence that education should turn to training students in various skills.

5. On the recent trend to understand the essence of the liberal state in terms of such neutrality, see Bruce Ackerman, *Social Justice in the Liberal State* (New Haven: Yale, 1980) and the book that is sure to become the *locus classicus* of this movement: John Rawls, *Political Liberalism* (New York: Columbia, 1993).

6. There are encouraging moves in this direction among the most recent liberal theorists. See William Galston, *Liberal Purposes: Goods, Virtues, and Diversity in the Liberal State* (Cambridge: Cambridge University Press, 1991).

generation to another and those, such as Robert Lipkin, who insist that its function is rather to serve as an institutional center for the radical critique of "normal culture."[7]

Interestingly, C. Vann Woodward affirms a vision of the university strangely similar to Lipkin's when Woodward argues *against* the new campus speech codes whose adoption is part of the diversification program Lipkin thinks that his own notion of the university endorses. Woodward writes: "The purpose of the university is not to make its members feel secure, content, or good about themselves, but to provide a forum for the new, the provocative, the disturbing, the unorthodox, even the shocking – all of which can be profoundly offensive to many, inside as well as outside, its walls."[8]

One wonders whether it is really necessary to have a forum for remarks and conduct whose *only* merit is that they are disturbing and shocking. One also wants to know why the university should never be interested in making the students "feel good about themselves." What if it were shown that some minimal measure of self-confidence could make learning easier for some people, traditionally excluded persons, for instance?[9] In any case, the dispute about self-esteem may be a straw man, at least in the context of calls for curricular diversification within the university (as distinct from the discussion of primary- and secondary-school curricula.) Influential advocates of multiculturalism at the university level deny that promoting student self-esteem is a major motive behind their proposals. Molefi Asante writes, "I know of no Afrocentric curriculum planner – Asa Hilliard, Wade Nobles, Leonard Jeffries, Don McNeely being the principal ones – who insists that the primary aim is to raise self-esteem. The argument is a false lead to nowhere because the curriculum planners I

7. For the former position, see two reports by chairpersons of the National Endowments for the Humanities: William Bennett, *To Reclaim a Legacy*, 1984; and Lynne Cheney, *Humanities in America*, 1988. For the latter position, see Lipkin's contribution to this volume.

8. Woodward, "Reply to Letters," *New York Review of Books* (September 26, 1991), pp. 75–76, where Woodward responds to criticisms of his favorable review of Dinesh D'Souza's book *Illiberal Education*. For an argument against speech codes similar to Woodward's, but from a stance of leftist radicalism, see Eugene Genovese's review of the same book, "Heresy, Yes – Sensitivity, No," *New Republic* (April 15, 1991), pp. 30–35.

9. For a thoughtful and historically informed (but quite unsympathetic) treatment of the use of history in bolstering the self-esteem of oppressed people, see Arthur Schlesinger, *The Disuniting of America: Reflections on a Multicultural Society* (Knoxville, Tenn: Whittle Books, 1991), esp. chaps. 3, 4.

am familiar with insist that the fundamental objective is to provide accurate information."[10]

According to the view suggested here, among the university's primary aims is the cultivation of intellectual and moral virtues, indeed, the cultivation of habits of mind that blend the two. This conception of the role of the university is not novel. It still frequently surfaces in universities' official statements of their mission, even when it does little to animate what actually happens on campus. A statement on the "Objectives of the University" at Georgetown, where I wrote this essay, states in part: "By its curriculum and educational policy, the University strives to develop the whole person through the cultivation and discipline of the will as well as by the formation of the intellect and by the sharing of factual information. . . . The University seeks to promote the highest development of the individual student and the most effective use of talent. . . ." Among the "specific ideals" to which the institution commits itself is "the perfectibility of society through the acquisition and practice by its members of the theological, intellectual, moral virtues and their derivatives, e.g., patriotism, loyalty, and social consciousness. . . ."[11]

If the academy is successful, its graduates should, among other things, possess intellectual humility and a related willingness to learn from others, a sensitivity to their own and others' failings and needs, a serious commitment to truth and a consequent loathing of what is false or meretricious, a joy in learning, and a dissatisfaction with what is either merely conventional or merely unconventional. It is puzzling to me that so many today think it a distinctive part of the university's mission either to defend or to attack the cultural *status quo*.[12]

---

10. Asante, "Multiculturalism: an Exchange," *American Scholar* (Spring, 1991). Reprinted in *Debating P.C.*, Paul Berman, ed. (New York: Dell/Doubleday, 1992), pp. 299-311, at p. 307. This valuable collection, on which I have relied heavily, brings together a number of pieces by some of the principal figures in the disputes over campus diversity.

11. See *1991-1992 Georgetown University Faculty Handbook*, pp. viii, ix. Admittedly, in this statement, Georgetown also dedicates itself to "uphold, defend, propagate, and elucidate the integral Christian and American cultural heritage [expressed in] the Declaration of Independence, . . . the American Constitution, and its Bill of Rights." The tone of this is rather disagreeably parochial, Americanist, and "monocultural." However, it should be remembered that the "Christian . . . cultural heritage" to which it refers is meant to capture truths about all humanity. The emphasis on patriotism and American heritage may be survivals from the Nativist epoch in American history, when Catholic institutions were especially anxious to combat their image as agents of a foreign potentate.

12. This should make it clear that I am in general agreement both with David Smith's account of the "academic virtues" of inquiry, honesty, and courage, and with his claim that it is the university's role to help its members increase knowledge (their own and others'), build character, and create community.

In recent disputes, three principal reasons have been offered why the university should, with only minor changes, retain the traditional "canon" of texts and themes: (1), they better enable students to understand "our" culture; (2), they have had such great historical impact; and (3), the texts manifest excellence and the themes are quite simply important.[13] The last of these claims has drawn special criticism from the more extreme elements of the diversification movement.[14] The concept of an education that dispenses with standards is, however, merely empty. Education must be guided by choices and those choices should be guided by what we know and reasonably believe. Still, while we need standards and must needs employ the ones that seem best to us, there is room for a certain modesty born of a recognition that our standards may, at the very least, have an element of the merely parochial. Some of what strikes us as less worthwhile may simply disturb prejudices whose status as mere prejudices might be revealed to us by provisionally taking some "inferior" works more seriously.

It is worth noticing that this sort of argument is an anti-skeptical one. It assumes that there are truths, including truths about values, and is an argument that appeals precisely to these truths about values in order to ground the claim that we should widen our field of investigation to include overlooked texts and ideas. Thus, this argument also rejects cultural relativism about values, in that it assumes that values can be understood and appreciated outside one's own culture. Indeed, when this assumption is denied, as it is by the more skeptical and relativist fringe of the diversification movement, it is hard to see much of a point to multicultural diversification. The debate is then reduced to a mere insistence that one group of people and texts be "exalted" by study rather than another, merely because, with no rational justification even offered, the speaker "sides" with a particular group. Let us set aside the silly and low-minded assumption that subjecting a text to rigorous study is mainly a matter of exalting it, as if *what* were being said about it (possibly some-

---

13. See John Searle, "The Storm over the University," *New York Review of Books,* December 6, 1990, pp. 34-42. Reprinted in Berman, pp. 85-123.

14. Stanley Fish maintains that "there is no such thing as intrinsic merit," and holds that "all preferences are principled" because they must all "derive from the norms inherent in some community." Fish, *Doing What Comes Naturally* (Durham: Duke University Press, 1989), pp. 164, 11. I owe these citations to Roger Kimball, *Tenured Radicals* (New York: Harper Collins, 1990), chap. 6. See also Dinesh D'Souza's report of a revealing interview with Fish in D'Souza, "Illiberal Education," *Atlantic*, March, 1991, pp. 51-79, at 72-73. In a similar vein, Kimball quotes Houston Baker as dedicating himself to the disappearance of the standards that people appeal to for their supposedly self-deceptive belief that artistic taste is different from preferring "a hoagy [to] a pizza." (Kimball, p. xiii.)

thing quite critical) didn't matter.[15] This is the sort of assumption that appeals to our publicity-driven time, in which it has become a given that, as Oscar Wilde said, the only thing worse than being talked about is not being talked about. Plainly, there is no basis on which to accede to the demand for diversification unless there can be *reason* to do so, and there can be no good reason to do so unless it can be shown that studying a diverse selection of texts is valuable because it will teach us something that is important for us to know and that is true.

The case for cultural relativism about values is weak for several reasons. In the first instance, we should remember that in the older, clearer, and more useful senses of the term "culture," not every set of customs that a group acknowledges, uses, or teaches will count as a culture. Culture, in this definition, is a process of tending and nourishing that results in individual growth and development. Certainly there can be differing cultures, inasmuch as there can be differing regimens, each of which helps a person's humanity to flourish. There is no good reason to suppose that the customs of every group will necessarily aid human development and flourishing.[16] Not all values, then, can be logically

---

15. Paula Rothenberg writes that "The traditional curriculum . . . calls books by middle-class, white, male writers 'literature' and honors them as timeless and universal. . . ." Rothenberg, "Critics of Attempts to Democratize the Curriculum are Waging a Campaign to Misrepresent the Work of Responsible Professors," *Chronicle of Higher Education* (April 10, 1991), pp. B1, B3. Reprinted in Berman, pp. 262-68, at p. 265.

16. On the historical development of the notion of "culture," see Raymond Williams, *Keywords*, rev. ed. (New York: Oxford University Press, 1983), s.v. "Culture."

It is likely that in many groups some customs will help and others will hinder human growth; and there is no reason to suppose that we could tote up all the pros and cons of the customs of each group, and then make a cross-cultural comparison in which the value of each group's set of customs, its "way of life," would come out exactly equal to that of every other group's set. Surely, even if such a calculation were possible, there is no reason to think we could know its result in advance, as the proponents of what is sometimes called "cultural equity" would have it.

Some philosophers have recently used human beings' ability to adapt to a variety of cultures with differing moral codes and ideals of the well-adjusted individual to argue against the "mono-moralist" thesis that one set of moral requirements applies to all humans. However, as Laurence Thomas has trenchantly observed, even if many different moral and psychological norms are compatible with human nature, that fact provides us with no basis for supposing that all fit human nature equally well. (See Thomas, "Review of Owen Flanagan's Varieties of Moral Personality," *Ethics*, (1993).) In any case, if we are to judge whether people are faring adequately in a society that calls upon them to conform to a certain moral and psychological model, we may well need to rely upon prior ideas about what constitutes faring well on the one hand, or living a shrivelled or warped life on the other. In that case, we rely on value judgments in justifying claims about human nature. Thus, there are limits to the extent to which appeals to human nature, including appeals to human diversity and malleability, can properly undermine our evaluative convictions. (That is not to endorse the non-naturalists' and non-cognitivists' insistence that, in the order of being, moral judgments cannot be derived from the facts of human nature. However, it does suggest that the proponents of "wide reflective equilibrium" are correct in claiming that, in the order of knowing, at least, our value judgments will influence our philosophical anthropology, as well as vice versa.)

identified merely as the norms of a certain culture. For some standards of what is good and bad for people must be presupposed if we are even to identify a group's customs as a "culture," that is, a social environment that cultivates people and helps them to thrive.[17]

Moreover, it is doubtful that there is much empirical evidence for the cultural relativity of standards. Proponents of cultural relativism sometimes neglect to distinguish between evidence that there is some measure of cross-cultural disagreement about what is good and what is true and evidence that goodness and truth are creatures of various cultures and inseparable from them. Finally, it is difficult to see just how the necessary empirical evidence could be amassed.

Let me try to explain why even in principle such a project would be difficult. Cultural relativism, in the forms with which we are concerned, can be understood as essentially involving:

a *relativity* thesis, holding that some evaluative judgments are relative in some significant way to the codes (or traditions or life-styles or something similar) of cultural groups;

a *diversity* thesis, holding that these groups' codes, life-styles, etc., are not entirely identical in what they commend and condemn; and

a *non-rankability* thesis, restricting the extent to which different codes, or opposed provisions drawn from different codes, can be ordered as better or worse.[18]

---

17. Of course, it remains open to think of values merely as those customs the group happens to use or teach. However, even this seems to be an external imposition on the social group that oftentimes will have a very different conception of their norms. They may well ground their norms in claims about human history, and about the natural or supernatural order. They may well understand their normative judgments not merely as the requirements of their group, but as truth-claims about what befits human beings in the light of a certain vision of human origins, or about what humans need if they are to prosper in a world thought to have a certain origin or purpose. It is difficult to see in what way it is respectful to the group to wrench these normative beliefs out of the context of the historical, anthropological, or religious belief that supports them, in order to treat them merely as means of social regulation, interesting only for what they indicate about the group, rather than as parts of a broader conception of human life that may be interesting for what it asserts about the world.

18. The idea and terminology for the first two theses I borrow from John Ladd, "Introduction," in *Ethical Relativism* (Belmont, California: Wadsworth, 1973), pp. 1-11. The idea, and awkward terminology, for the third is my own. I add this thesis to reserve the term "cultural relativist" for those who think that ultimately there is no legitimate and objective basis on which to rank and choose among cultures, and to distinguish such thinkers from "communitarians" who, while strongly linking morality to tradition, insist upon the ability for such rational appraisal and choice. My terminology is probably somewhat idiosyncratic, but not without rationale.

Each of these elements affords a dimension, which I shall label *judgmental scope*, *depth*, and *strength*, respectively, in respect to which any two relativist conceptions of evaluation can vary. Regarding the first thesis, consider the view of a person who endorses some form of cultural relativism in aesthetics yet thinks it doesn't apply to judgments about, say, religious ritual objects. That makes her relativism less *extensive* in scope than that of someone who holds that *all* aesthetic judgments are relativized. Regarding the second, consider the claim that some types of form are deemed ugly in every culture. Such a position displays a relativism that doesn't go as *deep* as that found in the view that there are *no* such (cross-culturally) universal aesthetic norms. Regarding the third, consider the position of someone who, while she thinks that aesthetic standards merely derive from a group's code, and that codes differ in content from group to group, nonetheless maintains that there are some standards (presumably, not aesthetic ones) that can legitimately serve as a non-relativized basis for saying that the standards of, say, Group Number One are better than those of Group Number Two, or that a particular standard in the code of the first group is superior to the corresponding standard in the other group's code.[19] Such a relativism is not so *strong* as that of someone who insists there are no such non-relativized standards by which different codes can properly be evaluated.

There are serious problems confronting any form of cultural relativism that has substantial judgmental scope, depth, and strength. Consider aesthetic evaluations. There is no reason to call any set of judgments in a society we encounter *evaluative* judgments unless they are recognizable as such. Moreover, we cannot recognize them as aesthetic unless they pertinently resemble what we ordinarily call aesthetic. But this pits some of the cultural relativist's claims against others, especially as her relativism becomes deeper and becomes more extensive in judgmental scope. This is because she needs the judgments and practices in question to be similar enough to our own to be recognizable as aesthetic, yet also wants them to be sufficiently different from

---

19. Any relativist who holds that terms of evaluation can be identified by their function would seem to be thereby *committed* to the existence of such non-relativized bases for evaluating codes, since some group's code may fulfill any such proposed function, for example, helping to perpetuate the group's customs and rituals, less effectively than does that of another group.

our own so that her relativity thesis becomes plausible.[20] Nor will it do for her to say that the judgments differ from ours in content but are similar in the rationale supporting them, for this will tend to mean that relativism evaporates as we approach the deeper evaluative claims that serve as our judgments' or practices' epistemic or justificatory basis. At that point, the cultural relativist's best hope is to insist upon some purely formal criteria for recognizing aesthetic judgments. The familiar forms of formalism are all problematic in the light of philosophical criticism in the last few decades and, in any case, merely beg the question against those who hold that no judgment should be counted as aesthetic unless it is similar in subject, content, and rationale to the only paradigms we have – that is, the aesthetic judgments we ordinarily make.[21]

It is also true, as Plato saw, that problems of vicious self-reference continue to plague cultural relativism. What can we make, for example, of the claim that there can be no universal truths on the grounds that truth is merely a matter of what wins local approval? Is this a universal claim about truth? If so, then some universal truths obtain, and the only dispute is about which ones, a matter that must be decided on its merits. If not, and the relativist's claim about truth applies only to certain conceptions of it, then it may be open for the rest of us to work with more embracing conceptions.[22]

---

20. Of course, it is notoriously unclear why relativists think that the diversity of moral opinion, even if it is a fact, should lend evidential support to their relativity thesis. That thesis is merely one of the available explanations for the diversity. Its superiority to other possible explanations needs to be carefully demonstrated, not presupposed.

By the way, it has been objected to my argument that it relies upon the implicit rejection of "holism." I have my doubts about this claim, but I do not think it can be understood or assessed until some fuller account of the relevant holism is offered, along with some reason to think that such holism is true. For an effort to bring some clarity to the variety of uses assigned this trendy term, see Jerry Fodor and Ernest LePore, *Holism: a Shopper's Guide* (Cambridge: Blackwell, 1992), esp. Introduction.

21. The arguments I make here are presented with a little more detail in my "Relativism and Moral Divergence" *Metaphilosophy* 19 (1988): 264-81. The general anti-relativist strategy resembles that of Donald Davidson's in his "On the Very Idea of a Conceptual Scheme," in *Relativism: Cognitive and Moral*, edited by Michael Krausz and Jack Meiland (Notre Dame: University of Notre Dame Press, 1982), pp. 66-80.-For a sophisticated treatment of truth-relativism and its problems, see Chris Soyer, "True For," in Krausz and Meiland, pp. 84-108.

22. See Plato's refutation of Protagorean relativism in *Gorgias*. It should not need to be added that my belief that Plato's cogent criticisms of the relativism of his day still have relevance today does not entail that I am a Platonist, a "foundationalist," an "absolutist," or some other hobgoblin from the neo-Pragmatist's demonology. Literary critic Barbara Herrnstein Smith seemingly wants to reduce truth to little more than what others will let us get away with saying. See Smith, *Contingencies of Value* (Cambridge: Harvard University

Finally, there is always an irony in people having recourse to the supposed relativity of values in pursuit of some normative goals, in this case, political ones. As Barbara Ehrenreich writes, taking a stance of politically critiquing this society is incompatible with the "position fashionable among some of our post-modernist academics, that there are no absolutes, no truths, and hence no grounds for moral judgement. . . . There can be no left where the only politics is [the] narrow politics of [group-]identity."[23]

Of course, the choice remains to abandon relativism in favor of a more radical position, perhaps the nihilistic thesis that no aesthetic standards

Press, 1989). This is dangerously self-referential in a number of ways. First, and most damagingly, by the very standard it proposes, it may well turn out not to be true. It depends on whether those of us in her communicative community will let her get away with saying this about truth. (I, for one, vote "no.") Second, even if it passes its own dubious test, it implausibly allows statements about things to pass from truth to falsity and back again, while the things remain the same and only people's conventions change. (Some proponents of such a view will, of course, deny that statements are about external things, insisting that our talk cannot refer to things but only to other pieces of language ("intertextuality"). There are philosophical arguments to be made against such positions, but we needn't pursue them here. (They will mostly consist merely in displaying the inanity of what is already patently silly.) Third, it borders on the obscurantist and the masturbatory in the self-obsessive manner in which it makes all study of the world into the study merely of our folkways. Such cynical parochialism cannot but run counter to the point and spirit of a humanizing education.

We should acknowledge that Smith responds to criticisms such as mine in her fifth and seventh chapters, but not, I think, in such a way as to allay fears about the coherence and plausibility of her position. She thinks, for example, that she can escape the problems of self-reference that plague relativism by insisting that her own views are not presented as assertions to be believed true but rather as "alternative descriptions" offered "for sale" in hopes that some intellectual "consumers" will "buy" them. (pp. 112ff.) Unfortunately for her, this gets nowhere. Descriptions themselves can be more nearly or less nearly true, closer to or farther from the full truth. Likewise, if "buy[ing]" is meant to be a doxastic matter, as in the colloquial expression to which Smith refers, then the prospective "buy[er]" must assess the quality of the "commodities" offered her by attending to their truth. (As traditionally understood, truth, in advertising or elsewhere, seems to have no role in Smith's marketplace.) I suspect that the discerning shopper will find Smith's intellectual products a bad bargain.

23. Barbara Ehrenreich, "The Challenge for the Left," *Democratic Left* (July/August, 1991). (Reprinted in Berman, pp. 333-38, at p. 337.) She is especially concerned lest cultural relativism deprive social critics of their ability to mount moral condemnations of the oppression of women in many Third World countries. For a journalist's elaboration of this point, see Cathy Young, "Equal Cultures – or Equality?" *Washington Post* (March 29, 1992) p. C5.

Cornel West agrees with Ehrenreich's general point: "As democratic socialists, we have to look at society in a way that cuts across race, gender, region, and nation." West, "Diverse New World," *Democratic Left* (July/August, 1991). (Reprinted in Berman, pp. 322-26, at p. 330.)

Edward Said helpfully discusses the way in which a "politics of [group -]identity," born in self-affirmation can become an intellectual strait-jacket and a metaphysical absurdity.

31

have validity, either across or even *within* cultures.[24] However, this move merely dissolves the humanities into the social sciences, and transforms texts, works of art, and arguments into mere ethnographic artifacts, of interest only for what they tell us about the people who made them and their way of life. This sort of view seems implausible on the face of it, and in any case I doubt many of the enthusiasts for the "new humanities" would happily embrace this rather unwelcome way of deconstructing their livelihood. Even here, of course, some non-relativized standards will need to be presupposed and others must needs emerge, as some "texts" will be more revealing than others, and some anthropological reports will be better than others in explaining what these artifacts have to tell us about their makers.

I conclude that, while it is a mistake for proponents of curricular diversification to take refuge in cultural relativism about values or truth to defend their position, any argument claiming that the traditional curriculum should be retained as is because of the excellence of the themes and works it treats is open to the criticism that certain non-traditional works may have excellence to which mere prejudice and self-satisfaction have blinded us.

The second rationale for rejecting the multiculturalists' suggestions to alter the traditional curriculum and its "canon" is that this tradition maintained and justly emphasized works and ideas of great or lasting influence. This is more problematic. There is a kind of noteworthiness that attaches to an influential work. However, just as Sherlock Holmes learned from the dog who didn't bark, we may also have much to learn from what gets

---

"Who benefits from leveling attacks on the canon? Certainly not the disadvantaged person or class. . . . [G]reat antiauthoritarian uprisings made their earliest advances, not by denying the humanitarian and universalist claims of the general dominant culture, but by attacking the adherents of that culture for failing to uphold their own declared standards, for failing to extend them to all, as opposed to a small fraction, of humanity." See Said, "The Politics of Knowledge," *Raritan* (Summer, 1991). Reprinted in Berman, pp. 172-89, at pp. 177ff., 188. For a stinging critique of the metaphysics of racial "essence," as manifested in the Negritude movement, see Charles Johnson, "Being and Race," in Johnson, *Being and Race: Black Writing Since 1970* (Indianapolis: Indiana University Press, 1988). In a singularly valuable contribution to this discussion, Irving Howe offers a useful summary of the importance of some of the traditional "Great Books" to influential radical thinkers in Howe, "The Value of the Canon," *New Republic* February 18, 1991. (Reprinted in Berman, pp. 153-71.)

24. I discuss the differences among relativism, skepticism, and nihilism as they apply within one field of evaluative discourse, the ethical, in "Relativism and Moral Divergence." That article also contains an earlier version of the argument presented here. For further discussion and application to the views of one relativist thinker, Alain Locke, see my "African-American Perspectives, Cultural Relativism, and Normative Issues," in *African-American Perspectives on Biomedical Ethics*, edited by Harley Flack and Edmund Pellegrino (Washington: Georgetown University Press, 1992).

ignored. Perhaps we can find out a good deal about Western history from works with something to say, but against whose influence the West immunized itself. Perhaps there is truth in Roger Kimball's assertion that "by virtue of its history, its political institutions, its major cultural affiliations, and its dominant language, the United States is essentially a Western society."[25] Nevertheless, it remains a fact that America's history, politics, and culture have been subject to diverse and neglected influences, ones that our institutions of higher education have largely ignored. What Kimball says provides no reason against turning more attention to "minor" affiliations and influences, including those of American minorities.[26] In any case, as we move into the twenty-first century, the growing influence of female and non-Western sources on American life and thought is something that becomes increasingly foolish to deny.[27]

The first rationale offered for resisting the multiculturalists' calls for reform is that tradition best enables students to understand "our" culture. I think this argument also fails. Increasingly, "we," that is, Americans, are not white people descended from recent immigrants from Europe. Even if the purpose of educating people were to enable them to achieve a better self-understanding, as this rationale seems to presuppose, then, given the diversity of the origins of the American people, and even of the European people, this purported rationale against multiculturalism undermines itself. For, as "we" are not homogeneous, the paths we take to historical self-understanding must necessarily diverge.[28] Moreover, I doubt many of the more thoughtful traditionalists would really want to rely on this conception of higher education. For one thing, it threatens to reduce what should be an ennobling experience, one that takes a person

25. Kimball, 205.

26. Searle, no devotee of what Kimball correctly labels "The New Sophistry," makes this point well in "Storm." Searle sensibly departs from Bennett and others to praise the recent revision in Stanford's curriculum as a reasonable response to a world, a nation, and a state (California), in which non-Western influences play an increasing role.

27. D'Souza, who is quite critical of much in the diversification movement, readily allows this. His concern, entirely proper, is that the forces that H. L. Gates calls "the cultural Left" distort the picture presented of the non-Western world and its history by, among other things: (a) ignoring what Third World cultures themselves see as most important, e.g., such religious scriptures as The Koran, and (b) viewing all events and interactions through the (possibly distorting) lenses of various Western intellectual fashions of nineteenth- and twentieth-century origin – class analysis, economic determinism, feminism, historicism, etc. Such approaches to diversification would themselves seem to be a form of the Western cultural imperialism their advocates decry. (See D'Souza, *Illiberal Education* (New York: Free Press, 1991), chaps. 3, 8.)

28. Note that even talk of "Europe" implies a unity that was imposed, and sometimes for political purposes. "But 'Europe' is an ideological construct. It doesn't exist other than in the minds of elites who tried to constitute a homogeneous tradition that could bring together heterogeneous populations – that's all it is." (West, pp. 328-29 in Berman.)

outside of her own time and place in order to explore the wider world, into something self-centered. For it is self-centered not only in its ultimate goal of developing a student's own humanity, but in its more immediate focus and themes.[29] Any form of "education for democracy" is, it should be noted, explicitly political in its aims and its goal of preparing people for the political role of citizen is significantly narrower than the traditional aim of helping to develop their humanity, even if one assumes that democracies are the most suitable political arrangements for developed human beings to live within. Henry Louis Gates, Jr. is, I think, close to the mark when he urges that universities "begin to prepare our students for their roles as citizens of a world culture, educated through a truly human notion of "the humanities" – rather than . . . as guardians at the last frontier outpost of white male Western culture, the keepers of the masterpieces."[30]

II. The Challenge of Diversity

If we think about ethics and the university as something aimed at developing humanity by communicating knowledge and cultivating intellectual and moral virtues, then how should we think of ethics *in* today's American state university? How should students, faculty, administrators, bureaucrats, legislators, and citizens respond to the challenges and choices posed by the "diversity issues" that serve as our subtext here? While I have nothing in the way of final answers, I will offer some thoughts in the hope of stimulating reflection and dialogue.

First, let us look at the calls for changes in the curriculum, as they con-

---

29. ". . . [T]he old monocultural education will not do. Monoculturalism represents a retreat into parochialism, and in a practical sense, is not a good preparation for living in this [that is, today's] world." Barbara Ehrenreich, "Challenge for the Left," *Democratic Socialist* 19 (July/August, 1991). Reprinted in Berman, pp. 333-38, at p. 334.

30. Henry Louis Gates, "Whose Canon Is It, Anyway?" in Berman, pp. 190-200. The ellipsis in the text marks my deletion of Gates' attribution to William Bennett and Allan Bloom of the cultural imperialist view he mocks. I doubt this is fair to Bennett and Bloom, and appears itself to be an instance of Gates succumbing to the tendency to cast these two, whom he calls "the dynamic duo of the new cultural right," in "the roles that George Wallace and Orville Faubus played for the civil rights movement, or that Richard Nixon and Henry Kissinger played during Vietnam – the 'feel good' targets who, despite internal differences and contradictions, the cultural left loves to hate." (Gates, pp. 190-91.)

There are also problems with Gates' formulation: citizens are citizens of a state, not of a culture. "Citizen" is an essentially legal and political term; "culture" is not. Moreover, the notion of "culture," if it is to be useful, should pick out a moral local environment. In any case, even if it makes sense to say the world could have a single "world culture," surely it won't have one for some time to come.

cern the basic *work* of the university community. Some traditionalists maintain that "the rhetoric of 'pluralism,' 'diversity' . . . [and multiculturalism] cloaks the abandonment of traditional humanistic culture. It belongs with the prattle about he humanities instilling dissatisfaction and the desirability of undermining the traditional canon."[31] I do not see why this should be so, why curricular diversification need be seen as "abandoning" traditional culture and "undermining the . . . canon." Surely, anyone who both recognizes her own ignorance and longs to know the truth will see the importance of going beyond her own time and place in search of insights and perspectives that might reveal to her aspects of reality otherwise hidden from her. Indeed, the image of "perspective" is revealing in this connection.[32] A person's visual perspective or point of view affords her a distinctive picture of things, but one that is, by its very nature as a perspective, limited and distorted by angle and distance. From one standpoint, the square table top appears rhomboid, from another one, it appears trapezoidal, and so on. We change our visual perspective, our standpoint, in order to help correct these deficiencies. What is interesting about taking seriously this now-common image of perspective is that it both gives us reason to seek out new and different viewpoints, and firmly anchors that reason in our overarching and guiding interest in overcoming distortion so as to arrive at a more nearly accurate conception of the properties of the thing viewed. Different perspectives afford us differing images of how a thing *looks*; their importance derives from how they provide data from which we can come to know how a thing *is*. Thus, we endorse the advice of some proponents of multicultural diversity so that we can broaden our horizons (to change the metaphor), but do so in a way that better positions us to reject the relativist, nihilistic, and latitudinarian rhetoric and rationales they offer.[33] The university's task, *pace*

31. Kimball, p. 63.

32. For a somewhat fuller exposition of this analogy and argument, see my "African-American Perspectives, Cultural Relativism, and Normative Issues."

33. The best critique of the extremist fringe of the diversification movement is in Searle, *op. cit.* See also the letters and Searle's rebuttal in *New York Review of Books*, February 14, 1991, pp. 48-50. Additional spirited debate against the new nihilism is in Tzvetan Todorov, "Crimes Against Humanities," *New Republic* July 3, 1989, and Kimball. Todorov nicely exposes the literally Orwellian nature of the anti-rationalists' attack on the notion of external reality, and the arrogant elitism of their insistence that the academy is somehow exempt from external criticism. (His discussion focuses on a pamphlet prepared in rebuttal to criticism from Bennett, and others: George Levine, et al., *Speaking for the Humanities* American Council of Learned Societies, Occasional Paper No. 7.) Kimball is a journalist with a scholarly background, not an academic, and one whose views I have criticized above. Nonetheless, it must be admitted that, unlike many of his professorial adversaries, Kimball has a keen logical mind and a healthy sense of the absurd. See especially his deflation of the deconstructionist's professed devotion to "close readings" in chapter four, and his admirable rebuttal, in his sixth and seventh chapters, of the assault that "The New Sophists" have launched against truth and objectivity.

some traditionalists, is not merely to transmit this culture. There may be much in this culture that needs to be altered or abandoned. Cornel West writes that "The political challenge is to articulate universality in a way that is not a mere smokescreen for someone else's particularity."[34] He is correct, but the challenge to the university is not merely, nor even in the first instance, political. Diversification of the curriculum is important, but important only insofar as it aids in the quest for truth. Once we abdicate that quest, diversification loses its most serious *intellectual* rationale. Why change what cannot be improved by making it more accurate? Why bother studying the differing ideas of others, if that study stands no chance of bringing our views closer to the truth? I am aware, of course, that answers have been offered – appeals to "solidarity," to continue the "conversation", etc. – but I know of no intellectual reason of notable seriousness.

There are other reasons as well to diversify the curriculum. One obvious pedagogical reason is that many students from groups historically excluded from the university may more readily "identify" with a work whose characters or author resemble her in respects she finds especially important in her own self-conception, or whose topics address matters internal to that self-conception. Of course, the university should not encourage a student to rest content with a narrow conception of her identity, one that reduces herself merely to her gender or race, for example, or in which those aspects play a defining role. To do so would be to acquiesce to one of social oppression's most dehumanizing assaults. However, all that is involved here is a familiar tension we encounter within pedagogy. How far should we go in taking measures to accommodate the material to the student, and when do we stop, lest we stoop to pandering to her uninformed preferences rather than meeting her educational needs?[35] The answer is not one that is easily stated in the abstract, but the question is by no means peculiar to the problem of curricular diversity. Students may come into the classroom constricted by shriveled self-images that assign inordinate importance to their race and sex. It will

34. West, p. 331 in Berman. He goes on to add that "we will trash older notions of objectivity, and not act as if one group or one community or one nation has a god's eye view of the world." Loc. cit. This suggests that we need new and better standards for objectivity, not the abandonment of objectivity in favor of a smug contentment with (or obsessive self-confinement to) a perspective afforded by some group.

35. The scholar and journalist Andrew Sullivan addresses this issue of reductionist self-conceptions as it arises for homosexuals. One of Sullivan's own concerns is to reconcile his traditionalist religious views and "neoliberal" to "neoconservative" political position with his homosexuality. See Maer Roshan's interview with him, "Andrew Sullivan Unedited," *NYQ* (February 9, 1992) pp. 25-31.

sometimes be necessary, therefore, to meet them and to appeal to them as they are if they are to leave the classroom with richer and more nuanced conceptions of themselves.

Let us now turn from integration of the curriculum to the second topic raised by proponents of diversification – affirmative action in hiring and admissions. This concerns the *composition* of the university community. Other contributors to this volume treat the legal issues in detail. I offer only a few thoughts. We may distinguish external goals served by programs of preferential hiring or admission from internal goals thereby served. The external goals are goals external to the university's mission of providing a humane education. A state university's adoption of a program of preferential student admissions, for example, might benefit society because the better educated minority population that results might generate a more equitable economic distribution, or a lessened incidence of violent crime. Internal goals are goals that are critical to the university's educational mission. For example, an institution might adopt programs of preferential admissions and appointment in the belief that students will learn better if they are exposed, both inside and outside the classroom, to students, teachers, and administrators who approach certain issues from a different point of view, in the sense of bringing beliefs, feelings, and projects influenced by experiences white males seldom have.

If this is correct, then we can avoid some of the worries that arise over whether preferential treatment policies replace the more qualified with the less qualified. For, insofar as some of the institution's goals in filling a certain slot are internal ones, for example, to help enhance its educational environment by making it more diverse, then considerations of race and gender can legitimately play a part in the evaluation process and thus become legitimate factors that help "qualify" some but not all applicants.

It is worth noting that, once again, our way of arguing for the position advanced by proponents of diversification undermines arguments offered by some of the more extreme elements within the movement. They maintain that persons admitted or hired under affirmative action programs are to be representatives of "the black point of view" or "the women's point of view."[36] However, to pigeon-hole these people would do them, their groups, and the institutions who accept them a grave disservice. It also does the people admitted or hired a disservice, because to pressure them to conform their thoughts to some pre-established norm or orthodoxy for members of their group is bound to hinder their individual

36. For a vigorous protest against this pressure to turn intellectuals from underrepresented minority groups into mere mouthpieces of the people, see Stephen Carter's *Reflections of an Affirmative Action Baby* (New York: Basic Books, 1991).

development as creative and independent thinkers. Moreover, it does the ethnic or gender group itself a disservice because it tends to deprive them of the sort of original thinking from which good leaders are most likely to emerge. It constrains the best educated among them to *follow* the thought of those they might lead. Most important for our purposes, as it concerns the aims of the university, to undertake programs of preferential admissions and hiring with such an objective does a disservice to the institutions themselves. It ill serves them, because it frustrates their aim of cultivating such intellectual (and sometimes moral) virtues as originality, creativity, independence of judgment, and intellectual courage.[37]

Points of view properly reside in individuals, not in groups, as conservative and liberal individualists rightly remind us. Moreover, an individual's point of view, that is, the assumptions, concerns, etc., she takes in thinking about a matter will be influenced by a variety of factors, some universal, some idiosyncratic, and some deriving from experiences she has had *because* she belongs to this or that ideological, or religious, or eth-

---

37. In contrast, a report from a budget committee of the faculty of the University of California at Berkeley suggests that the university's hiring policy target putting faculty members from underrepresented minority groups into ethnic studies programs, a move which threatens to ghettoize both the professors and their areas. (See Stephen Barnett, "Get Back," *New Republic*, February 18, 1991, p. 24.) Similarly, in a statement written for a coalition of Black teachers at the University of Texas at Austin, such faculty are explicitly assigned the "work" of "produc[ing] and teach[ing] specific knowledges [sic];...and contest[ing] dominant knowledges [sic]." (Ted Gordon and Wahneema Lubiano, "Statement of the Black Faculty Caucus," *Daily Texan*, May 3, 1990. Reprinted in Berman, pp. 249-57, at p. 254.) This suggests that African-American teachers, for example, are to teach "Black Knowledge" and to contest "White Knowledge." Now, in common sense and, standardly, in epistemic logic, it cannot be that if I know p you can know not-p, so Black Knowledge could not contradict White Knowledge. However, one sometimes fears that logic and common sense are to be discarded with other suspect forms of rationality in the new university. Paula Rothenberg, for one, warns ominously against the traditional curriculum's tendency to take "abstract, oppositional thinking as the paradigm for intellectual rigor." (Rothenberg, p. 266 in Berman.)

The Texas statement, by the way, seems to be an example of the tendency we mentioned above, and which D'Souza warns against, the temptation to insist that Third World cultures be viewed through interpretive schemes from nineteenth- and twentieth-century Western thought. It recommends, for example, that students study one (apparently, non-American) culture with "attention to the ways in which issues of social formations (race, gender, class, and sexuality) are played out. . . ." (p. 256) Similarly, "multiculturalism . . . requires study of race, gender, class, and sexuality" and is said to be about "how power is wielded between cultures. . . ." (p. 255) Here the controversial theses that race, gender, and even sexuality (presumably they mean heterosexuality, homosexuality, and perhaps other possibilities as well) are all "social formations" are not merely presupposed but are taken as presuppositions that should guide the construction of the curriculum. Similarly, it seems to be assumed that the most important or interesting thing about a culture is not how it does its work of cultivating the individual but simply what power arrangements it incorporates and sustains. And again, this highly debatable thesis is not merely endorsed, but is taken to be so securely established that it can properly shape and direct the curriculum.

nic, or gender (or other) grouping. However, while the point of view is the individual's, and will have been affected by diverse aspects of her life and thought, it remains true that *some* of these influences will be experiences neither universal nor idiosyncratic, but shared by and even characteristic of members of her racial or gender group. To the extent that one individual's point of view is especially shaped by such factors, we can identify a sense in which, perhaps, we can intelligibly say that her point of view is characteristically female or African-American or Hispanic (etc.). Note, however, that having such a point of view, as we conceive of it here, is a matter of *how* a person thinks, and of *why* she thinks as she does. What counts is the extent to which her reflection has been influenced by her intellectual response to experiences characteristic of, or especially common among, people of this or that group. Beyond this, it is doubtful that there is or can be such a thing as, for example, "thinking Black," where that is defined as a matter of content (unless what one means by it is only the uninteresting "thinking what Black people statistically tend to think"). However, it is possible for a person's thinking to be more or less influenced by things that happen to her, or that she does, or situations she is in, because she is Black.[38] This means that having, say, a perspective on an issue, a perspective that can meaningfully be called an African-American one, is not a matter of *what* the individual thinks, but *why* she

---

38. It may be relevant to mention a parallel possibility of "female thinking." In an important and influential book, Carol Gilligan has argued that, in our society, there may be modes of moral thinking females are more apt to employ than are men, especially ones emphasizing connectedness and caring over individualism and rights. (See Gilligan, *In a Different Voice: Psychological Theory and Women's Development* (Cambridge: Harvard University Press, 1982).) However, even some of her most thoughtful and sympathetic readers think the real value and insight of her work lies in its returning to our attention aspects of *any* sensible person's moral thought that regnant moral philosophy and psychology have, to their detriment, neglected. The importance of such work, then, is not to sketch out a map of "female moral thinking" to which a woman can advert lest she stray too far from her gender's norm, but better to enable us to devise comprehensive and adequate moral theories, ones that take due account of elements and types of moral thought our old theories disregarded. I think that something similar will likely hold true for ethnic perspectives. They may be important, but, if they are, their chief importance will lie in their enabling us better to recognize and to transcend the limitation of any such point of view. ". . . [J]ust to be an independent postcolonial Arab, or black, or Indonesian is not a program, nor a process, nor a vision. It is no more than a convenient starting point from which the real work, the hard work, might begin." Edward Said (in Berman), pp. 180-81. He later elaborates, "One of the great pleasures for those who read and study literature is the discovery of longstanding norms in which all cultures known to me concur: such things as style and performance. . . ." (p. 188) We might only add that the search for further universal values, and for values whose absence from certain groups is a tragedy for them, is one of the great motivations for a study of diverse ways of living and dying.

thinks it – of how her thinking is affected (if it is affected at all) by things she has done or experienced because she is African-American.[39]

In thinking about preferential admissions, it also vital that we remember the crucial difference between the discrimination James Meredith faced when, as a black man, he sought to desegregate the University of Mississippi in the early 1960s, and such "reverse discrimination" as it is alleged Allan Bakke faced a decade later when race-based set-asides at the medical school of University of California at Davis may have helped block his admission there. Meredith was, and Bakke was not, a victim of

---

39. This is a point obviously lost on some of those who so vociferously opposed President Bush's recent nomination of Justice Clarence Thomas to the United States Supreme Court. Some suggested, for example, that there could be no legitimate reason for the president to appoint a black person to the court if he or she was a neo-conservative. (Arch Puddington attributes such a remark to Eleanor Holmes Norton in Puddington, "Clarence Thomas and the Blacks," *Commentary*, February 1992, pp. 28-33.)

A claim of this latter sort is more a partisan posture than an intellectual position. Still, even if one treats it with undeserved seriousness, one line of response is obvious: it may be desirable to have someone on the court who informs its decision-making process with reflections influenced by common elements of African-American experience, because these may be important things for the judges to take account of. The court may, of course, come to the same decision as it otherwise would, if the African-American appointee shares their jurisprudential philosophy, but the court affects our polity not only by what it decides, but also by how it reasons and by how well and to whom it can persuasively defend its conclusions. Such niceties will not matter, of course, to those to whom only results are important. But that merely shows the poverty of their normative thought.

It may be that some ways in which one's ethnic experience might affect a person's thought are profoundly undesirable, of course. Shelby Steele, often unwillingly labeled a neoconservative, discusses a number of supposed psychological mechanisms he thinks operate in Black people he deems over-sensitive on racial issues – emotional "recomposition," "compensatory grandiosity," "race-holding," "integration shock," etc. (See Steele, *The Content of Our Character* (New York: St. Martin's Press, 1990), esp. chaps. 2, 3, 4.) On the other side, for a different group of Black thinkers, it is those they find insufficiently "conscious" of their Blackness who get the theoretical couch treatment. The press reports that Price Cobbs describes a disorder he calls "Token Black Syndrome," whose victims (mainly first-generation status-achievers) endorse negative stereotypes about most Black people from whom they consequently strive to maximize their difference, and Ronald Hall thinks that he has discovered a similar "bleaching syndrome," whose "symptoms" include a total repudiation of other Black people and identification with White ones. (See Jack E. White, "The Pain of Being Black," *Time*, September 16, 1991, pp. 25-27.) There is ample reason to be skeptical of all this. Much of it seems merely to be an effort to psychologize politics by identifying supposed mental disorders in people with whose politics the various authors disagree. This bait-and-switch tactic allows one to speculate airily before one's audience about what mechanisms drive an intellectual opponent to think as she does, thus distracting that audience from one's failure to have done the hard intellectual work of rebutting *what the opponent has said*. Such a ploy is always tempting, since it offers the false hope of enabling one to dispense with the necessity of having to defend one's own ideas on their merits, and psychologists from Freud on have succumbed to it. Nonetheless, however suspicious we should be about these claims, there is always a chance that some element of truth may lurk behind all the bluster about "syndromes." Whether or not such disorders actually exist, their possibility can serve to remind us that race can affect thought for the worst.

state policies rooted in vicious racial animosity. This is the core evil of racism, I think, a fact obscured by the term's frequent misuse as a synonym for "racial prejudice." Racial prejudice – that is, pre-judgment on the basis of race – is a cognitive matter, one that takes on moral import, on those occasions when it bears moral import, from the racial hatred that disposes some people too readily to form negative opinions about members of a particular race. Understanding racism in this way, as fundamentally a failure of the heart rather than a failure of reason, helps us better to fathom what it is to discriminate *against* a group or against a member of a group on account of her membership.[40] An act of racial discrimination (that is, race-sensitive discrimination) occurs when one makes a distinction on the basis of race. (This need not always be conscious. The real reason you do not rent me a room may be that I am Black – that may be what it is about me that turns you off – even if you convince yourself it was for some other reason.) Racial discrimination is wrong whether race hatred directly motivates the distinction, as in the Jim Crow laws, or indirectly, as when, for example, a person's racist antipathy leads her to believe that the school's moral or academic level will be unduly lowered by admission of Black people.[41] It is in such cases that we can properly talk of discriminating *against* certain people, and against the groups to which they belong, for it is in these cases that the agent's discriminatory

40. This way of thinking about racism and discrimination occurred to me in the course of reflecting on Anthony Appiah's subtle exposition of a doxastic conception of racism in Appiah, "Racisms," in *Anatomy of Racism*, ed. David T. Goldberg (Minneapolis: University of Minnesota Press, 1990), pp. 3-17. I critically examine several recent accounts of racism, including Appiah's, and develop an alternative approach in two papers now nearing completion, "Current Conceptions of Racism" and "The Heart of Racism," respectively.

Both my view and Appiah's are plausible to the extent that they allow persons of any class or race to be racists. However, nowadays some prefer to conceive of racism in terms of systematized relationships of economic power. When racism is defined in such a way, it turns out that, while a disempowered "person of color may discriminate against white people or even hate them, his or her behavior or attitude cannot be called 'racist.'" (Paula Rothenberg, *Racism and Sexism: An Integrated Study* (New York: St. Martin's Press, 1988), p. 6). That sort of view has little to recommend it, beyond the dubious advantage of offering some measure of comfort to those bigots and apostles of racial hatred who are Asian or Black. It seems to stem from the mistakes, mentioned earlier, of collapsing moral categories (here, racism) into political ones, and reducing all political matters to relationships of (usually, economic) power. In contrast, just a few decades ago, even the radical left conceded the possibility that, when racism is systematized (as, *contra* Rothenberg, it need not be), its victims might respond with what Sartre called their own "anti-racist racism." (See Appiah, "The Conservation of 'Race,'" *Black American Literature Forum*, vol. 23 (1989), pp. 37-60, at p. 58 note 9.)

41. For a subtle discussion of this phenomenon, see Adrian Piper, "Higher Order Discrimination," in *Identity, Character, and Morality*, edited by Owen Flanagan and Amelie Rorty (Cambridge: MIT Press, 1990).

behavior is motivated in part by her hostility to the interests of members of the affected group.

This gives us reason to suspect that rhetoric about so-called "reverse discrimination" against Whites trades unfairly on the association of the term "discrimination" with the racist discrimination against Blacks that people like Meredith contested. The new racial discrimination, if that is what it is, is not *racist* discrimination; that is, it is not based in race hatred. This does not make it morally acceptable, of course, but it does mean that it is not unjust in the way that Jim Crow discrimination was. A new moral argument is needed, and my suspicion is that some people hope to trade on the negative connotations that the term "discrimination" inherited from the civil rights movement's struggle against racism in order to avoid their having to supply, defend, and articulate the argument they need for their criticism of affirmative action.[42]

On the other hand, we should admit that defenders of affirmative action tend to mount an inadequate response to the charge that preferential treatment programs are unjust because they deprive some people (usually Whites or males) of benefits on account of their race or gender. It is an inadequate response to this, the most serious of the arguments against preferential treatment programs, to say simply that such programs are chiefly intended neither to reward the deserving nor punish the guilty, but are aimed at serving the sound social goal of public

---

42. On the view taken here, many forms of preference will turn out to be licit, and even supererogatory. Schools with special histories, identities, and commitments – historically Black institutions, women's colleges, universities with strong denominational affiliations, etc. – will understandably and properly employ special criteria in determining what makes for a desirable member of the university (student, faculty, and administrator). The same can be true of programs within a school. Once properly understood, talk of unjustly discriminating *against* members of group A will often get no purchase in these contexts, where the point is rather specially to seek out members of group B. It is, of course, a mistake to infer from the fact that a policy favors members of group B the conclusion that it discriminates against members of group A.

Of course, sometimes what is presented as preference for those in one group is really only disguised animus against members of a different group, as is likely to be the case in White Students Unions. (For a journalistic report on this recent campus phenomenon, see Valerie Richardson, "'Whites' seek multicultural niche," *Washington Times*, March 28, 1992, pp. A1, A8. At some point, should multiculturalism become the order of the day, there maybe valid reason for specialized study of then-neglected Euro-American cultures. Right now, however, this movement seems to be grounded more in racial resentment and antagonism.) My major point is simply that there is a moral difference, one which today's loose talk of "discrimination" tends to conceal, between, on the one hand, policies genuinely motivated by a special concern for, or interest in, members of one group, and, on the other, group-hatred masquerading as favoritism. That does not commit me to claiming that this difference will always be easy to discern. However, I should also add that it will not always be so difficult to tell real and morally unobjectionable favoritism from the phony.

utility.[43] It may be that such policies are best advocated on such for-ward-looking grounds, rather than as reparations for past injustices. Nonetheless, such a rationale does nothing to convey why this means of pursuing the goal is not unjust to the Whites or males who lose out under affirmative action programs.[44] Similarly, it will not do merely to point out the many other exceptions within the university to merito-cratic evaluation – slots reserved for the children of alumni or donors, etc. Even if these other exceptions are all morally unobjectionable, which is open to question, the opponents of affirmative action think that depriving people of benefits because of *racial* classification is espe-cially troublesome morally, even as the Supreme Court has held that it requires "strict scrutiny" in the law. More direct, but ultimately even less successful, is the strategy of confronting the charge of injustice head-on by denying that those who lose out under preferential pro-grams are "innocent victims," because they have inherited undeserved advantages from the discriminatory structures and practices of the past.[45] Unfortunately, however true this premise may be, the necessary con-clusion does not follow. "Innocent" properly contrasts either with "guilty," as in its legal use, or with "currently engaged in doing harm," as the term's etymological root in "nocent" (harming) indicates. However, the fact that a person such as Allan Bakke may have inherit-ed a comparatively advantaged socio-economic position from his fore-bears entails neither that he was guilty of any wrongdoing nor that he was, at the time he applied to medical school, engaged in doing harm.[46] So, this line of response cannot avail.

---

43. For an argument of this sort, see Robert Fullinwinder's contribution to this volume.

44. Fullinwinder may think that he has responded to this worry by pointing out that such "victims" of preference programs as Allan Bakke are randomly selected, not invidi-ously singled out. However, this strategy surely takes too far the post-Rawlsian tendency to reduce justice to fairness. One could as well (that is to say, as poorly) defend the decision to kill you for the good of the group if we could just show that we have good reason to offer up *some* sacrifice and assure you that your name was randomly selected, say, because it was drawn from a hat containing everyone's name.

Tom Beauchamp cites some recent empirical studies to support his contention that preference programs are justified as correctives against the likelihood of present-day race-based discrimination. This is an appeal to justice, not merely to social utility, but not to backwards-looking considerations of justice. (See Beauchamp, "Goals and Quotas in Hiring and Promotion," a paper presented to the Kennedy Institute of Ethics at Georgetown University, February, 1992.)

45. For this strategy, see Sharon Rush's contribution to this volume.

46. One might protest that Bakke *was* doing harm. Wasn't he keeping others down, after all, by holding more than his fair share? But suppose he was. These still were not things he was "engaged in doing," because these were not actions of his (even if we elect to use action-imagery and the active voice in describing them).

What is needed instead is a challenge to the assumption that depriving someone of a benefit because of race or gender is *eo ipso* unjust. This assumption, after all, is not obvious on its face. What motivates it primarily is the now-spontaneous condemnation of the sort of race-based deprivation against which the civil rights movement fought. However, if, as I have argued, the wrong of Jim Crow is best understood as having been grounded in the racial antipathy that motivated its practices and laws, then a differently motivated program may well pass moral muster, even if it is true that, under its regime, racial classifications will sometimes play a role in some people's missing out on some social benefits.[47]

The third of the topics pertaining to campus diversification that we will treat concerns campus speech and conduct, and the codes for their regulation. This involves the *behavior* of the members of the university community in their dealings one with another. Virtuous people are sensitive to others' sensitivities, to their vulnerabilities. Moreover, one way in which we learn to be virtuous is by acting as a sensitive person acts. Thus, a community properly expects its members to conduct themselves in a certain way and finds certain other ways unacceptable. We cannot change hearts, the real business of ethics, solely or even chiefly by imposing rules of conduct, of course. Indeed, to the extent that a school enforces such rules, it manifests its failure adequately to assist its members in the formation of such virtues as civility, respect, and sensitivity. Nonetheless, it is worth noting that even if a regulation cannot generally be enforced, due to the way in which its enforcement would endanger liberties, it still may make an important contribution.[48] Simply having a standard codified can show that the group takes

---

47. Recently, many have urged race-blind ways of increasing the numbers of students, faculty, and administrators from underrepresented groups. (The sociologist William Julius Wilson is known for his advocacy of this position, and his has lately been joined by several other voices, both liberal and conservative, from academia and politics. See the brief journalistic account of the neoliberal thought by Anthony Flint, "Kerry speech springs from new school on race," *Boston Globe* April 5, 1992, p. 24. For a political conservative's defense of this position, see D'Souza, *Illiberal Education*, chap. 8). Given the ugly history of racial classification in this country, there may be good social reasons for preferring such race-blind programs, when they can be effective. However, some scholars have called this condition into question. Using statistics on ethnic and economic distributions of higher Scholastic Aptitude Test scores, Andrew Hacker argues that such policies are unlikely to work. "Let us suppose that the nation's most selective colleges set aside a total of 75,000 scholarships for low-income students, to be bestowed on a race-blind basis, according to academic merit. If SAT scores were used to assess that capacity, virtually all of these awards would have to go to Asians and whites." (Hacker, "Playing the Racial Card," *New York Review of Books* (October 24, 1991), pp. 14–18, at 18.) If he is correct, then arguments like mine that race-based favoritism need not be morally objectionable become more important.

any violations quite seriously, something that in principle *justifies* punishment.[49] These codes, as I envision them, ought to concern themselves both with *what* thoughts are expressed and with *how* they are expressed. The latter breaches are, I think, better candidates for a punitive response. A sensible person who holds a belief that members of this or that group are inferior, for example, may remain open to hearing arguments that her belief is false, even if she holds this belief because of some intellectual/moral vice. One who contemptuously expresses this opinion, however, indicates not simply an opinion, but also a callousness that calls not merely for reconsideration but for penitence and reform.

In this connection, it is worth observing a salient difference between hate speech and speech that is merely offensive. Whether your saying something constitutes offensive speech depends on what its (actual or probable) effects are. You say something offensive only if what you say does (or reasonably would) offend. This is, as philosophers say in other contexts, a forward-looking and an outward-looking consideration; it is a matter of the speech act's results.[50] In contrast, to determine whether, in making a certain utterance, I engaged in *hate* speech, we must look to

48. Ehrenreich claims to have found a "culture" of "political correctness" on campus that encourages students "to rely on administration-enforced rules to stop offensive speech and to enforce a new, and quite admirable, kind of civility. . . . [T]he problem is: rules don't work. If you outlaw the use of the term 'girl' instead of 'woman,' you're not going to do a thing about the sexist attitudes underneath. . . . The only route is through persuasion, education, and organizing." (Ehrenreich, p. 335 in Berman.) My quarrel with this is that rules, even seldom-enforced ones, can themselves play a part in this educational endeavor, and the processes of drafting, adopting, explaining, and defending such rules can constitute an important forms of organizing and instruction.

49. The continuing influence of some early modernist legal theory, with its reduction of *liability* to punishment to the punishment's *probability*, and its understanding of law as merely enforced commands, obscures several purposes that a restriction may legitimately serve. It may, for example, be largely educational. Drawing a line to demarcate those forms of conduct the group or institution deems intolerable may help the group to define itself, to achieve greater self-understanding, and to commit itself to certain ideals. The restriction can serve these goals even when, because of the ways in which strict enforcement may endanger proper liberty of expression, breaches are seldom punished. The aims of self-definition and commitment may be advanced merely by the restriction's solemn affirmation that these forms of conduct *deserve* punishment. (The classical sources for legal positivism, of course, are John Austin's *Province of Jurisprudence Determined* and the legal writings of Jeremy Bentham. More recent, revisionist treatments of positivism, such as H.L.A. Hart's *Concept of Law* (Oxford: Oxford University Press, 1960) and Joseph Raz's *Concept of a Legal System*, 2nd ed. (Oxford: Oxford University Press, 1980) have some measure of success in avoiding the excesses and inadequacies that attend simplistic reductionism.)

50. In J.L. Austin's terminology, verbally offending someone is a perlocutionary action, one that we perform *by* (rather than *in*) saying what we say. (See Austin, *How to Do Things with Words*, rev. ed. (Oxford: Oxford University Press), 1975.) For an application of Austin's theory of speech acts to the topic of campus regulation of hate speech, see Andrew Altman's contribution to this volume.

45

why I said it. This is a backward-looking and an inward-looking inquiry. For it is its motivation that makes what I do an act of hate, just as it is their motivation that makes some actions acts of kindness, of revenge, and so on. Hate is fundamentally a will to injure. Thus, it follows that we cannot pick out a certain verbal formula and say that to utter it is *eo ipso* to engage in hate speech. That will have to depend on why I utter it, specifically, on whether I do so from hate. Of course, the use of some verbal formulas, we are entitled to presume, is motivated by hate. This applies most saliently to expressions involving what Andrew Altman calls "slurs and epithets."[51] *How* I said what I said can be an important clue to *why* I said it. Someone who says that homosexuality is a disease *may* be performing an act of hate. It may well be an act of hate, for example, if she says it in order to injure homosexuals in their self-esteem. It may also be an act of hate if it has a more complicated origin. Suppose the speaker hates homosexuals because they are homosexuals, and this hatred predisposes her to believe the worst about them, perhaps because of psychological pressure to justify her antipathy to herself. In that case, although she may say what she does without any intent to injure, she will still be acting from hatred, in that her words will still have hatred in its motivational history and structure. However, another person may assert the same proposition without committing an act of hate at all. Perhaps she is merely voicing a reasonably held opinion in medical taxonomy, deriving perhaps from her own scientific consideration.[52] Plainly, to dismiss her utterance (or, worse yet, to dismiss *her*) as "homophobic", without further investigation, is unjustified.[53]

Those whom the academy has historically excluded may be more vulnerable to incautious remarks, and may well need special protection. Still, the establishment of special protection for some groups must be done in a balanced way, lest a proper aversion to "blaming the victim" render an institution incapable of blaming wrongdoers. Note that someone who occupies the passive status of victim in one set of relationships – say, as a

51. See Altman's contribution to this volume.

52. A case of this sort was discussed at the Baltimore conference. In it, as I recall, the speaker was a science student.

53. This is not to deny that there will be contexts in which it is legitimate to suspect that an individual's eager embrace of unflattering opinions about homosexuality (or about Africa, femaleness, etc.) results from a general antipathy to homosexuals (or to Black people, or women). My point is simply that in the absence of abusive language, it is itself both prejudiced and unfair to jump to the conclusion that the speaker suffers from "homophobia." Surely, the university is ill-served when proper concern for the sensitivities of historically marginalized peoples forecloses legitimate study of such topics as the medical and moral status of homosexual conduct.

victim of racism – may nevertheless be the victimizer in another, as when she treats a member of the more advantaged group insensitively. People often say that "the personal is political", meaning that even intimate relationships should be analyzed using such traditionally political categories as power, equality, rights, and autonomy.[54] However, I think the deeper truth is that the political is personal. By this I mean that even in evaluating interactions between the dominant and the oppressed, in these or in other cultures, we would do best to look mainly at whether the participants are responding with kindness, respect, good-will, gentleness, and other personal virtues. It is to these matters that we must direct our atten-

Indeed, using the pseudo-medical term "homophobia" to characterize a speaker's moral or social criticism of homosexuals or homosexual conduct is itself instructive. It implies that the speaker's beliefs stem from a phobia, that is, from a disordered and irrational blend of fear and hatred. If there is such a mental disorder, then it may be true that, in a given instance, it motivates an individual's thought and speech. However, to justify such a "diagnosis" one would actually have to carry out the investigation into the individual speaker's rationale and motivation. Too often, however, the term "homophobic" is used as a rhetorical smear, designed to obviate the need to ask for and seriously listen to the speaker's reasons for her opinion.

It would, I suspect, be best to dispense with the term altogether. Marshall Kirk and Hunter Madsen urge use of the more precise term "homohaters." They write, "'Homophobia' is a comforting word, isn't it? It suggests that . . . all who oppose, threaten, and persecute us [that is, homosexuals] are actually scared of us! . . . [However, f]ear need have noting to do with it. A well-designed study by researchers S. Shields and R. Harriman . . . demonstrat[ed] that although some 'homonegative' males respond to homosexual stimuli with the 'tell-tale racing heart' of phobia, plenty of others don't." They condemn "the specious 'diagnosis'" of homophobia as a "medically exculpatory euphemism," and offer a proposal: "Let's reserve the term 'homophobia' for the psychiatric cases to which it really applies, and find a more honest label for the attitudes, words, and acts of hatred that are, after all, the real problem." As for their own linguistic procedure, "when we really do mean 'fear of homosexuals,' [then] 'homophobia' it will be; when we're talking about hatred of homosexuals, we'll speak (without the hyphen) of 'homohatred,' 'homohating,' and 'homohaters.' We urge the reader to follow suit." (See Kirk and Madsen, *After the Ball: How America Will Conquer Its Fear and Hatred of Gays in the '90s* (New York: Doubleday, 1989), pp. xxii-xxiii.) This is sensible advice, though some caveats are in order. First, we should bear in mind that not every fear is a phobia. Second, even the quasi-scientific term "homonegative" tends to lump together such very different matters as (1) a person's personal aversion to her own engaging in homosexual activities; (2) her concern over perceived social effects of other peoples' homosexual conduct; and (3) her holding the belief that such conduct is morally impermissible. Hatred of homosexual persons is normally immoral (although, as Kirk and Madsen point out, to see it simply as a medical condition tends to exculpate). Disapproval of homosexual practices, whether on medical, moral, or religious grounds, is a different matter, however, and it may often be an unrelated one. Third, to use the prefix "homo" to mean "homosexual" is objectionable for obvious reasons, so it seems preferable to speak of "homosexual-haters" and "homosexual-hatred," retaining the hyphen.

54. For an intelligent journalistic treatment of some recent feminist thought on the relationship between the personal and the political, see Karen Lehrman, "The Feminist Mystique," *New Republic*, March 16, 1992, pp. 30-34.

tion if we are serious about ethics, whether inside the university's walls or beyond them.[55]

My aim here has been to defend much of the new program of multi-cultural diversification in a way that can appeal to liberal (and even to neoconservative) thinkers who embrace a traditional conception of the university's mission. At the same time, my effort has been to save the multiculturalist movement from its more extreme and vocal advocates, the ones who rely on various combinations of nihilism, relativism, skepticism, and anti-rationalism to make what often turns out to be an incoherent and discreditable case.[56]

55. In a book in progress, Michael Slote develops a promising account of morality as "agent-based," that is, such that claims about what moral duty requires and about what ultimately constitutes human welfare are to be understood in terms of human virtue.

56. I am grateful to the University of Baltimore's Hoffberger Center and its directors for inviting me to contribute. I am also indebted to David DeGrazia, to Laura Garcia, and to audiences at the University of Baltimore, at Georgetown University's Kennedy Institute of Ethics, at Boston College, and at the College of Saint Francis in Illinois for stimulating discussion and suggestions when I later read versions of the paper. During the time I worked on this project, I received generous sabbatical assistance from Georgetown University, and fellowship support from the National Endowment for the Humanities (grant #FA-30573) and from Harvard University's Program in Ethics and the Professions.

4
Pragmatism, Cultural Criticism and the Idea of the Postmodern University

Robert Justin Lipkin

If we see knowing not as having an essence, to be described by scientists and philosophers, but rather as a right, by current standards, to believe, then we are well on the way to seeing *conversation* as the ultimate context within which knowledge is to be understood.

Richard Rorty[1]

The pursuit of learning is not a race in which the competitors jockey for the best place, it is not even an argument or symposium; it is a conversation. And the peculiar virtue of a university (as a place of many studies) is to exhibit it in this character, each study appearing as a voice whose tone is neither tyrannous nor plangent, but humble and conversable. A conversation does not need a chairman, it has no predetermined course, we do not ask what is it "for," and we do not judge its excellence by its conclusion; it has no conclusion, but is always put by for another day. Its integration is not superimposed but springs from the quality of the voices which speak, and its value lies in the relics it leaves behind in the minds of those who participate.

Michael Oakeshott[2]

We cannot permanently divest ourselves of the intellectual habits we take on and wear when we assimilate the culture of our own time and place. But intelligent furthering of culture demands that we take some off, that we inspect them critically to see what they are made of and what wearing them does to us.

John Dewey[3]

1. R. Rorty, *Philosophy and the Mirror of Nature* 389 (1979).
2. M. Oakeshott, *The Idea of a University* in *The Voice of Liberal Learning: Michael Oakeshott on Education* 95, 96 (T. Fuller, ed. 1989) (hereinafter cited as M. Oakeshott, *The Voice of Liberal Learning*).
3. J. Dewey, *Experience and Nature* 35 (1929).

For every voice you've ever heard, there's a thousand without a word.

Fleetwood Mac[4]

Introduction

American society is presently in the throes of a vast cultural war,[5] a war that seeks to define what it means to be an American.[6] The parties to this conflict are diverse and unrepentant; and the war is being fought on many different levels in diverse contexts.[7] The complexity of this cultural war strongly resists systematic explanation, let alone any obvious theoretical solution. Still, it might be possible to provide a theoretical framework for analyzing the problems underlying this conflict that might in turn suggest possible solutions. No doubt any theoretical framework will oversimplify by stressing certain features of the controversy to the exclusion of others.[8] Though a theoretical framework to the controversy inevitably has these failings, it may nonetheless illuminate the issues involved. At least, that is my hope in this article.

The American cultural war is between two familiar adversaries.[9] One party seeks to restore traditional values such as God, the family, patrio-

4. *Blue Letter, Fleetwood Mac* (1975).

5. R. Bork, *The Tempting of America: The Political Seduction of the Law* 10 (1990).

6. J. Davison, *Cultural Wars* 50 (1991) (arguing that this cultural war is an attempt to define "the meaning of America, who we have been in the past, who we are now, and . . . who we, as a nation, will aspire to become in the new millennium." This cultural war is a "struggle to redefine the national identity." A. Schlesinger, *The Disuniting of America* 2 (1991). Consider:

The schools and colleges of the republic train the citizens of the future. They have always been battlegrounds for debates over beliefs, philosophies and values. Today our educational institutions face intense pressure to revise academic curricula to meet the needs – and demands – of an increasingly pluralistic society.

What students learn in schools vitally affects other arenas of American life – the way they see and treat other Americans, the way they conceive the purpose of the republic. The debate about the curriculum is a debate about what it means to be an American. What is ultimately at stake is the shape of the American future.

Id. at 2-3.

7. This suggests that it might be more accurate to call the present conflict a series of cultural wars. In a conflict of such vast proportions, each side commits excesses, mistakes, and at times exhibits bad faith. This should not dissuade the unaligned from taking sides. Partisanship is warranted just as long as everyone keeps in mind that taking sides does not commit one to each and every claim endorsed by that side.

8. In this regard, I cannot discuss every important aspect of the controversy even as they pertain to the issues I do discuss. For example, I do not discuss whether a multicultural program satisfies its goals when alternative cultural perspectives are presented in a core curriculum, though Western culture remains dominant. Similarly, I do not explore whether

tism, and orthodoxy as the defining characteristics of American culture. According to this perspective, traditional values are all that is needed to resolve the social problems plaguing contemporary life.[10] Alternatively, their opponents see hierarchy and domination as the source of these social problems and seek instead a resurgent commitment to equality and liberty in order to give the downtrodden and excluded a fairer share of the social pie.[11] This war between traditionalists and progressives pervades all aspects of contemporary social life.[12] In some quarters these adversaries have become enemies, no longer interested in persuading the other, but instead directing their diatribes at the unconverted and unaligned.

In the American experience, traditionalism and progressivism have been vying with one another for control of the dominant culture since

multicultural education precludes Western culture playing a central role in humanistic studies. Moreover, I do not discuss whether Western culture is sufficiently self-critical to make the argument in this paper otiose. Perhaps, more importantly, I do not discuss multiculturalism in primary and secondary education. Indeed, I believe the argument in this essay has different implications for pre-university education than it does for university education. Neither do I discuss the implications multiculturalism has in providing a hospitable educational environment, inculcating values of mutual respect, generating self-confidence, self-respect, and self-esteem. For a thoughtful discussion of these values see Robert K. Fullinwider, *Multiculturalism Education*, 1991 *U. Chi. Leg. For.* 75. Additionally, I do not explore the possibility that one or both parties stick to their position on grounds of self-interest. See M. Kempton, *Another Kind of Multiculturalism*, *N.Y. Rev. Bks.* (arguing that opponents of multiculturalism are intransigent because they do not welcome the amount of work required to become proficient in the literature, say, of non-Western cultures).

9. The question of how many parties are involved in this controversy is itself controversial and dependent upon the level of generality at which we describe the conflict. On its most general level I believe there are two parties. When we describe the controversy in more concrete terms, the number of possible parties increases. Matters are compounded if we insist that the parties to these cultural wars divide nicely into the left and right. See John B. Judis, *Telling the left from the right in these times*, *In These Times*, vol. 15, p. 2 (1991). The matter is usually more complex than such a dichotomy permits.

10. Traditionalists generally contend that their values are the only true values, and, therefore, should prevail over conflicting values. Usually, traditionalists believe that it is not sufficient for *them* to abide by their values. Others, even those opposed to traditional values, must also adopt them whether they want to or not. For example, it is not good enough for Christians to abstain from buying alcoholic beverages on Sunday. In their view, no one should be able to buy them. In this way, traditionalists seek to control the value choices, indeed the value environment, of others.

11. On a more abstract plane, traditionalists and progressives both might agree that equality and liberty are fundamental values shared by all. But such abstract agreement is compatible with disagreement over concrete cases; hence, agreement on abstract matters gives us much less than we might have otherwise desired.

12. It is a struggle that is "taking place . . . in our politics, our voluntary organizations, our churches, our language – and in no arena more crucial than our system of education." A. Schlesinger, *The Disuniting of America*, *supra* note 6 at 2-3.

the inception of the republic.[13] Currently, two factors in this ongoing cultural struggle, however, have seriously exacerbated the tension between these competing ideals. First, in the last century, and especially in the past two decades, the homogeneity of the American population has changed drastically. We will soon no longer be a mostly Caucasian, mostly European people.[14] The question naturally arises as to how our essentially Western or European culture should accommodate these novel, diverse, and sometimes antagonistic cultural perspectives. The second element is the relatively widespread belief that we have entered a postmodern phase of historical development.[15] For those who resist nihilism and radical skepticism, pragmatism, of one form or another, typifies the constructive intellectual tenor of the postmodern age.[16]

As an antimetaphysical and antiepistemological perspective, pragmatism counsels us to revise our conception of the roles truth, knowledge, and reality play in our world views. Rather than insisting on a foundationalist picture – that an indubitable reality grounds our knowledge of science and ethics – pragmatism counsels us to seek as many different kinds of objections to our beliefs and values as possi-

13. In a perfectly trivial sense orthodoxy always wins this battle. Since if the dominant culture is challenged by progressivism, and progressivism wins, short of total revolution, orthodoxy coopts the progressive challenges, and these changes then become orthodoxy.

14. The question here is whether it makes sense to speak of Western culture as one tradition, or whether it really is a compilation of several different, often incompatible, traditions. See C. West, *Diverse New World* in *Debating P.C.* 326, 327-28 (P. Berman, ed. 1992) [hereinafter *Debating P.C.*] Although it is true that a comprehensive analysis of the terms "Western culture" and "European culture" will reveal multifarious strains of disparate cultural elements, I do not believe that this dissolves the usefulness of these terms for present purposes. However, I cannot argue this point here. Suffice it to say that the terms "Western culture" and "European culture" are, in my view, posits, the utility of which vary in different contexts. In this context, I submit, these posits are useful, enabling us to critically examine whether the central role of the university should be to inculcate the dominant culture's values, or, instead, to provide the most sophisticated and comprehensive critique of these values possible. Similarly, using these terms for the purposes I intend does not preclude recognizing the problems associated with a "center-periphery model" of culture. See H. Gates, Jr., *Loose Canons* 191 (1992).

15. Postmodernity rejects faith in reason as a neutral methodological device for conducting cultural inquiry; consequently, postmodernity is antifoundationalist, antimetaphysical, and antiepistemological. Instead, it emphasizes the contingent, the particular, and the efficacious.

16. This claim concerning the relationship between pragmatism and post-modern intellectual inquiry is not obvious or uncontroversial. Some writers believe that some form of radical skepticism or nihilism typifies the postmodern imagination. Although I cannot argue for my conception of the relation between pragmatism and post-modernity here, the conception of cultural criticism developed in this essay should have a special hold on individuals who are sympathetic to pragmatism and see it as the penultimate form of post-modern inquiry. For an interesting argument against post-modern pragmatism, see C. Norris, *What's Wrong with Postmodernism: Critical Theory and the Ends of Philosophy* (1990).

ble. In this view, a belief or value is justified and reliable only when it has successfully overcome the best objections a particular era has to offer.[17]

Pragmatism has implications for cultural criticism and cultural criticism is designed to replace cultural warfare. Foundationalism regards the health of a culture to be a function of how well it represents the social and physical world.[18] Pragmatic cultural criticism, on the contrary, regards a culture to be healthy when it successfully survives all criticism to which it is subjected. The notion of a healthy culture in contradistinction to an unhealthy or pathological culture, is not intended as a rigid oppositional dichotomy capable of classifying cultures into those that are exclusively healthy and those that are exclusively pathological. The distinction is not absolute but is contextual and heuristic. In short, it is use-

---

17. There is no way to provide a formal explication of the notion of the "best" criticism; instead, this notion must remain intuitive and contestable.

18. There are two important types of foundationalism: strong foundationalism and weak foundationalism. Strong foundationalism maintains that reason and reality justify our beliefs and values. In this instance, reason and reality are metaphysical presuppositions of truth, the apprehension of which is established epistemically. Weak foundationalism, on the other hand, maintains that reason and reality are a logical (and therefore trivial) consequence of having justified beliefs and values. Reason and reality are explicated epistemically as features of justified beliefs and values. For the strong foundationalist, reason and reality justify our beliefs and values, while according to weak foundationalism our beliefs and values are justified by some other factor, such as coherence. Both views are foundationalist in that they contend that reason can in principle settle controversial issues in science and ethics.

Denying foundationalism does not, as some suggest, involve contradiction. My view is *not* that there is a rationally compelling argument showing that reason is inadequate. Indeed, I believe that reason, understood broadly to include deductive and inductive logic, experience, imagination and so forth, helps us resolve many important questions. However, reason is limited by the values that drive it. And no one has even come close to demonstrating that there are a complete set of values that it is contrary to reason to ignore. Consequently, reason is too thin a conception to help us resolve the important controversial issues presently confronting society. See Robert Justin Lipkin, *Beyond Skepticism, Foundationalism and the New Fuzziness: The Role of Wide Reflective Equilibrium in Legal Theory*, 75 Cornell L. Rev. 811 (1990).

Nor does abandoning foundationalism mean that inquiry must come to a halt. Rather, on pragmatic grounds, inquiry flourishes, with this single qualification. We need to seek consensus, and there are many ways to try to persuade people to adopt a particular view, for example, art, narrative, information, and appealing to values your adversary shares with you. What pragmatism insists upon, however, is the inevitability of inquiry coming to an end concerning certain controversies without necessarily persuading your adversary to change his mind. Moreover, it comes to an end without either you or your adversary violating any of the important elements of inquiry. Pragmatism, together with certain assumptions about the world, entails an ineliminable form of skepticism concerning the possibility of finding rationally compelling answers to many important practical controversies. *Id.* Unlike traditional skepticism, however, pragmatism finds value in continuing to converse about our differences in a non-threatening, open, and undistorted fashion.

ful to describe some dominant cultures as relatively healthy and others as relatively pathological.

Interestingly, traditionalism or orthodoxy has just as much riding on maintaining a healthy culture as progressivism. Therefore, orthodoxy should always welcome radical critique. A pragmatic conservative, like a pragmatic progressive, should realize that in abandoning philosophical and political foundationalism, and taking the pragmatic turn, the only thing that makes the dominant culture reliable is how well it defends itself against alternative cultural perspectives. Therefore, conservative and progressive pragmatists alike should seek an institutional expression for the radical criticism of the dominant culture.[19]

The university finds itself to be a central battleground in this cultural war.[20] In this essay, I present a conception of cultural criticism and healthy cultural change. According to this account, the university should be a bastion of progressive or radical critique of the dominant culture, irrespective of the particular substantive content of that culture. In calling the university a bastion of radical critique, I intend to emphasize the pragmatic legitimacy of the university as the chief institution responsible for systematic cultural criticism of the dominant culture.

The notion of a bastion of radical critique also suggests that theoretically the university, as a cultural critic, provides an adequate and unitary, though not exclusive, rationale for many of our intuitions about the role of the university in American society. Consequently, at least in principle, the idea of the university as a cultural critic can give conceptual coherence to the curricula by providing a rationale for academic policy decisions in favor of diversity.

Lest this point be misconstrued, the notion of the university as a bastion of radical critique does not entail that only radical critics should be part of the university; indeed, it entails that "[n]o proposal will work that fails to make a place for those who will inevitably resist any single philosophy."[21] Nor does it entail that radical critics should *dominate* university life. Consequently, this notion does not entail that the university become

19. Even nonpragmatists can be included here. If you're a nonpragmatist you probably believe that the best defended position is more likely to reflect reality than a less well defended one, and so, you too will seek a healthy culture. In both views a healthy culture is one that survives the best criticism and, so, on both views, a healthy culture is desirable, though for different reasons.

20. One feature of cultural warfare is the lack of consensus on just how to characterize the issues. No doubt some parties to this conflict might find tendentious my characterization of the conflict as a contest between traditionalists and progressives.

21. G. Graff, *Teaching the Conflicts* in *The Politics of Liberal Education* 57, 70 (D. Gless and B. Herrnstein eds.) (1992) (hereafter *Liberal Education*).

the "fortress of the left." Nothing could be more inconsistent with the notion of the university as the appropriate institution for sustained radical critique of the dominant culture. For while the university should be free and open, it should see its task as the *free and open criticism of the dominant culture*. In this fashion, the university functions as both a reforming and stabilizing institution in cultural inquiry. When radical critique of the dominant culture prevails, the dominant culture should be reformed; when it fails, the dominant culture should be defended.

The conception of the university as a bastion of radical critique states that among the chief institutions in a democratic society, the university and the university alone provides the stability and resources to function as the institution most able and most inclined to provide systematic, persistent, and progressive criticism of the dominant culture. This conception of the university's role in postmodern America specifically addresses the contemporary controversy over multiculturalism in the core curriculum as well as the problems concerning hate speech, affirmative action, and political correctness. In fact, this conception provides a rationale for a progressive interpretation and resolution of these issues.

In part one of this Article, I critically examine the standard conception of the university's role in liberal education. Part two sketches a pragmatic conception of cultural criticism, cultural health, and cultural change, suggesting that a multiculturalist curriculum should be a primary aim of the university. Further, this pragmatic conception of cultural criticism warrants constraints on hate speech, strong affirmative action programs, and a university environment that includes some notion of civility or "political correctness." My argument serves two general purposes. First, it creates a framework for justifying the cultural left's position on many of these issues.[22] Second, and more surprisingly, the argument shows why the cultural right should endorse this role for the university despite the fact that conservative ideology would be the target of such criticism in the prevailing cultural context.[23] The cultural right should endorse this view because the only indicator of the health of a culture is whether it successfully answers the criticism of different, even antagonistic, cultural perspectives. Moreover, for the cultural right to answer these criticisms

22. No doubt the notion of "the cultural left's" position on any issue is highly problematic. I use the term as a shorthand for a variety of positions purportedly in favor of the "victim's revolution."

23. Although there may be pockets of progressive control, progressivism must overcome the prevailing cultural paradigms before it even gets a fair hearing. The reason for this resistance is that many of the prevailing cultural paradigms are anything but open and undistorted.

there must be some intellectually respectable and effective institution producing the most trenchant statement of what is wrong with the dominant culture. Only then will the cultural right have any assurance that when progressive objections to the prevailing cultural paradigms are defeated, the dominant culture will be seen to be healthy and reliable. Before getting ahead of the argument, however, let us critically examine the traditional conception of the role of the university in American society.

I.

In the American context, the standard conception of the role of the university and of a liberal education includes a foundationalist conception of human inquiry. According to this conception students should be taught to acquire a value-free method of inquiry that reveals truths about the universe as well as about human existence. These truths are often enigmatic, requiring considerable ability in separating the wheat of reality from the chaff of appearance. What anchors our system of beliefs and values is an independent reality that when apprehended provides an inter-subjective procedure – consisting of reason or nature – for evaluating beliefs and values. This procedure then provides a politically neutral perspective from which we can comparatively evaluate different, and sometimes radically different or incommensurable, cultures. In this view, culture and education must be devoid of politics.[24] Conversely, the error of multiculturalism is to interject politics into what should be an apolitical academy.[25]

The standard view conceives of reason or nature as a principle of criticism by which we arrive at truth and knowledge.[26] The goal of criti-

---

24. This essentially conservative claim simply masks the dominant conservative dimension of culture and education. It implies that once "culture [and education] [were] uncontaminated by politics; but for [the conservatives] politics can only mean left-wing politics. Their own politics is not politics." R. Jacoby, *The Last Intellectuals* 200 (1987).

25. Gerald Graff succinctly exposes the hypocrisy of two vocal critics of multiculturalism, Lynne Cheney and George Will, when he writes "[t]he assumption seems to be that when you say 'the American system is the best in the world' you are just stating a fact; whereas when you 'advocate social change' you are being political and therefore don't deserve public funds. Change is political but patriotism is not." G. Graff, *The Nonpolitics of PC*, 6 *Tikkun* 50, 51 (1991). Graff sees a possible benefit from the unwarranted concern over multiculturalism: "If the PC scare produces any good result, it will be in smoking out and exposing the hypocrisy of such apolitical claims, so that people who have up to now been taken in by the shell game played with words like 'political' and 'politically correct' will start to see the double standard it depends on." *Id.*

cism, in this view, is to understand the world in which human beings find themselves. Criticism refers to something external to the human community and to human culture. This transcendental perspective functions as a standard according to which everything else can be evaluated. The standard conception tells us that truth is valuable for its own sake, irrespective of whether it solves social or political problems. Truth is a relation that connects us to the external, objective world. If truth solves social and political problems, so much the good. If it fails to find a solution, it is still valuable in its own right.[27]

This conception of inquiry implicitly supports the dominant culture.[28] Because truth should be neutral with respect to controversial moral and legal questions, intellectual inquiry should likewise be neutral. The pursuit of this inquiry in an institution such as the university should be devoid of substantive political commitments. Because the standard view regards human intellectual inquiry as politically neutral, the university as the temple of human inquiry must therefore also be politically neutral.

Some adherents of the standard view contend that political neutrality is not the goal. Instead, we should look for the one true conception of the good life and express that conception in our cultural institutions. Allan Bloom endorses this view, insisting that the ancient Grecian conception of the good life is the appropriate foundation for cultural institutions, especially the university. In Bloom's view, excellence, perfection, and superiority are perfectly natural, just, and good. Indeed, opponents of

26. One version of the standard view is the "marketplace of ideas" theory. According to this view, ideas should flourish because only then do we have reason to trust our beliefs and values. Only when these beliefs and values clash with alternative beliefs and values can we be warranted in what we endorse. The surviving beliefs and values are more likely to reflect the external, objective world than beliefs and values that do not survive. Once we abandon the standard notion of inquiry, we can no longer have any reason to believe that certain beliefs and values and not others are more faithful to an external objective reality. We might still believe that a clash of ideas is good. But if we do, it will be for pragmatic reasons.

27. It could be objected that truth is a metaphysical, not an epistemic, notion. According to this objection, truth is tied to reality, while only by *discovering* the truth of reality do we have knowledge. Truth, as a metaphysical notion, presupposes the independence of truth and verification, or, in other words, it insists that it is conceivable that there exists "truth beyond all verification." B. Loar, *Truth Beyond All Verification* in *Michael Dummett: Contributions to Philosphy* 81 (1987). This nonepistemic conception of truth maintains that a proposition is true or false independently of our permanent inability to prove it true or false. A. Goldman, *Epistemology and Cognition* 148 (1986).

28. The notion of a "dominant culture" consists of those norms and values that are expressed most readily by institutions which govern society. A dominant culture usually reflects what a majority of individuals, or at least a majority of the most powerful individuals endorse, though not necessarily. The dominant culture controls the way we understand ourselves and our relation to others; if we repudiate the dominant culture we are often at war with ourselves as well as society.

such a view are responsible for the disintegration of the true basis of American culture. Characterizing his opponents' point of view Bloom writes:

> We should not be ethnocentric. . . . We should not think our way is better than others. The intention is not so much to teach the students about other times and places as to make them aware of the fact that their preferences are only that – accidents of their time and place. Their beliefs do not entitle them as individuals, or collectively as a nation to think they are superior to anyone else. . . . [I]ndiscriminateness is a moral imperative because its opposite is discrimination. This folly means that men are not permitted to seek the natural human good and admire it when found, for such a discovery is coeval with the discovery of the bad and contempt for it. Instinct and intellect must be suppressed by education. The natural soul is to be replaced with an artificial one.[29]

This natural good, once appreciated, informs all worthwhile human activities. Cultures inconsistent with this foundation of human society are bad and, if possible, ought to be eliminated. Similarly, liberal education should reflect and nurture this natural foundation of human society. For Bloom, "[a] good program of liberal education feeds the student's love of truth and her passion to live a good life."[30] Bloom's view is that truth and goodness exist independently of the human community and human culture. Or, if they are dependent upon culture, they are dependent on the one true culture. In this view, a culture is correct or healthy only when it reflects the natural good.[31]

29. A. Bloom, *The Closing of the American Mind: How Higher Education Has Failed Democracy and Impoverished the Souls of Today's Students* 30 (1987) (hereinafter A. Bloom, *The Closing of the American Mind*).

30. *Id.* at 345.

31. Something beyond culture must exist and philosophy is our ticket there. Consider:

> Men cannot remain content with what is given them by their culture if they are to be fully human. This is what Plato meant by the image of the cave in the *Republic* and by representing us as prisoners in it. A culture is a cave. He did not suggest going around to other cultures as a solution to the limitations of the cave. Nature should be the standard by which we judge our own lives and the lives of other people. That is why philosophy, not history or anthropology, is the most important human science. Only dogmatic assurance that thought is culture-bound, that there is no nature, is what makes our educators so certain that the only way to escape the limitations of our time and place is to study other cultures. History and anthropology were understood by the Greeks to be useful only in discovering what the past and other peoples had to contribute to the discovery of nature.

A. Bloom, *The Closing of the American Mind* at 38. If Bloom would countenance cross-cultural comparisons, for Platonic reasons, then he would, like the pragmatists, embrace multiculturalism. In this event, Bloom's reason for consulting other cultures would be because knowledge of other cultures assists us in discovering the nature of reality, while the pragmatist's reason is to have the most critically scrutinized view possible. Still, in these circumstances, both views embrace multiculturalism, but not the same conception of multiculturalism.

Bloom gripes about the failure to appreciate the Platonic conception of liberal education, namely, assisting people to correctly perceive permanent truths upon which learning and culture depends. Due to the influx of anarchistic, democratic, and nihilistic approaches to learning, contemporary liberal education is in an acute state of crisis. Essentially, "the crisis of liberal education is a reflection of a crisis at the peaks of learning, an incoherence and incompatibility among the first principles with which we interpret the world, an intellectual crisis of the greatest magnitude, which constitutes the crisis of our civilization."[32] The real crisis of liberal education, according to Bloom, is "not so much in this incoherence, but in our incapacity to discuss or even recognize it."[33] The appropriate form of liberal education "flourished when it prepared the way for a discussion of a unified view of nature and man's place in it, which the best minds debated on the highest level."[34]

Curiously, in a work on "the closing" of the human intellect, Bloom offers this rather tendentious view of liberal education.[35] For in Bloom's view, unless one professes a belief in a final truth and a final good towards which appropriate human inquiry and education aspire, one has embraced nihilism.[36] But, of course, Bloom's framework hardly exhausts the possibilities. Human life might not have any one final good and yet

32. *Id.* at 346.
33. *Id.*
34. *Id.* at 346-47.
35. Indeed, Bloom's contention that liberal education has succeeded in "closing" the American mind is a misdescription even from his point of view. What Bloom wants to say or should want to say is that the American mind has become empty. Consider Sir Moberly's characterization of the distinction between a closed mind an empty mind:

> [Education and intellectual inquiry] involves the avoidance of two extremes, the closed mind and the empty mind. It is possible to hold preconceptions in such a way that one's mind is not really open to entertain any fresh evidence that seems to contradict it. This is the notorious fault of the dogmatist; and for one open and avowed dogmatist there are half a dozen who are dogmatists unconsciously but quite as effectually. The great advances in [intellectual inquiry] have generally been made by [people] who were ready to take interest in, and to concentrate attention on, the unexpected, and, if need be, to jettison all presuppositions. On the other hand simply to jettison all presuppositions is not only impossible but absurd. What is required is, to integrate the new and the old, and not to ignore either.

Sir Walter Moberly, *The Crisis in the University* 66 (1949). According to this characterization, Bloom is a dogmatist complaining about modern and post-modern nihilists who have tried to jettison from their minds just those classical presuppositions to which Bloom dogmatically clings.
36. Rorty observes that "Straussians [like Bloom] typically do not countenance alternative debatable interpretations of [Aristotle, Hobbes, Locke, Rousseau and Kant], but rather distinguish between their own 'authentic understandings' and others' 'misunderstandings.'" R. Rorty, *The New Republic* 28, 29 (April 4, 1988).

59

there still might be the possibility of intellectual inquiry and even of nobility. Bloom appears to maintain that you either believe in one final good or you believe in nihilism, without stopping to consider that there may be multiple goods, even incompatible goods, that human beings must discover or create and choose between.[37] Truth and goodness can be contextual or relational without being relative.[38]

Bloom also insists, like the ancients, that humanity's final good is found in nature and is not the product of human needs and desires.[39] Nowhere does Bloom explain the historical failure of the best minds and hearts of our civilization to make intelligible and plausible the notion of a final good that is fixed and independent of human community. Moreover, Bloom's insistence that the ancients have already got things right suggests a dogmatic cleaving to the past, not the openness of an authentic intellectual or philosopher. Nonetheless, Bloom insists that his rather narrow conception of human inquiry harkening back to ancient Greece is the one true and "open" view. In fact, the "closing of the American mind" more nearly describes Bloom's own view than those of his opponents'.

John Searle, though formally dissociating himself from Bloom's conception of educational culture, endorses a similarly foundationalist conception of human inquiry.[40] In the traditionalist's view, according to Searle, "education is by its very nature 'elitist' and 'hierarchical' because it is designed to enable and encourage the student to discriminate between what is good and what is bad, what is intelligent and what is stupid, what is true and what is false."[41] Of course, in one generous interpretation of these remarks, they are uncontroversial. Problems arise when these remarks are understood to imply some univocal set of value-free standards that can distinguish the good from the bad, the intelligent from the stupid, the true from the false – a set of standards that itself is politically neutral.

Searle's foundationalism suggests that judgments of value are themselves neutral with respect to the texts they evaluate. Furthermore, if you do not adopt the appropriate Archimedean standards you are a dolt. And once you adopt the appropriate standards (probably Searle's) you, of course, are on the side of the angels even when these standards lead you to a substantively different conclusion from mine.

37. See, I. Berlin, *The Crooked Timber of Humanity* (1991).
38. S. Hook, *Allan Bloom's Critique of American Education: A Noble Failure*, in *Convictions* 120-21 (1990).
39. *Id.* at 125.
40. J. Searle, *The Storm Over the University*, 37 N.Y. Rev. Bks 34 (Dec. 6, 1990) (hereinafter J. Searle, *N.Y. Rev. Bks.*).
41. *Id.* at 36.

Rather than appreciating that reason and the standards of evaluation it entails are themselves expressions of political values, Searle insists that reason is the final arbiter of all theoretical and practical intellectual controversies. But what else can reason be but a commitment to an actual historical conception of human inquiry? And how can such a commitment avoid the political?

Searle appears to believe that there is some way to avoid the political commitments associated with the concept of reason. Similarly, Searle believes that we can avoid the political element in evaluating great texts. In a public television interview, Searle repeatedly appealed to reason as the non-political vehicle for arriving at the truth. In reality, however, a commitment to reason and truth is nothing more (nor less) than a rhetorical device designed to make certain actual historical strategies of evaluation appear natural and inescapable. Rather than being dedicated to an open form of human inquiry, reason and truth – when understood in this fashion – represent an artificial restriction and distortion of human intellectual inquiry. Searle seizes on an Enlightenment conception of inquiry and represents it as natural, fixed, and non-historical. Yet no one, including Searle, has ever made intelligible what such a conception could mean.

Roger Kimball commits the same mistake in diagnosing the present crisis of the university.[42] According to Kimball, the decadence of the contemporary academy is due to the corruption of traditional educational ideals.[43] The symptoms of decay are apparent.

> It is one of the clearest symptoms of decadence besetting the academy that the ideals that once informed the humanities have been corrupted, willfully misunderstood, or simply ignored by the new sophistries that have triumphed on our campuses. We know something is gravely amiss when teachers of the humanities confess – or, as is more often the case, when they boast – that they are no longer able to distinguish between truth and falsity. We know something is wrong when scholars assure us – and their pupils – that there is no essential difference between knowledge and partisan proselytizing, or when academic literary critics abandon the effort to identify and elucidate works of lasting achievement as a reactionary enterprise unworthy of their calling.[44]

42. R. Kimball, *Tenured Radicals: How Politics Has Corrupted Our Higher Education* (Harper and Row: 1990) (hereinafter R. Kimball, *Tenured Radicals*).

43. *Id.* at 165. Kimball gives the uninitiated the impression that he is correctly revealing an important, fatal problem with contemporary academia, namely, the takeover by the radical left. However, when one examines the issues more carefully, it becomes obvious that Kimball has distorted more than he reports accurately. This has led one participant in this controversy to characterize Kimball's view as "his hallucinated vision of American academia run by a radical conspiracy." Peter Brooks, *Tenured Radicals, Times Literary Supplement*, p. 15, Col. 1, April 19, 1991.

44. R. Kimball, *Tenured Radicals, supra* note 42.

What's worse, for Kimball "the most troubling development of all is that such contentions are no longer the exceptional pronouncements of a radical elite, but have increasingly become the conventional wisdom in humanities departments of our major colleges and universities."[45] On its face, Kimball's view has some appeal. Obviously, some texts assert the truth, while other texts do not. But upon closer inspection we see his position for the foundationalist political view that it is. Instead of characterizing some texts as important, even sublime, because of the way they address important human needs, Kimball implies that there is some Archimedean standpoint equally accessible to Harvard undergraduates, poor whites, blacks, latinos, gays and lesbians, women, and the homeless.[46] What is more, this standpoint guarantees to certain texts truth and importance once and forever.

Kimball's view also distorts the pragmatic temperament,[47] for pragmatists are certainly able to distinguish between true and false claims. Similarly, pragmatism can distinguish between "knowledge and partisan proselytizing." The critical locution is "there is no *essential* difference between knowledge and partisan proselytizing."[48] It hardly follows that there is no important difference at all.

What pragmatism asserts is that the difference between "knowledge" and "partisan proselytizing" is something that we cannot know in advance. There are no *a priori* litmus tests, no neutral perspectives that can be used to evaluate a speaker's remarks. No general theories exist for distinguishing between belief and delusion, and all we can ever hope for are piecemeal investigations together with the acute intellectual anxiety and curiosity that usually accompany these activities. No doubt demagogues and demons abound. But nothing can guarantee that we can know the demagogue or demon in advance. Pious buzz words such as Truth, Reason, Knowledge, Impartiality, Disinterested Inquiry, and so forth uttered by the killer B's – Bennett, Bloom, and Bellow – cannot prove that *they* are on the side of the

---

45. *Id.*

46. I do not deny that one factor in evaluating a text is its aesthetic dimension. But this is only *one* factor among others. And indeed, it is far from apolitical. The bottom line is even if the aesthetic dimension includes no political stance, whatever that means, by doing so it *rejects* addressing political views and social problems. And if that is not a political point of view nothing is.

47. I do not suggest that Kimball had the pragmatist in mind as the target of these remarks. However, since pragmatism, as I understand it, rejects Kimball's view, this is as good as place as any to present the pragmatic rebuttal.

48. R. Kimball, *supra* note 42 at 165. (Emphasis added)

angels.[49] Indeed, the rhetoric of the killer B's is driven by a passionate conviction to destroy the cultural left. Certainly, such a conviction can in no way be accurately regarded as apolitical.

Michael Oakeshott contributes an interesting version of the standard view. A university, for Oakeshott, does not have an antecedent purpose or goal. Rather, "[a] university is a number of people engaged in a certain sort of activity . . . 'the pursuit of learning.'"[50] For Oakeshott, "[w]hat distinguishes a university is its special engagement in the pursuit of learning."[51] The pursuit of learning occurs in the context of a wide ranging conversation with things past.[52]

This conversation bestows upon the student "the most characteristic gift" that is "exclusive to the university and is rooted in the character of university education as neither a beginning nor an end, but a middle. . . . The characteristic gift of the university is the gift of an interval."[53] During this period, an individual can avoid the slings and arrows of commitment to causes whether noble or pedestrian, a time for "suspending judgment" and pursuing learning just for the sake of the pursuit. According to Oakeshott, "[o]ne might . . . reduce this to a doctrine about the character of a university; one might call it the doctrine of the interim."[54] A concern for technical knowledge, for social justice, or even for grasping the meaning of life is, for Oakeshott, anathema to the doctrine of the interim. Enthusiastic, but detached, participation in the conversation is the salient feature of Oakeshott's university. On the other hand, a committed education distorts this conversational process. There can be no ulterior motive for imparting the body of knowledge to new generations except that it is our cultural legacy and therefore is inherently valuable.

A liberal education should indeed be a conversation, but not directed exclusively at things past. Instead, students who have imbibed things past with their mother's milk should be exposed to deep and comprehensive critiques of the dominant culture. The presupposition always should be:

49. William Bennett, former Secretary of Education and former federal drug czar, Allan Bloom, and Saul Bellow, the novelist, have been named "the killer Bs" for their strident, irritating, and sometimes infuriating distortion of multiculturalism. For example, it is reported that Saul Bellow once exclaimed that when the Zulus have a Tolstoy we will read him.

50. M. Oakeshott, *The Idea of a University* in *The Voice of Liberal Learning, supra* note 2 at 95, 96.

51. *Id.* at 96.

52. *Id.*

53. *Id.* at 126-27.

54. *Id.* at 128.

here is our culture, now let's see what's wrong with it. This is the only pragmatic way to have any reason to believe that what remains after such critique is reliable and useful.[55]

Does this preclude the pursuit of learning? If that means having the time and resources within which to *explore* avenues of learning patiently, without the need for immediate profit, the answer is clearly "no" for those so inclined. If the pursuit of learning means structuring the university to preclude the possibility of commitment, passion, and devotion to a political cause, or to a particular conception of the meaning of life, then it isn't obvious that "the pursuit of learning" is an unqualified good. Certainly, an Oakeshottian view is antithetical to intellectual pluralism, the view that a multiplicity of reasons for pursuing education is legitimate and desirable. Moreover, if we were concerned with the best reason for a university education, I shouldn't think that Oakeshott's reason would prevail over a passionate devotion to understanding human life and our place in the universe. What better reason could one have for embarking on a course of university education? Certainly not the impartial pursuit of learning, whatever that means.

Oakeshott is disturbingly uncharitable to alternative visions of university education. In his view, the crisis of the universities is due to "men of power who desire that the universities should be flooded with exactly the sort of undergraduate, whose character they admire; they have the intention of transforming the universities into places designed and planned to provide what these undergraduates suppose they need."[56] Oakeshott offers this admonition:

> [W]hen the pressure of change in this direction becomes irresistible, the universities will suffer a destructive metamorphosis from which recovery will be impossible. The problem today is *not* 'how to translate the ideal of the cultivated gentleman into democratic terms and combine an intensive and relentless pursuit of excellence with a new sensitiveness to the demands of social justice.' In the past a rising class was aware of something valuable and enjoyed by others which it wished to share; but this is not so today. The leaders of the rising class are consumed with a contempt for everything which does not spring from their own desires, they are convinced in advance that

55. Of course, to engage in radical criticism of the dominant culture entails that students are sufficiently well-versed in what the dominant culture is and how it got to be dominant. Radical criticism can come about in at least one of two ways. First, a course can specifically set out to criticize some portion of the dominant culture. Second, a course can "ignore" the dominant culture and simply discuss alternative cultures.

56. M. Oakeshott, *The Idea of a University* in *The Voice of Liberal Learning, supra* note 2 at 130.

they have nothing to learn and everything to teach, and consequently their aim is loot – to appropriate to themselves the organization, the shell of the institution, and convert it to their own purposes. The problem of the university today is how to avoid destruction at the hands of men who have no use for their characteristic virtues, men who are convinced only that "knowledge is power."[57]

On pragmatic grounds, however, Oakeshott has it wrong. Certainly, if Anglo-American society *is* racist, sexist, classist, and imperialistic, then the contempt of the "rising class" is warranted.[58] In these circumstances, pragmatic fallibilism should seek out the arguments justifying the contempt. Either such arguments are sound or they are not. Instead of belittling the inclination to invalidate tradition, an Oakeshottian argument should seek to hear the arguments and rebut them. But first they have to be heard. And the standard view is bent on silencing these voices.

I think this is what explains the sometimes extreme and intransigent position taken by some on the cultural left at least in the United States. The dominant culture does not offer them a fair hearing in churches, in the media, nor in public and private associations and ceremonies. Thus, when they achieve *some* power in academic settings, in rare instances they exhibit totalitarian tendencies.[59] But nowhere in the cultural war is this the rule rather than the exception.[60] Moreover, it is the totalitarianism of the cultural right that causes this intransigences.

Due to the emotional tenor of this controversy even the traditional pragmatic conception of social intelligence can go awry. Sidney Hook, "one of the chief heirs"[61] of Deweyan pragmatism, contends that "the epistemology of the criticism of Western culture is primitive and mistaken especially in the demand that faculty be recruited from 'women and people of color' to study ideas and aspects of culture that involve them."[62] In human inquiry first-hand experience or empathy is not required. Consider his reasons:

57. M. Oakeshott, *The Universities* in M. Oakeshott, *The Voice of Liberal Learning, supra* note 2 at 105, 130.

58. Oakeshott's analysis applies to the British context, but an Oakeshottian argument can be redeployed in the American academic cultural wars.

59. Any cultural perspective can exhibit totalitarian tendencies. Basically, you endorse a totalitarian viewpoint when you believe that some group – either the majority or minority – has the right to impose its views simply because it is that group. I am sure that the cultural left has its totalitarians, but so does the cultural right.

60. What about the "rising class" frightens conservatives so much? If the conservatives are pragmatists they should welcome the influx of new or different ideas and encourage experiments in creating new forms of life.

61. P. Kurtz, *Introduction*, in S. Hook, *Convictions* 7 (1987).

62. S. Hook, *An Open Letter to the Stanford Faculty* in *Convictions* at 133, 137.

One does not have to be German to study Luther or the German Reformation or be sympathetic to the Nazis to study Hitler. As well argue that men cannot be gynecologists, that only women are best to study family law, or that only fat physicians can study obesity or hungry people the phenomenon of starvation as that only people of color and women are uniquely qualified to do justice to the place, achievement and oppression of minorities and their culture, wherever relevant in Western culture. . . . Race, color, religion, national origin, and sexual orientation are neither necessary nor sufficient conditions for the fruitful study of the humanities or any subject matter . . . The quest should always be for the best qualified.[63]

This seems unconvincing. Certainly, being X *is* neither a necessary nor sufficient condition for studying, understanding, or representing X. Justices Sandra Day O'Connor and Clarence Thomas are probably *not* qualified as spokespersons for either women or African-Americans. If they are qualified, their qualifications certainly do not depend on their gender or their race. But that is irrelevant to the question of whether having first-hand experience as a member of an excluded, dominated, or ridiculed group is *one* factor, all things being equal, for having a *better* understanding of the problems facing that group than do outsiders.[64]

As a stutterer I would want a recovered stutterer to teach a course in public speaking. This does not mean that non-stutterers cannot understand a stutterer's plight,[65] or that we should consider stuttering to be the norm, or even a perfectly alternative way of speaking. It is just that a teacher who is aware first hand of the problems stutterers face in this society is *likely* to be more sensitive to these problems than a non-stutterer. The critical term here is "likely," not "necessarily." Fluent speakers are usually unaware of the problems stutterers face, and so in reacting to

63. *Id.*

64. Hook also overlooks the fact that excluded or stigmatized people often find learning experiences more inviting when not confronted by authority figures who in their mind represent those who have excluded them.

65. My sister, Julia R. Fischel, a speech therapist and a non-stutterer, is sensitive to the plight of stutterers and understandably more knowledgeable than ordinary people about the causes of stuttering. For example, the conventional view about stuttering is that it is a psychological, not a physical, problem. M. Schwartz, *Stutter No More* 19 (1991). Recent discoveries, however, suggest that the ultimate cause of stuttering is due to the locking of the vocal cords, a physical condition. *Id.* at 14. When the vocal cords vibrate, a person *cannot* stutter. That's why you cannot stutter when you sing, even if you are Mel Tillis. Should we investigate the dynamics of all other "disabilities" so that we might be more knowledgeable and sensitive to the obstacles other people face in dealing with circumstances we take for granted?

stutterers, or designing discussion groups, and so forth are often guilty of "fluentism."[66]

I take this to be obvious, especially from a pragmatic perspective. Hook's remark's can then only be understood as an atavistic reflection of a foundationalist picture of human life, where truth reflects an external reality to which anyone, however inexperienced, has equal access, just as long as he is smart enough and a good enough investigator. Such a picture of human inquiry is completely insensitive to the vagaries suffered by people having atypical natural abilities, and who, because of these abilities, are themselves regarded as marginal, weird, or disabled.

Insensitivity, however, is not uncommon among the critics of multiculturalism. In commenting on the "ambitious projects" of some universities "to rearrange admissions and curricular requirements to foster such values as 'tolerance' and 'diversity,'"[67] as if these were necessarily and obviously bad, Dinesh D'Souza writes:

> Over the past few years, presidents and deans on most campuses have assembled task forces to set their agenda for "multiculturalism" or "pluralism," and have then incorporated several of their recommendations into official policy. Diversity, tolerance, multiculturalism, pluralism – these phrases are perennially on the lips of university administrators. They are the principles and slogans of the victim's revolution.[68]

What can possibly be wrong with diversity, tolerance, or pluralism? Have we plummeted so far from the American conception of civic virtue and duty that these terms signify nothing but leftist code words? Is that really plausible? Remember, part of the history of the United States *is* the history of victimization.[69] Accordingly, what can D'Souza mean by

---

66. Fluentism assumes that everyone is equally able to speak in public settings. The Association of American Law Schools, among other institutions, is guilty of fluentism in designing its workshops. Typically, at the beginning of each "small group" session, the leader asks each member of the group to introduce himself. As a stutterer, and a sometime member of these workshops, take my word that this seemingly innocuous request sometimes gives a stutterer reason to avoid participating in these workshops, or, at least, to avoid attending the small groups discussions.

67. D. D'Souza, *Illiberal Education: The Politics of Race and Sex on Campus* 17 (1991) [hereinafter D. D'Souza, *Illiberal Education*].

68. *Id.*

69. I do not see how one can quarrel with the contention that Native Americans, African-Americans, women and others have been systematically victimized in American society. This hardly entails the rejection of American culture as a relatively better place to flourish than other areas of the world. But it does suggest that the American revolution of achieving equality and liberty for everyone is radically incomplete.

labelling diversity, tolerance, multiculturalism, and pluralism "principles and slogans of the victim's revolution?" Does he intend to show that there is no need for a victim's revolution?[70]

Even if you share D'Souza's perception – that the United States is a basically democratic, fair, and morally acceptable society – does this mean that there is no need for a "victim's revolution?"[71] Rather than denigrate multiculturalism, D'Souza (and the other critics) should show that there is no need to redress the grievances that multiculturalism allegedly redresses, or, if there is such a need that traditional culture is perfectly capable of doing the job.[72] If D'Souza appreciates the nature of pragmatic cultural criticism, he should want the universities to support the victim's revolution whether or not he saw the need for it. Because by having the university serve as the victim's representative in criticizing the dominant culture can D'Souza have any reason to believe that the dominant culture is healthy.

Consequently, the standard view is defective, on pragmatic grounds, since it places something external to human inquiry toward which inquiry is directed. Even shorn of foundationalist pretensions, the standard view still attempts to provide an external perspective as the arbiter of conflicts arising in the context of inquiry. But how do we determine when a putative standard is legitimate? Only by appealing to an additional meta-standard that is sufficiently neutral to arbitrate between competing first-order standards. The regress here is apparent. Either we never reach a neutral perspective as a means of deciding between competing standards or we find a neutral standard only by begging the question against skepticism as well as against our enemies' standards.

70. In light of the Rodney King verdict and the ensuing riots, is such an argument even faintly plausible? Denigrating the notion of a "victim's revolution" suggests that "D'Souza could do with a few more walks on the hard side of struggle." C. Stimpson, *Big Man on Campus*, *Nation* September 30, 1991 Col. 3.

71. I enjoy living in the United States. Indeed, I think that the United States is probably more conducive to human flourishing than any other society. (Alas, I have never lived in any other country.) Yet I simply do not understand why anyone would want to concentrate on what's good about the United States. I could understand this if the ills plaguing the United States were trivial. But they are not. So let's love the United States by extirpating its non-trivial ills. Let's not spend our lives adoring anything. Rather, let's spend it improving everything.

72. One can regard cultural history in the United States as an attempt to integrate more and more excluded groups into the dominant culture. It could be argued that only by such a principle of expansion does the moral community become more and more inclusive, more compassionate, and more just. Robert Justin Lipkin, *The Theory of Reciprocal Altruism*, 30 *Phil. Stud.* (Ireland) 108, 119 (1984). On pragmatic grounds, given what we know empirically about human nature, there can be no alternative to working towards the most inclusive moral community.

In other words, we have the following choice: we can look for coherence and simplifying redescriptions of our actual strategies for conducting inquiry, or we could ask for a meta-strategy external to the process by which we can justify or legitimize the actual standards we use. The latter choice is obviously bankrupt because we have no way of legitimizing the external standard, except by some further external standard or by appealing to the very practices the external standard was designed to validate. In the first instance, our argument commits us to a regress, while in the latter case the argument is obviously circular. The traditional view depends upon the notion of an external validating standard according to which we demonstrate the ineluctability of our actual strategies for resolving cultural controversies. But such a standard is impossible. Consequently, any such view that depends on an external notion of truth, knowledge, and justification is pragmatically pointless.

If, however, no external standard is available, won't our reliance on actual inquisitional strategies inevitably reject progressive change? The answer is "yes" in circumstances where we have a restricted or impoverished notion of inquiry. In these circumstances in which we have an impoverished notion of inquiry, however, the question of progressive change usually doesn't arise. On the other hand, in circumstances in which we have an abundantly rich notion of inquiry, we have all we need for progressive change. In these circumstances we can redescribe and reconstruct actual patterns of inquiry to achieve new ends.[73] I attempt such a reconstruction in the following section of this essay.

II.

In this section I want to sketch a pragmatic conception of cultural criticism. Pragmatic cultural criticism includes the notion of cultural health and change and is committed to multiculturalism. However, before describing this mode of inquiry let me first make some preliminary remarks about the notion of "culture."

---

73. This presupposes that pragmatism contributes to progressive social change. I think it does. But its effect can only be understood after resurrecting traditional forms of inquiry in pragmatic dress. I argue this in greater detail in *Pragmatism — The Unfurnished Revolution: Doctrinaire and Reflective Pragmatism in Rorty's Social Thought*, 67 Tulane 1561 (1993). For an important exchange on the issue of pragmatism's efficacy, see L. Baker, *"Just Do It": Pragmatism and Progressive Social Change*, 78 Va. L. Rev. (1992) and R. Rorty, *What Can You Expect from Anti-Foundationalist Philosophers: A Reply to Lynn Baker*, 78 Va. L. Rev. 719 (1992).

A culture is a comprehensive response to certain inevitable problems in social interaction. Cultures typically take some stand on the relationship between the individual and the state or some other dominant group. Typically, cultures have complex conceptions of work, religion, family, play, sanity, education, personal or sexual ethics, and customs. Generally, "[a] culture . . . is a continuity of feelings, perceptions, ideas, engagements, attitudes, and so forth, pulling in different directions, often critical of one another and contingently related to one another so as to compose . . . a conversational encounter."[74] A culture "reaches us, as it reached generations before ours, neither as long-ago terminated specimens of human adventure, nor as an accumulation of human achievements we are called upon to accept, but as a manifold of invitations to look, to listen and to reflect."[75] Cultural understanding presents itself as "specific invitations to encounter particular adventures in human self-understanding."[76] Similarly, understanding one's self is "inseparable from learning to participate in a 'culture.'"[77]

A culture usually has some conception of what counts as legitimate inquiry, though this might not be explicitly formulated or presented in general terms. A cultural system is the general unifying structure of multifarious forms of life; "each authentic culture has its own unique vision, its own scale of values."[78] An individual reflects these values. The simpler the culture, the more transparent the individual. The more fragmented or complex the culture, the more complex the individual. Cultures include paradigms or models, consisting of instructions, for resolving social conflicts and social crises, and cultural inquiry and criticism involve critically evaluating these models to assess their continuing viability.

---

74. M. Oakeshott, *A Place of Learning* in *The voice of Liberal Learning* at 28. Oakeshott's remarks continue:

> [Our culture], for example, accommodates not only the lyre of Apollo but also the pipes of Pan, the call of the wild; not only the poet but also the physicist; not only the majestic metropolis of Augustinian theology but also the "greenwood" of Franciscan Christianity. A culture comprises unfinished intellectual and emotional journeyings, expeditions now abandoned but known to us in tattered maps left behind by explorers; it is composed of lighthearted adventures, of relationships invented and explored in exploit or in drama, of myths and stories and poems expressing fragments of human self-understanding, of gods worshipped, of responses to the mutuality of the world and of encounters with death.

Id. at 29.
75. *Id.*
76. *Id.*
77. *Id.* at 28.
78. I. Berlin, *Giambattista Vico and Cultural History* in *The Crooked Timber of Humanity*, *supra* note 37 at 59.

In the spirit of contemporary pragmatism, cultures should be evaluated and compared only in antifoundationalist, antiessentialist terms. No Archimedean perspective exists for evaluating cultures that is not itself a cultural product. No Platonic or Kantian standards of cultural criticism exist. Nevertheless, cultural criticism is still possible. First, pragmatic cultural criticism pits a culture against itself – is the culture sufficiently free of inconsistencies? Do its deepest principles pervade all significant dimensions of the cultural system?[79] Are the underlying values of the culture expressed non-arbitrarily and with sufficient force and clarity throughout the culture?

Second, one culture can be played off other cultures. Once we understand how culture A and culture B purport to resolve problems in kinship relations, for instance, or free speech, we can pragmatically assess each culture's solution in familiar, common sense terms. Does A or B better deal with the problems we need solved? The fact that we can assess the relative merits only in terms of the culture in which we find ourselves is no more damaging than saying I solve the myriad problems of my life in terms of the person I am. What more could one expect? Once I understand culture B's solution to the problem, I can assess it well enough. Indeed, even if on pragmatic grounds I always initially choose my own culture's solution, I should at least be willing to try culture B's solution in the event that my solution fails.

At this juncture, let me introduce an analytic construct concerning cultural criticism that I believe to be quite useful in understanding cultural development and change. Cultural processes can be broadly divided into two general categories: normal culture and revolutionary culture. More perspicuously, we should distinguish between two modes of cultural inquiry: normal cultural inquiry and revolutionary cultural inquiry.[80]

---

79. Cf. R. Dworkin, *Law's Empire* (1986).

80. This distinction is designed to reflect Thomas Kuhn's distinction between normal and revolutionary science, and not to indicate some independent position about revolutionary change in some Marxist or other radical sense. T. Kuhn, *The Structure of Scientific Revolutions* (1971) (distinguishing two different forms of scientific inquiry), see also, R. Rorty, *Philosophy and the Mirror of Nature* (1980) (distinguishing two different forms of discourse); Robert Justin Lipkin, *The Anatomy of Constitutional Revolutions*, 69 Neb. L. Rev. 811 (1989) (distinguishing two different forms of constitutional adjudication); Robert Justin Lipkin, *Indeterminacy, Truth and Justification in Constitutional Theory*, 69 Fordham L. Rev. 645 (1992). Indeed, in my view, revolutionary culture should be a permanent and non-violent feature of contemporary society, though this does not preclude in principle the need for revolutionary cultural inquiry to be transformed into revolutionary military struggle. Though a conceptual and moral possibility, in my view, revolutionary military struggle is usually inadvisable. Further, in democratic societies, revolutionary military struggle should have as its goal the restoration of a more just, normal culture.

Normal culture consists of those norms and values that individuals share and through which they understand themselves and others as well. A normal culture "has its own pattern, its own characteristic arrangement of its constitutent energies."[81] Its structure, imbibed subliminally by human beings, has one salient commitment: its own perpetuation.[82] This structure guides the cultural norms and values to form the psychological counterpart of biological conditions.[83]

The fact that we share these norms and values with others does not in itself entail that normal culture is necessarily good. Indeed, normal culture, when it is dominant and bad, should be transformed. This essay's theme is that on pragmatic grounds the university should be an institution that radically criticizes the normal and dominant culture. Only in this manner can a pragmatist reasonably rely upon the culture of her society.

Normal cultural inquiry comes about when individuals agree on the relevant paradigms for resolving cultural problems and conflicts in a particular cultural area. A cultural paradigm is a principle or rule for determining legitimacy in that area of the culture. Suppose, for instance, a culture is fully or completely individualistic. In such circumstances, the question of social welfare should be resolved according to what the paradigm of individualism entails. In normal cultural inquiry individuals agree on the appropriate cultural paradigms. In these circumstances, dissent that promises to disrupt normal inquiry without justification should be suppressed. Unless the dissenters can explain, for example, why lining up at a bus stop is wrong, pushing oneself to the front of the line should not be tolerated as being faithful to the paradigm. However, there can be no automatic suppression of dissent because the conditions warranting suppression will themselves be contestable.[84] Consequently, the analytic distinction between normal and revolutionary cultural inquiry is not fixed and absolute; nonetheless, adopting this pragmatic construct is useful.

Normal cultural inquiry along with the judicious suppression of dissent that makes normal inquiry possible, permits the inquirers to achieve the goals and purposes that the paradigm makes possible. Furthermore, normal cultural inquiry encourages individuals to stabilize, refine, and perfect the paradigm in order to deal with unforeseen cultural difficulties. For once problem solving under a particular cultural paradigm falters,

81. J. Dewey, *Freedom and Culture* 23 (1989).
82. *Id.*
83. *See Id.* at 24.
84. I owe this point to Barbara Herrnstein-Smith in correspondence.

dissent and revolutionary cultural inquiry occurs. In such circumstances, a cultural crisis or series of crises exists, and a cultural crisis is typically resolved by resurrecting the old paradigm or by replacing it. Resurrecting a paradigm involves re-conceptualizing the paradigm's structure, while replacing a paradigm involves rejecting the old paradigm and the problems it sought to resolve along with it. By replacing the old paradigm, therefore, the new paradigm creates a new set of problems *and* a new set of possible solutions.[85]

Normal culture consists of beliefs and values upon which there is relative agreement. Revolutionary culture, on the other hand, consists of proposals for important changes in normal culture upon which there is relatively little agreement. Let me hasten to add that this analytic construct does not reflect a fixed and rigid dichotomy between two qualitatively different categories, namely, normal culture – what we hold in common – and revolutionary culture – what we do not. No interesting, controversial, substantive judgment of value is shared by everyone.[86] Still, there are many values concerning murder, theft, and fraud as well as competitiveness, work, and play that are commonly shared and no one would try to devise a *moral or political argument* denying these values. This does not imply that these values are uncontestable once and forever. Anything *can* become contested; but *some* values are simply *not* contested. Most importantly, some cultural values must be held to be beyond controversy at least temporarily in order for cultural war to exist in the first place. For there to be cultural war you need opponents, and to have

85. When this occurs it might be asked what happened to the old paradigm and old problems. The answer is that they might be abandoned or they may be assimilated into the unconscious fund of knowledge, expectations, and assumptions of cultural life.

86. Consequently, I believe Stanley Fish is generally right that conclusions concerning what we have in common are usually contestable and, therefore, there is no rigid dichotomy between what is common and what is not. *See* S. Fish, *The Common Touch, or, One Size fits All* in *Liberal Education, supra* note 21 at 241, 244-47. I do believe, however, that some of these conclusions are much less contestable than others, and there are times when some values are virtually uncontestable, for example, that it is wrong to eat human beings for the fun of it, Jeffrey Dahmer and Hannibal Lecter notwithstanding. This qualification is instructive. Every important cultural or political value is less than universally accepted and perhaps even less than universally acceptable. Universalists, however, reply that there are values shared by everyone, at least when characterized on the appropriate level of generality. For example, no serious arguments exist supporting Jeffrey Dahmer's life style of killing and eating people. Perhaps we have made some moral progress since prehistoric times. Particularists hedge by responding that such "commonly" shared values are not interesting because they do not have significant implications for resolving our cultural wars. But that is precisely because they are commonly shared values. Cultural wars arise in the context of individuals sharing many important substantive values, values that at one time might have been controversial, but are no longer so. This agreement is limited, however, leaving the field open for disagreement on many contemporary issues.

opponents you need individuals who agree on many values, but whose agreement is seriously incomplete. It is inconceivable for there to be a cultural war between opponents who hold nothing in common. In such circumstances you could not even characterize your opponent as having a culture that is hopelessly different from yours.[87]

Healthy, normal cultural inquiry solves problems according to a stable cultural paradigm generating little or no dissent. For example, special, gender-linked courtesy to women was at one time part of a stable cultural paradigm. At that time, challenging the paradigm was deemed boorish. Cultural crisis and illness become evident when such challenges cannot be suppressed as happened in the feminist revolutions in the middle of the twentieth century. The failure to suppress dissent means that normal inquiry cannot be accommodated on its own terms. At this point, the only way to re-establish a healthy, normal cultural perspective is by *encouraging* dissent, although this time dissent becomes a full-blown, global criticism of the particular area of the culture. In this situation, the present cultural paradigms must endure revolutionary cultural criticism. The result is either continued crisis, the re-establishment of the original paradigm with significant or trivial modifications, or the abandonment of the old paradigm in favor of a new one. Cultural war is the result of the inability to settle a cultural crisis by restoring normal cultural inquiry.

A culture is healthy or normal when it consists of a paradigm or set of paradigms that permit the normal resolutions of social, political, and legal controversies. According to the prevailing paradigm, suppression of dissent is perfectly legitimate in such circumstances so as long as the proposed cultural change is relatively non-controversial. However, because

According to Fish, the conservative's view is "part of a (doomed) effort to stay the replacement of one historically produced 'common ground' by its inevitable successor." S. Fish, *The Common Touch* in *Political Education in Liberal Education, supra* note 21, at 264. Since "values and standards are themselves historical products, fashioned and refashioned in the crucible of discussion and debate, there is no danger of their being subverted because they are always and already being transformed." *Id.* Conservatives then want to put an artificial brake on a process that cannot be stopped; saying "no" to history will inevitably be an abject failure. What Fish fails to appreciate is that taking the cultural right's position on cultural change represents one major tenet in American political life. And though history cannot be stopped, it can be thwarted and distorted. The fundamental tenets of cultural conservativism will be transformed only to the extent required by historical transformation itself, shaving off dried skin and redeploying principles of meritocracy and competitiveness in a cosmetically more attractive fashion. This is the ultimate goal of conservatives such as Bennett and Cheney, and far from being impossible, their strategy is in fact working. From this conservative perspective, making as few changes in one's cultural values as is necessary to keep one's ideology going is, in effect, saying "no" to history.

87. For a similar point, but pertaining to radically different languages, see D. Davidson, *On the Very Idea of A Conceptual Scheme* in *Post-Analytic Philosophy* 129 (J. Rajchman and C. West, eds. 1985).

no culture is ever completely normal or healthy, cultural criticism is essential and ought to be a perpetual and systematic element of the cultural system. If this is granted, the next question requires us to determine which social institution or institutions promises to provide the most efficient form of revolutionary cultural inquiry – that is, the most efficient and plausible form of cultural criticism.

Normal culture is the dominant process through which an individual becomes the person she is. Understanding oneself is "inseparable from learning to participate in what is called a [normal] 'culture.'"[88] Furthermore, normal culture is the dominant force by which individuals live out their lives, providing the dominant tools for dealing with problems of work, play, spirituality and so forth. Additionally, it provides the means for resolving personal dilemmas as well as for solving a multifarious range of interpersonal and social problems. Normal culture is the force that permits us to understand and resolve the problems we face. Without normal culture there would be no self-understanding and no medium through which to understand others. Normal culture involves such pedestrian customs as lining up at the supermarket check out, as well as such complex qualities as gratitude, courage and fortitude. Normal cultural inquiry involves piecemeal criticism of means and ends relations, but stops short of more general or global attempts crtiticizing the goals and purposes of our cultural system. Normal cultural criticism therefore seems inadequate as a means of providing this more comprehensive type of cultural criticism. Instead, normal cultural criticism needs to be Burkean in its insistence on piecemeal, incremental social change in response to concrete problems – social change that is tailored to resolve nothing more than the particular problem at hand.

When no endemic process exists for resolving cultural controversies, normal culture – shorn of revolutionary cultural inquiry – tends to atrophy. Since, on pragmatic grounds, cultures are "experiments in living," a vital feature of cultural institutions is lost when nothing prods them to defend themselves. A culture is "healthy" only when it has the capacity to expand and develop, and to resolve standard as well as atypical problems. This process in turn requires some mechanism to prompt normal culture to take stock of itself.

Revolutionary culture is thus the process through which normal culture stays healthy. Moreover, cultural criticism often involves demonstrating how sub-cultural groups are unjustifiably excluded from the dominant culture. Cultures that refuse to accept the influx of new ideas,

88. M. Oakeshott, *A Place of Learning* in *The Voice of Liberal Learning* at 17, 28.

attitudes, and values, along with cultures that forbid the inclusion of marginal groups, have a tendency to wither and die. Because revolutionary cultural inquiry cannot pervade every area of cultural life, a healthy, normal culture will seek an institutional means for permanently, but safely, expressing revolutionary cultural criticism and inquiry. Several institutions are possible candidates for the permanent home of revolutionary cultural inquiry: the church, the media, and the university are three chief examples of such institutions. Although the church is sometimes a catalyst for social and cultural change, the daily operations of religious institutions in American society follow normal cultural paradigms. In these institutions, paradigms and rules for settling controversies are fixed and dissent is suppressed.

The media are arguably a much more likely candidate to function as the institutional bastion of cultural criticism in a liberal democratic society. Generally speaking, the media function as an institution of criticism within the context of normal cultural inquiry. At best, the American media function as a mirror of normal culture.[89] The media evaluate claims made through normal cultural inquiry. Journalists try to discover whether our political and social leaders are living up to the spirit of our cultural paradigms. Rarely do the media challenge the paradigms themselves.

Can the media function in the way required by the concept of a healthy, normal culture? Well, while a critical media can contribute to the health of a normal culture, journalists historically have not operated in American culture as an impetus for revolutionary cultural criticism.[90] And perhaps there are good reasons for this. Mass culture is concerned with it's own perpetuation, and thus the media cannot function as a source of radical criticism. Mass cultures cannot tolerate revolutionary criticism from within, since for normal cultural inquiry to progress there must be an enormous degree of consensus on a myriad of important moral, legal, and political problems.

To carry out a sustained critique of the dominant culture, an institution should exhibit the following characteristics: first, it should be relatively independent and insulated from the dominant, normal culture. I stress the word "relatively" because no institution is totally independent and insulated from the wider culture, if only due to its own social and economic interpenetration. Nevertheless, some institutions must be significantly independent of and insulated from the wider culture. This is both an institution's strength and weakness. It is its strength because an

89. At its worst, the media are libelous, sensationalist, and trashy.
90. It could be argued that the media in Europe are more likely to engage in revolutionary cultural inquiry than their counterparts in the United States.

institution significantly, though not absolutely, independent of and insulated from the wider culture can exercise the opportunity to criticize the wider culture. An institution whose activities are largely tutelary and preparatory is ideally suited for this sort of criticism. But this is its weakness too, because such an institution does not have the capacity for directly affecting the everyday operations of the wider culture. The results of this criticism will have only an indirect, though powerful, effect on changing the wider culture.

Second, the institution should have the depth of intellectual resources to provide a wide array of criticism of every aspect of normal culture. Third, it should provide the best intellectual and theoretical minds in the nation to formally carry out this radical cultural critique. Finally, the institution should have the capacity, in its sequestered environment, for carrying out or putting into practice actual experiments in social interaction that follow from its intellectual critique of the wider culture. The university can be a safe testing ground for certain ideas, even when these experiments might not, and perhaps should not, be tolerated in the wider society. For example, ordinances against hate speech might be perfectly reasonable in the institutional setting, while not practicable in the wider society.

III.

The conception of the university employed in this essay exists in sharp contrast to the notion of education as apolitical. Indeed, education in a liberal democracy serves a civic function;[91] it must prepare individuals for the full and equal citizenship that is required by the liberal democracy. This requirement is naturally tied to social and cultural criticism.

The university serves as the most likely permanent institution capable of sustained cultural criticism.[92] The university – especially the tenure

91. Manfred Stanley defines a civic institution "as any institution central to the production or maintenance of goods defined by a large majority of citizens as vital to the material and moral prosperity of the commonwealth." M. Stanley, *The American University as a Civic Institution*, 2 *The Civic Arts Review* 4, 5 (1989). Thus, preserving the general health of the dominant normal culture entails subjecting its basic presuppositions to sustained radical critique. This approach also entails a preservative function. E. Green, *Education For A New Society* 116-17 (1947). Radical critique preserves those values that survive its criticism.

92. I do not discuss the role of the arts in this essay because the arts as a social institution are too diverse, diffuse, and remote from the dominant culture to provide the appropriate pragmatic cultural criticism. Of course, an artist should consider one of her central goals the testing of standard cultural icons, but the university should function as a conduit through which the arts critically affect the dominant culture.

system – provides the necessary independence for theorists and scholars, thereby enabling them to engage in a wide array of criticism of the wider culture.[93] Consequently, the conservative charge that American universities are failing because they are controlled by tenured radicals is invalid on its face. The university *should* be the natural home for "tenured radicals."[94] If a university has no tenured radicals, it is delinquent in its role as cultural critic. Let us now examine what it means minimally for the university to function as an institution of cultural criticism of the wider culture.[95]

First, in order for the university to function formally as an institution of cultural criticism, it must have a diverse – multicultural – array of faculty and students. Different perspectives in varying degrees of depth and commitment must be part of the everyday operations of the university. Second, in order to subject the dominant – normal – culture to revolutionary criticism, the university must formally and informally familiarize its students with the foundations and structure of normal culture.

This is why the present debate over the core curriculum – or canon – seems so disingenuous. No one suggests in this debate that it is appropriate for the university to teach courses reflecting only non-Western cultures. The typical proposal for reform suggests that along with the core curriculum, non-Western courses should be provided to serve as an alternative perspective on many of the attitudes and aspirations taken as normal in Western culture. Furthermore, while it is useful to compare American culture with alternative perspectives from non-Western bourgeois cultures, it is also useful to contrast American culture with non-Western cultures that are non-capitalistic as well. By doing so, we perform a greater service to the dominant culture in the United States.

This is why Dinesh D'Souza's diatribe against I. Rigoberta Menchu is so wide of the mark.[96] For presenting a bourgeois, capitalist, Guatemalan view, while worthwhile in providing an alternative perspective, is not nearly as effective for cultural criticism as presenting a view that challenges the basic tenets of capitalism. And you do not need to be a socialist, Marxist, or revolutionary to endorse this position. All you need to be

---

93. Consider D'Souza's remarks: [I]f radical solutions may not be contemplated in the university, where else should they be considered? Because they are sanctuary institutions, universities can be a philosophical testing ground for programs of revolutionary transformation. . . . D. D'Souza, *supra* note 67 at 250.

94. R. Kimball, *Tenured Radicals, supra* note 41.

95. This will, of course, involve the tenured critics being self-critical as well.

96. D. D'souza, *I. Rigoberta Menchu: An Indian Women in Guatemala* in *Illiberal Education, supra* note 67 at 59.

is a pragmatist who understands that healthy cultures typically survive and remain healthy only by subjecting themselves to systematic criticism that compares their perspectives to other cultural perspectives. Furthermore, the more opposed the perspective is the more healthy is the dominant normal culture in considering it.

In order to represent and reflect the normal, dominant culture, a core curriculum must have a sufficient number of traditional courses in the sciences and humanities. But keep in mind that the normal, dominant culture is already embodied in a student's self-conception when she arrives at the ivy halls. Any native individual who did not reflect the dominant culture at least partially, would be more than mad: she would not be a person. Consequently, the dominant culture has an enormous head start on any alternative perspective. This might imply that in certain circumstances, the university can place a weighted hand on formal and informal means of exposing students to alternative cultural perspectives. Without becoming authoritarian, some non-dominant perspectives may require special treatment in order to assist the university in its role as a bastion of radical cultural criticism. Nothing is wrong with such an affirmative action strategy regarding *ideas*.

Though university students are already familiar with the dominant culture, students still need to achieve a reflective understanding of the roots and structure of the cultural system that defines them as people.[97] Without such a background, a sustained radical cultural criticism of the dominant culture is impossible. To achieve this, radical cultural criticism must also include systematic exposure to perspectives from sub-cultures, that is, from normal, non-dominant cultures within our own society. This can take many forms. University policy might include such normal multicultural perspectives in each traditional course. Alternatively, a core curriculum might include certain traditional courses without comparing alternative perspectives, while at the same time setting aside a certain number of courses explicitly designed to present the alternative cultural perspectives that form an integral part of cultural criticism.

Second, a liberal education should include courses specifically designed to criticize the dominant culture, courses in comparative cul-

---

97. Of course, cultural criticism is not the only reason for restricting the role of Western culture in core curriculua. An additional reason is simply civility, to avoid insulting non-Westerners by insisting that their cultures are somehow second-rate or marginal. While the cultural right appears not to be sensitive to this point, it is difficult to understand why. Wasn't a similar insensitivity responsible for the European influx to the Americas in the first place? Oppression and insensitivity are simply two sides of the same prejudiced coin.

tural perspectives as well as courses specifically and exclusively dealing with other cultures.[98] Understanding other cultures in their own terms contributes to a pragmatic validation of our normal culture. Multiculturalism in the university is thus a necessary commitment of an anti-foundationalist pragmatic conception of cultural criticism.

Multiculturalism does not preclude studying a Western canon. In fact, studying a Western canon is unobjectionable all things being equal. But in the context of present American demographic conditions, having a mostly Western canon suggests that the cultural norm, or even the cultural ideal, is Western culture. Inevitably this is an endorsement of the status quo politically, educationally, and morally. Accordingly, one wonders how Sidney Hook could deny this fact when he asserts that "[f]ar from leading to a glorification of the status-quo, as their ignorant detractors charge, the knowledge imparted by such courses, properly taught, is essential to understanding the world of our own experience regardless of whether one seeks to revolutionize or reform or preserve it."[99]

Besides being simply rude, this remark reveals an enormous insensitivity to the process whereby ideas become accepted. For Hook, a narrow, impoverished conception of rational persuasion is the sole vehicle for accepting a belief or value. But, in fact, the assumptions with which we address an issue often determine what our conclusions will be. Hence, regarding Western culture as somehow sacrosanct does contribute to preserving the status quo and makes revolution and reform that much more difficult. Furthermore, Hook's remarks fail to appreciate that once a student invests the enormous amount of time and energy required to understand her own experience, experience that typically is embraced by one's family, friends, and social heroes, it is only the remarkable student who can also develop the tenor of mind to subject this experience to radical criticism. Hook's reactionary condemnation of those challenging his position is itself existential confirmation of their position. For if Sidney Hook can be so patently blind to the problem of institutionalizing truly radical criticism, how can we expect the ordinary undergraduate to do any better? The problem with Hook's view is that once the average student takes a series of such courses, "taught properly," there is almost no chance for her to devel-

---

98. One way to achieve this, perhaps, is to create a critical studies department consisting of courses in philosophy, literature, history, anthropology, medical humanities, and law. A critical studies department should have as its central goal assisting students in understanding their culture's strengths and weaknesses.

99. S. Hook, *The Attack on Western Civilization* in *Convictions* at 139, 141.

op the tools necessary for reform or revolution. Instead, the natural predilection is rather to preserve the familiar.[100]

In a similar vein, E.D. Hirsch states that it is paradoxical to claim that "cultural literacy" preserves the status quo because "traditional forms of literate culture are precisely the most effective instruments for political and social change."[101] In Hirsch's view:

> All political discourse at the national level must use the stable forms of the national language and its associated culture. . . . Radicalism in politics, but conservatism in literate knowledge and spelling: to be a conservative in the *means* of communication is the road to effectiveness in modern life, in whatever direction one wishes to be effective. . . . Conservatives who wish to preserve traditional values will find that these are not necessarily inculcated by a traditional education, which can in fact be subversive of the status quo.[102]

Certainly, "traditional education" does not *necessarily* lead to traditional values; but it certainly makes criticism of the dominant culture more difficult. Similarly, using our "national language and associated culture," with its allegedly meritocratic principles of distributing goods, makes it difficult for radical egalitarianism to even get a fair hearing. Finally, where radical change requires revising political consciousness, conservatism in language, even if only a means, often impedes such change. For example, radically revising linguistic conventions by replacing the canonical use of "he" with the exclusive use of "she" or perhaps the random use of "she" and "he," and other similar changes, may be required if radical feminism is to get a fair hearing. The conservative (linguistic) view that "he" stands for either gender embodies an ideology that sometimes is almost impossible to overcome.

Given the diverse political reasons for insisting on "cultural literacy" (some of which are not unreasonable), it should not be mysterious why the cultural left is incensed by Hirsch's views. Yet Richard Rorty is troubled by the left's reaction to Hirsch. According to Rorty, the left benefits from culturally literate high schoolers because

---

100. The point here is that the typical student is usually exposed subliminally and formally to the dominant culture only. How then can we pretend that such exposure is merely a necessary condition to changing or preserving the dominant culture? Instead, this exposure is a very sophisticated and insidious form of brainwashing. Did *Sidney Hook* really miss this point? Of course, the words "properly taught" are weasel words. In this view, "properly taught" means learning the appropriate critical skills. But if the appropriate critical skills preclude multiculturalism, the argument begs the question against Hook's critics, while if these skills include multiculturalism, Hook's argument concedes the very point at issue.

101. E.D. Hirsch, *Cultural Literacy* 22 (1988).

102. *Id.* at 23-24.

[i]t is, after all, easier to teach Shakespeare in a Stephen Greenblattish, quasi-Foucaldian way to students who recognize the names of Shakespeare's plays, easier to explain possibilities of social transformation to students who know that the French Revolution antedated the Russian, easier to talk about sexism to students who recognize the term 'women's suffrage' and the name 'Betty Friedan,' easier to talk about homophobia to students who have heard of Oscar Wilde, and so on.[103]

The problem with Rorty's defense is that when cultural literacy is presented to the general public as *the minimum* knowledge any literate person should have, it never fully comes off as *only* that. Instead, it is received as the immutable core of cultural life. This core material comes steeped in the political culture of the status quo, or more dangerously, it inculcates the basic individualistic, competitive, meritocratic principles embedded in the dominant culture. This, of course, not only means that students reach self-understanding in terms of this political culture. More importantly, it also means that *most* students will never even take the cultural left's views seriously.

Multiculturalism can be viewed as a form of inquiry specially adapted for a pragmatic liberal education and having implications for such issues as ordinances against hate speech, affirmative action, and political correctness. Before discussing these issues let me characterize multicultural academic inquiry as a type of conversation pervading every area of university life.[104] Academic cultural conversation should be a continuing process through which diverse members of the academic community learn about themselves and express who they are and what expectations they have of others. Academic cultural inquiry as conversation includes the metaphor of a seminar or conversational table that conveys the idea of mutually disinterested people engaging in a joint activity for mutual advantage. This metaphor helps us describe certain moral and political qualities that should be incorporated into the idea of academic cultural inquiry as a conversation. Let's explore these qualities.

Conversationalism, in its broadest outline, is typically conceived of as a replacement for traditional conceptions of human inquiry.[105] As a

103. R. Rorty, *Two Cheers for the Cultural Left* in *Liberal Education, supra* note 21 at 233, 236. And so it is.

104. My notion of conversationalism differs from Oakeshott's in at least one significant respect. Conversationalism is an activity that is driven by and about human community and culture. Oakeshott's use of "conversation" appears to be more concerned with the intelligent pursuit of whatever intellectually appeals to the participants. Urgency in understanding oneself and one's relationships with others surround my notion of conversationalism, but not Oakeshott's notion of "conversation."

105. See Robert Justin Lipkin, *Kibitzers, Fuzzies and Apes without Tails: Pragmatism and the Art of Conversation in Legal Theory*, 66 *Tulane L. Rev.* 69 (1991).

postmodern form of inquiry, conversationalism has instrumental and intrinsic features. I have discussed these features elsewhere.[106] Here I only want to stress some of the instrumental features. Conversationalism, and its metaphor of a seminar table, permits both friends and enemies to face and take direct stock of one another. In doing so, it permits important psychological and phenomenological factors – which aid in mutual understanding – to become operative.[107] Ordinarily this method permits enemies to take one another more seriously.

Furthermore, the metaphor of a seminar table is uncontroversially egalitarian. Each voice must be present at the table and must have the same opportunity to speak. The atmosphere around the table must be such that each voice feels free to speak if she chooses. There must be no obstacles to speaking, nor recriminations afterward. This notion of conversation is especially suited to university life.

For we must consider cultural criticism of the dominant culture not as a diatribe but as a conversation among and between the dominant normal culture and other perspectives.[108] Conversationalism operates as it should only when all significant voices are represented at the seminar table. Affirmative action, then, is a requirement of cultural criticism on two grounds: first, if the goal of a healthy culture is a culture that hears all voices, then all voices must be represented at the seminar table. Second, if a healthy culture is one that survives the criticism of alternative voices, then alternative voices must sit at the seminar table. Consequently, members of minority and marginalized groups must be present at the seminar table in order for the dominant majority culture to be a healthy one.

This goal of inclusion entails that both faculty and students include members of minority and marginalized groups. In principle, this might entail that less than qualified faculty and students be recruited in order for marginalized voices to be present at the table, even if these voices are weak or inarticulate. However, because American society has sufficient numbers of qualified students and qualified faculty to represent the minority and marginalized view points, we fortunately do not face this problem. Nonetheless, the principle is a crucial one, namely, that there are *cultural* reasons for affirmative action that complement but are distinguishable from the moral and legal reasons for affirmative action.

---

106. *Id.* at 109.

107. Under certain circumstances, these instrumental benefits can become perverted, thereby distorting and even disrupting the conversation.

108. Conversation, or the method of inquiry and discussion I have elsewhere called "conversationalism," is a useful way to understand the kind of context in which cultural criticism takes place. *See supra* note 105.

Consequently, in this view, liberal education as a conversation requires the presence of members of minority and marginalized groups, whether qualified or not.

Ordinances against hate speech contribute to the university's role as cultural critic and liberal education's role as a conversation in other ways. Members of minority and marginalized groups must function in an environment that is as stigma-free as possible. Although, it is no doubt quixotic to insist upon a completely stigma-free university environment, the university has an obligation to provide physical and psychological security for all groups, especially minority and marginalized groups. For purposes of the argument in this essay, this obligation is neither moral nor legal. Instead, the university has a *cultural* obligation to provide this security given the university's special role as an institutionalized bastion of cultural criticism. Ultimately, the obligation derives from the university's role in helping procure the health of the dominant culture.

The fundamental concern here is with the character and operation of the cultural conversation as it occurs in every aspect of university life. Protecting minority and marginalized groups dissipates the unfettered power of pranksters, bigots, and racists. Such protection makes members of minority and marginalized groups feel less stigmatized in two ways: first, it reduces the total amount and degree of stigma.[109] Second, and perhaps more importantly, it shows that the university itself publicly and formally stands behind them and against stigmatization. This public role is fundamentally important even when it doesn't reduce the total amount of stigmatization, for it sends a message that as far as the wider university community is concerned, the conversation will be shorn of bigotry and racism.[110] In short, the message of civility pervades the seminar table.

What role does "political correctness" play in conversationalism? The term itself doesn't have much to recommend itself, especially given its portrayal by the media. However, the notion that there are certain forms of discourse and conduct that are inappropriate does have a strong foothold in the notion of cultural criticism. If cultural criticism is instrumental in procuring a healthy, normal, and dominant culture, then the notion of appropriate discourse and conduct is a salient component of the concept of the university as an institutionalized form of revolutionary

109. However much protection the university gives these groups, there will always be a residual degree of stigmatization that cannot be eradicated without imposing draconian totalitarian measures, and perhaps not even then.

110. The university must take a *stand* against invidious discrimination. As a minimal condition, an ordinance, even a weak ordinance, is required to support this stand. *See* Grey, *Civil Rights vs. Civil Liberties*, 8 Soc. Phil. & Pol'y 81, 104-7 (1991).

cultural criticism. What pragmatic conservatives and progressives alike should be concerned with is the access to and fluid operation of the conversation around the seminar table. Hence, members of dominant groups should show a greater sensitivity to members of groups traditionally excluded from this table. This might be exemplified in general considerations concerning how we refer to various groups or how we assess the feasibility of introducing new courses or programs. At any rate there should be in general a heightened sensitivity to excluding minority and marginalized groups from the conversation across all facets of the university.

Our discourse and conduct reveals our attitude towards the nature and expansiveness of the seminar table. Consequently, how we refer to people reveals the value that our culture and language place on them. Perhaps there is no better example than referring to someone as "queer." What could this possibly mean except that the qualities most characteristic of human beings are absent? Consequently, unless we are willing to say that gays and lesbians, women, African-Americans and so forth are not human, we better devise a method for revising our vocabulary along the lines of civility.

This conclusion has serious implications for the concept of the university as a bastion of cultural criticism. It is a short jump from viewing someone as queer to concluding that he or she should not have access to the seminar table. Consequently, the seminar table might require that civil discourse eschew such terminology. I view this as simply an implication of the general view widely accepted in normal culture that we be courteous or at least civil to one another. Courtesy requires that you do not berate others as fat, stupid, gimpy, ugly, and so forth.[111] If political correctness is no more than civility, it has an obvious place in the conversation that structures a liberal education.[112]

It should be pointed out that the metaphor of a liberal education as a conversation around a seminar table does not guarantee, nor does it even make very much more likely, the resolution of all or most important cultural conflicts. But it does show that there are two very different ways of

111. The question of which speech to suppress is essentially a question of what sort of political culture we wish to create. In these terms, civility might dictate that we chill speech like "nigger," "cunt," "kike," and "faggot." S. Fish, *There's No Such Thing as Free Speech, and It's a Good Thing Too in Debating P.C.*, *supra* note 14 at 231, 244.

112. Ultimately, this conception of cultural criticism must confront First Amendment arguments against enforced civility. Of course, the constitutional guarantee of equal protection is a possible counterpoise to those arguments. Moreover, contrary to conventional wisdom there is nothing conceptually sacrosanct about the constitutional protection of free speech. No doubt free speech is central in a truly fair and democratic society; but protecting people against the hurtful, stigmatizing "free" speech of others might be just as essential. *See* Fish, *supra* note 111 at 245.

conceiving of cultural inquiry. One way conceives of cultural inquiry as directed outward toward some external independent reality that validates cultural development and change. The second conception of cultural inquiry is directed inward toward coherence, community and when possible, consensus.

The first view, a form of externalism, follows from a foundationalist or neo-foundationalist conception of inquiry, while the second view, a form of internalism, eschews foundationalist conceptions of cultural inquiry and instead seeks fraternity and solidarity. Indeed, the first view is explicable only in terms of some such foundationalist presuppositions. The internalist contends, on the other hand, that we should turn to others for a continuous undistorted dialogue concerning which cultural paradigms to create, and that our goal should be to understand ourselves in terms of our interactions with other people. The externalist denies the inherent importance of community and other people, while retreating into the external reality she champions, a "reality" that ultimately becomes a form of solipsism. The internalist makes human individuality and community the central tenets of human life. If you give up externalism, you can easily reject solipsism. However, there are risks. We risk not being able to achieve the appropriate form of consensus even when taking others seriously.

There are, however, other risks as well. Perhaps the most devastating one is the risk of totalitarianism, namely, forcing others to accept the group values simply because they are the group's values. What is more, this seems to be precisely the thrust of the right wing diatribe against radical cultural criticism and political correctness. The charge is or should be that the tenured left forces everyone to accept its fashionable left-wing values. That is, in saying that we ought not to call others "fat" or "queer" or "a piece of ass," we are imposing our values on them and coercing them to accept what we accept.

Two replies are in order. First, any culture has a sense of courtesy and civility that it imposes upon others. This sense of courtesy was once characterized as "good breeding" or "common decency." To say that a university cannot insist on common decency is preposterous. Some forms of speech and conduct are so inimical to communication and inquiry that they are precluded by the very purposes of these activities as aspects of conversational interaction. Second, the possibility of the charge of totalitarianism also permits the abuse of the charge. But let's be careful here. Whenever we say that someone *falsely* makes a charge that if true should tip the moral scale in her favor, we had better ask what benefits and burdens are involved in making such a false charge. Falsely charging rape, for instance, has such high burdens that few people would be willing to risk making the charge. But what risks does the charge of totalitarianism have when lodged by foundationalists and conservatives? I think very few indeed, and the benefits to these groups in a society not attuned to the importance of cultural criticism are bountiful.

Accordingly, conversationalism as a replacement for traditional foundational cultural inquiry might turn out to be a monumental failure in traditional terms. Instead, let's shift the goal of cultural inquiry. No longer should we hope to guarantee consensus on all controversial issues. Instead, we should simply provide a vehicle for continuing the conversation in such a way that all groups feel the capacity to express themselves to the extent enjoyed by other groups. At times this might entail skewing the conversation in favor of minority or marginalized groups; at other times it might not.[113] In any event, this is, I believe, a crucial commitment of anti-foundationalist cultural inquiry.

Pragmatism insists that there are no external perspectives from which to ground cultural inquiry and that, moreover, the results of inquiry are never known with certainty. Nonetheless, pragmatism insists that we can always do better, and that the only way to do better is by subjecting our culture to the widest possible criticism. Rather than denigrate the university as a bastion of progressive cultural criticism, pragmatism, whether of the left or the right, ought to celebrate this role. For whether you believe the dominant culture should reflect orthodox or radical values, pragmatists should want the dominant culture to receive the best criticism available. Only then can they have any confidence in the health of the dominant culture.

Accordingly, a well-educated American university graduate should have the following characteristics:[114] she should know enough about the

---

113. Even in a free society, the dominant culture favors itself. Consequently, for other voices to be heard we might need to skew the conversation in favor of minority and marginalized groups.

114. I will make only general remarks here. Searle, on the other hand, lists six categories of a well-educated person. J. Searle, *N.Y. Rev. Bks.*, *supra* note 40 at 42. Searle includes such knowledge as "a smattering of knowledge of the general and special theories of relativity, and an understanding of why quantum mechanics is so philosophically challenging. You need to "understand what a trade cycle is. . . ." *Id.* Also, "you need to know at least one foreign language well enough so that you can read the best literature that language has produced in the original, and so you carry on a reasonable conversation and have dreams in that language." *Id.* The most important reason for this is that "you can never understand one language until you understand at least two." *Id.* These are astounding as minimal conditions for a well-educated person. In Searle's view, then, many very effective university professors and some highly talented scholars, despite their effectiveness as teachers or scholars, are not even well-educated people. Quite an astonishing view.

dominant culture – including its science, social science, and humanities – to identify the dominant culture as a subject of criticism. Second, she should be trained in the analytic and critical skills necessary to thoroughly evaluate the dominant culture and to compare it with other cultures. Third, other cultures should be studied on their own in order to understand as many experiments in human flourishing as possible. These are general goals. If our well-educated person is a conservative she should know how to subject the dominant culture to the most impressive objections available in order to refute them and preserve the status quo. If she is a progressive, she should also know how to subject the dominant culture to these objections so that she can begin to reform the world according to her progressive vision. In either case, multiculturalism in a liberal education and the conversation that drives it should be endorsed by everyone.

Conclusion

This essay maintains that cultural health and reliability require continuous, institutionalized cultural critique of the dominant culture, and that more than any other social institution the university provides the most likely place to house this criticism. Accordingly, the university has a special role to play concerning such issues in the cultural war as ordinances against hate speech, affirmative action, political correctness, and multiculturalism. Its place is to provide the institutional setting for carrying on the pragmatic enterprise of radically criticizing the dominant culture through a continual cultural conversation. Ultimately, this conversation warrants either our confidence in the health of the dominant culture, or the judgement that the dominant culture is in need of repair. A reliable judgment that either the dominant culture is healthy or that it is in need of repair should be a goal toward which both conservatives and progressives aspire.[115]

115. I am deeply grateful to Barbara Herrnstein-Smith, Gerald Graff, and Giles Gunn, who, in responding to my unsolicited entreaties for critical feedback, revealed their supererogatory collegiality to someone unknown to them. I am also indebted to Edward Sankowski, Christopher Ake and Anne Shapiro for their very helpful comments on an earlier draft of this article. Robert Hayman and Rodney Smith also deserve my gratitude for sharing with me their ideas on the culture wars.

5
Neutrality, Politicization and the Curriculum★

Robert L. Simon

I remember being struck some time ago by an article on the ethics of teaching in which a philosophy professor declared that his goal as a teacher was to "save students from their parents."[1] At the time I agreed strongly with the statement, but as my children grew I began to have increasing doubts, and by the time they had entered college I had rejected it entirely.

I suspect that part of what troubles me about the statement is its suggestion (perhaps not intended by the author) that philosophy professors should function primarily as saviors whose principal aim is the undermining, perhaps by whatever means necessary, of the presumably more traditional and therefore presumably incorrect values students have inherited from their families.

More recently, many have argued that significant revision of the college curriculum, particularly in the humanities and social sciences, is necessary if students are to be saved from the cultural blinders allegedly imposed by the dominant groups and traditions within their society. Indeed, the curriculum of colleges and universities has become a contested area in the various ideological and cultural disputes currently being waged about higher education in America. Concerns about multiculturalism, the debate about political correctness, and demographic shifts in the ethnic composition of student bodies and the American work force, all have or are claimed to have significant implications for the curricula of colleges and universities. In this family of debates and controversies, proponents of more traditional conceptions of the curriculum have tended

---

★Sections of this paper appear in slightly different form in Robert L. Simon, Neutrality and the Academic Ethic, Rowman and Littlefield, 1994

1. Richard Mohr, "Teaching as Politics," *Report from the Center for Philosophy and Public Policy*, vol. 6 (1986) p. 9. I discuss this example in my "A Defense of the Neutral University," in Steven M. Cahn, ed., *Morality, Responsibility, and the University* (Philadelphia: Temple University Press, 1990) pp. 247-48.

to accuse opponents of politicizing the curriculum, of trying in effect to "save" students by inappropriate and unjustified means. Those in favor of revisions have frequently replied that the curriculum always has been politicized anyway. In what follows, I want to explore certain issues that arise from the charges about politicization of the curriculum, especially issues having to do with the meaning and justification of such claims.

According to many of those who wish to fundamentally restructure the curriculum, whom I will call revisionists, the charge of politicization functions only ideologically.[2] The function of the charge of politicization, in this view, is to allow proponents of the traditional forms of the curriculum, whom I will call traditionalists, to unfairly accuse the revisionists of importing politics into what had previously been a politically free zone devoted to objective scholarship and the pursuit of truth. Many revisionists would reply that the curriculum always has been politicized. Because past politicization involved values taken for granted by traditionalists, traditionalists were able to see educational choices as being free of political bias, even though such choices simply reflected the values of dominant groups. Thus, political scientist Ronald Walters argues that:

> many who are prepared . . . to do battle against the new Afrocentric and multicultural curricular ideas and to raise the flag of objectivity and factuality are doing the same as those who are attempting to assert the integrity of African civilization. . . . Which is to say that on both sides the advocates are partisans in an intellectual struggle . . . pious pretense to the contrary. The curriculum that we have today in American society is a by product of power. The effort to change the current curriculum is an effort to destroy the political orthodoxy which has established itself through power.[3]

But are curricular debates over Afrocentrism and multiculturalism merely disputes about power or are there genuine intellectual conflicts about the merits of conflicting positions? Do claims about the politicization of the curriculum function only ideologically or do they sometimes raise issues of substance? Perhaps the best way to make a start at dealing with these questions is to separate some of the issues raised by the whole topic of politicization of the curriculum.

2. The use of the term "revisionist" is not meant to deny that there are significant differences among those, such as multiculturalists, who recommend such fundamental change. Thus, revisionism is a term for a family of positions, not just one position. Moreover, the use of the term is not meant to deny that its scope is unclear. How much change must one advocate to be properly termed a revisionist is a difficult question, but one I do not explore in this paper.

3. Ronald Walters, "A Different View: 'Afrocentric' Means Providing the Neglected Black Perspective," *American Educator*, vol. 15, No. 3 (Winter, 1991) p. 26.

I. Politicization: What are the Issues?

Claims about politicization clearly raise a host of conceptual and normative issues.[4] For example, what does the charge of politicization amount to? What counts as politicization? Is politicization of the curriculum good or bad? Is it avoidable or unavoidable? Is politicization incompatible with objectivity and concern for intellectual merit? Would an unpoliticized curriculum necessarily be committed to traditional subject matter or to what has been called the "canon" in literature and the humanities?

We can begin by asking what function the charge of politicization serves. Clearly, it often is used as a conceptual weapon to discredit rival approaches to the curriculum, for revisionists are often accused of making the curriculum into an ideological tool that presumably it is not supposed to be. Conversely, traditionalists are often accused of failing to recognize their own ideological blinders, and thereby failing to appreciate not only that the curriculum always has been politicized but that it couldn't help but be politicized in the first place.

But why does the claim that the curriculum is politicized function as a criticism of other views? The charge of politicization does not function purely as an epithet. On the contrary, it can only function critically precisely because it makes some claim about the curriculum to which it is applied. But what is that claim?

Unfortunately, as we will see, it is unlikely that all those who speak about the curriculum being politicized have the same conception of politicization in mind. As with other important concepts in political philosophy, such as equality, justice, and fairness, different conceptions or theories of each notion are in the field.

While all of these different conceptions cannot be discussed here, at least some of the parties to the debate over the curriculum are advancing the view that what is politicized is neither neutral nor fully objective – perhaps not rationally justifiable at all. Thus, traditionalists, by claiming that the more extreme revisionists are politicizing a previously pure curriculum, are charging revisionists with departing from the ethics of objective scholarship in order to engage in political action. By responding that traditionalists ignore their own past politicization, many revi-

4. Politicization, whatever it is, can pertain not only to what is taught but to how it is taught, and to why it is taught, i.e., the reasons for teaching it. Clearly, traditionalists would regard even the teaching of the most classic texts as politicized if the reason for employing them was only to discredit anything Western, and if the method selected for accomplishing that aim was the indoctrination of students.

91

sionists are implying not only that the curriculum never was objectively defensible to begin with but that any choice of curriculum is more a matter of power politics than rational educational choice. When pressed to the limits, this account of politicization undercuts the claim that curricular decisions ever can be defended in terms that impartial people of good will, reasoning from diverse political perspectives, would find defensible. In this extreme interpretation, rational discourse itself becomes an ideologically contested notion, interpreted differently by those from different political, cultural, or socio-economic backgrounds.

Let us begin examining the family of conceptions that tend to characterize politicization in terms of lack of neutrality, objectivity, or impartiality, by considering the charge that politicization is unavoidable. For the idea that curricular struggles are really political battles in which claims of objectivity and neutrality play only an ideological role is at least suggested in the passage by Professor Walters quoted above. Again, such a view is at least suggested by the authors of the ACLS report, "Speaking for the Humanities," when they assert that

> traditional claims to disinterest, to the humanities as the realm of "sweetness and light," reflected unacknowledged ideologies. . . . The best contemporary work in the humanities strives to make clear both its critique of the ideologies of previous work, and its own *inevitable* ideological blindspots.[5]

Is politicization unavoidable? Is it a necessary element of contemporary political debate between traditionalists and revisionists? In considering such questions, we can also begin to distinguish at least some of the different conceptions of politicization employed in current discourse about the curriculum.

II. Is Politicization of the Curriculum Unavoidable?

As we have seen, if a politicized curriculum is unavoidable, then traditionalists who object to what they regard as revisionist politicization of the curriculum simply miss the point. If the unavoidability thesis is true, then revisionists are simply replacing one politicized or ideologically loaded curriculum with a different but equally politicized and ideologically loaded one.

---

5. George Levine, et.al., *Speaking for the Humanities: ACLS Occasional Paper #7* (New York: ACLS, 1989) p. 11, italics my own.

What reasons can be given for thinking the curriculum is unavoidably political? Perhaps by distinguishing the different reasons that can be given in support of such a view, we can also distinguish the different conceptions of politicization at work in this area.

According to one argument, the curriculum is inevitably political because it cannot be value-free. Thus, Henry A. Giroux, speaking to a conference of what has come to be called "the cultural left" asserts

> . . . the institutions of higher education regardless of their academic status represent places that affirm and legitimate existing views of the world, produce new ones, and authorize and shape particular social relations: . . . . The university is a place that is deeply political and unarguably normative.[6]

Arguing along similar lines, Henry David Aiken has also maintained that "to depoliticize the university would require the exclusion of all normative social and political studies."[7]

In these views, the curriculum is unavoidably normative so long as it contains normative studies (Aiken) or, more broadly, so long as it legitimizes certain world-views and shapes social relations (Giroux). Although I am not entirely clear what Giroux means by "legitimatizing world views" and "shaping social relations," he seems to be suggesting that at a minimum, the curriculum endorses some positions rather than others as worthy of examination and debate and so is value-laden. Because a value-free curriculum is no more possible than a four-sided triangle, and because a value-laden curriculum is unavoidably political, an apolitical curriculum is impossible as well.

Can the curriculum be value-free? I suspect that it cannot. Values can inhere in what is taught, how it is taught, and why it is taught. Clearly, a curriculum devoted solely to the classic texts, explored in an attempt to find universal truths or principles, is just as committed to values as one focused solely on texts critical of the classical tradition and skeptical of the existence of universal truths or principles. Surely the goals of searching for truth and the promoting study of the classical curriculum are as much values as are hostility to what some call "the canon" and skepticism toward traditional ideas of truth and objectivity.

---

6. Henry A. Giroux, "Liberal Arts Education and the Struggle for Public Life: Dreaming About Democracy," *The South Atlantic Quarterly*, vol. 89, No. 1 (1990) – Duke University Press, p. 114.

7. Henry David Aiken, "Can American Universities be Depoliticized," *Philosophic Exchange* (Summer 1970) reprinted in Sidney Hook, *Convictions* (Buffalo: Prometheus Books, 1990) p. 256.

Values, as Giroux maintains, are unavoidable in education. But what are the implications of this conclusion? In particular, is Giroux's inference from "the university is unarguably normative" to the "university is political" valid?

Clearly, if the absence of value neutrality implies the curriculum is politicized – unavoidably value-laden, the curriculum cannot avoid being politicized. But what is the significance of this conclusion? The clause of the United States Constitution forbidding an establishment of religion is value-laden, as it places a value upon religious liberty, but that does not prevent it from requiring government neutrality towards specific religions. Similarly, a good referee at a basketball game is enforcing the norms laid down in the rules of basketball, but this does not preclude the referee's being impartial towards the contesting teams. A stance of value commitment, then, while perhaps "political" in the broadest possible sense, does not preclude an absence of politicization in narrower and perhaps ethically more significant senses as well.

Although any curriculum must be permeated with values that guide decisions as to various levels of analysis of what is taught, how it is taught, and why it is taught, all values may not be equally partisan. Some values may be more narrowly partisan than others and perhaps less justifiably employed in educational contexts. Similarly, referees who enforce the rules of basketball may be enforcing certain values built into the rules, or into their interpretation of the rules, yet they are non-partisan compared to referees who makes decisions because they favor a specific team. Likewise, state neutrality towards religion may reflect a normative stance but is less partisan than a state policy that favors one religion over another.[8] In a parallel fashion, traditionalists who claim that revisionists are politicizing the curriculum may agree that any curriculum is value-laden but then go on to argue that what they object to is the particularly partisan nature of the values they claim the revisionists are employing.

In a sense, then, saying that the curriculum is unavoidably political because it is value-laden is trivial, for it obscures the need to make important distinctions among the kinds of values at stake. Moreover, saying this risks stretching the concept of the political so broadly that it

---

8. It might be objected that the Establishment Clause is narrowly partisan relative to some controversies. For example, it favors advocates of a liberal pluralistic society over those who favor a theocratic state. Although the issue of tolerance for the intolerant does raise complex issues, it can be replied that although the Establishment Clause does favor (and express) certain controversial values, any alternate provision would also do the same. The Establishment Clause is neutral, however, in that the reasons justifying its adoption do not rest on judgments as to which specific religious tradition deserves official recognition and support by the state.

makes no useful contrast and hence obscures narrower senses in which politicized and non-politicized curricula can be contrasted.

Aiken's claim that the curriculum is inevitably politicized so long as it deals with normative topics is open to similar sorts of objections. One might as well argue that basketball referees are inevitably partisans of one specific team or another simply because they engage in discussions of how the rules ought to be interpreted or changed.

Perhaps more to the point, there is a large gap between showing that a curriculum is normatively loaded, on one hand, and demonstrating that it is narrowly partisan, biased, or in some other way cognitively defective on the other. The premise that the curriculum is inevitably value-laden does not imply that it should be structured or presented so as to support a particular partisan ideology, whether on the left or right. Rather, among its normative goals might be acquainting students with enough critical tools and knowledge of major works that they are in a good position to make intelligent ethical and political choices for themselves. Accordingly, the jump from the normative character of the curriculum to the conclusion that it is therefore inevitably political, in any non-trivial sense of that term, seems far too hasty and is at best highly suspect.

Perhaps a second view of the politicization of the curriculum might have more to offer. This view suggests that politicization has to do not with the mere presence of value judgments but with the particular value judgments that are included in the curriculum. In this view, traditional forms of the curriculum are political because they express, or include, or support a particular selection of values: namely, those endorsed by dominant social groups. The curriculum is politicized, in other words, when it is value-laden in a biased manner. In this view, revisionists seek to broaden the traditional curriculum by broadening the selection of values supported by it, perhaps by including the perspectives of those excluded by more traditional approaches, particularly the voices of women and racial minorities. The politicized curriculum from this perspective is thus a biased or unrepresentative curriculum, one favoring the outlook of dominant social groups.

This approach may have more promise than those considered earlier, perhaps because it is plausible to think the content of the curriculum has been more greatly affected by the values of the relatively powerful than by those of the relatively powerless. However, this view too needs to be considered with care. It can be asked, in particular, in what way does it show the curriculum is *unavoidably* political? In fact, rather than supporting the claim that the curriculum is unavoidably political, it conflicts with it. That is, if revisionists claim to be replacing a curriculum originally biased towards a particular and presumably not fully adequate set of values with a less biased, more adequate substitute, then surely what they are claiming is replacing a more politicized curriculum with a less politicized one.

If so, that claim needs to be defended in critical debate by appealing to acceptable standards of justification and not presenting it simply as the replacement of one ideology by another. In particular, which changes in the curriculum ought to be considered improvements rather than simply the replacement of one highly politicized perspective by another?

Surely revisionists as well as traditionalists only lose if they view curricular arguments as merely power struggles for representation in an unavoidably politicized curriculum. If new curricular proposals cannot be plausibly presented as being educationally better than others for all concerned, what reason have those skeptical about the new proposals been given for changing their minds? Moreover, if power is all that is at stake, why should traditionalists change their minds at all? The critique of traditional political values itself becomes simply another political technique that, while perhaps effective, cannot claim to be rationally superior to the position it is critiquing.

Accordingly, then, if the claim that the traditional curriculum is politicized can best be understood as asserting that the traditional curriculum is biased in favor of the values of dominant social groups, that claim does not tally with the claim that all curricula are unavoidably politicized, particularly when that claim is interpreted in turn as something undermining the possibility of objective rational discourse about curricular choice. Rather than giving us any rational basis for choosing among many curricular options open to us, this claim is best understood as presupposing that an unbiased apoliticized set of curricular options is available to us. That claim may be true or false, justified or unjustified, but it can be debated and examined by critical standards accessible to both traditionalists and revisionists alike.[9]

Nonetheless, while it may be plausible to think that charges of the present curriculum's being biased presuppose the concept of an unbiased curriculum, advocates of the unavoidability thesis may claim that matters are not so easily resolvable. For although we may have the concept of an

---

9. The claim that the curriculum should be representative raises a host of problems itself. Who gets represented and how much representation is due? Is the goal "a curriculum that looks like America" and if so how is that to be implemented? Should groups be represented in the curriculum in rough proportion to the percentage of the community they constitute? If that is absurd, and qualitative standards of representation are to be applied, what standards are likely to be justified?

unbiased curriculum, each and every particular conception of it can become controversial. (Similarly, although we may share a common concept of justice, no one conception in all its particulars is likely to be shared by all.)

Thus, we need to consider a third account of why politicization of the curriculum is unavoidable. According to this "perspectivist" approach, traditionalists who speak of the need for objectivity, impartiality, and disinterested scholarly pursuit of truth ignore the degree to which criteria of objectivity, impartiality, and truth are embedded in the contexts of particular cultures, traditions, or socio-economic perspectives. Thus, a "Eurocentric" education takes for granted conceptions of objectivity, impartiality, and truth that may be challenged from other perspectives. In a more complex view, such as that suggested by Alasdair MacIntyre in *Whose Justice? Whose Rationality?*, Western culture itself is fragmented into diverse traditions, each with its own criteria of rationality, objectivity, and justice.[10] In some cases, criteria of objectivity, for example, may even be linked to gender. Thus, in her widely discussed book, *In A Different Voice*, Carol Gilligan reinterprets the empirical surveys conducted by psychologist Laurence Kohlberg and suggests that the impartial perspective, often identified by theorists with the moral point of view itself, tends to be associated more with male than female reasoning while females tend to reason from what has been called the perspective of care.[11] Although the relationship between the perspective of impartiality and that of care is debatable, in some interpretations what may count as objective reasoning from one of these points of view may be seen as defective moral reasoning from the other.

The idea that criteria of objectivity, rationality, impartiality and the like are embedded in specific perspectives or traditions suggests a third way in which the curriculum inevitably is politicized. In this view, the curriculum inevitably includes materials from specific traditions or perspectives, and thus is biased in favor of the criteria of objectivity, rationality, and the like that they contain. Such a bias is political because the criteria of some groups, traditions, or perspectives are given status, even canonical status, through inclusion in the curriculum while the criteria of other traditions or groups are denied such status through exclusion.

In its crudest form, the criticism is that the standard curriculum embodies a "white male point of view." More sophisticated theorists,

---

10. Alasdair McIntyre, *Whose Justice? Whose Rationality?* (Notre Dame, IN: The University of Notre Dame Press, 1988).
11. Carol Gilligan, *In A Difference Voice* (Cambridge: Harvard University Press, 1982).

such as MacIntyre, recognize the radical diversity of traditions making up Western culture, but their analysis still suggests that conceptions of impartiality, rationality, and objectivity must be understood within specific contexts, perspectives, or traditions. This lends itself to the thesis that the curriculum is inevitably politicized because the choice of traditions or perspectives to be taught invariably includes some conceptions of objectivity, rationality, and the like while excluding others.

While this analysis is of considerable interest, this kind of perspectivism does not fit easily into much of the critique of the traditional curriculum. After all, the critics of the traditional curriculum presumably want to say that their suggestions for revision improve the curriculum, make it better than it was, and therefore that their suggestions are justified. But perspectivism, at least in its less sophisticated forms, implies that judgments of better or worse, more or less justified, objective or unobjective, can only be warranted locally within a particular perspective or tradition. Thus, in a perspectivist analysis, what reason is there for those from other traditions or perspectives to accept the revisionists' critique of the traditional curriculum? According to perspectivism, no universal or interperspectival reasoning can be provided that is normative for all those who approach the curriculum in a multiperspectival society.

Perspectivism, at least in its cruder forms, seems to leave us with a model of the debate over the curriculum as at best a sort of Tower of Babel. The disputants engage in a debate in which adjudication or even mutual understanding seems impossible. In other words, this view of the unavoidability of the politicization of the curriculum seems self-defeating. It undermines the claims of the revisionists themselves to have justifiable and well-reasoned objections to the traditional curriculum that should be plausible to well-intentioned people from a wide variety of perspectives.[12] The trouble with perspectivism, at least when crudely understood, is that is seems to imply a self-defeating form of curricular relativism.

Perhaps, however, some forms of perspectivism do not lead to the kind of curricular relativism criticized above. Consider briefly MacIntyre's attempt to avoid the kind of relativism to which perspectivism seems committed. According to MacIntyre, although all criteria of rationality are embedded in particular perspectives, some by virtue of their survival and development in the face of epistemological crisis prove better than others over time. As MacIntyre argues,

12. Indeed, Gilligan, who appears not to be an epistemological perspectivist, explicitly rests her case in *In A Different Voice* for the existence of different gender-linked moral perspectives on empirical evidence open to and presumably persuasive to anyone.

> Every tradition, whether it recognizes the fact or not, confronts the possibility that at some future time it will fall into a state of epistemological crisis recognizable as such by its own standards of rational justification . . . the adherents of a tradition which is now in this state of fundamental and radical crisis may at this point encounter in a new way the claims of some particular rival tradition . . . they may find themselves compelled to recognize that within this other tradition it is possible to construct . . . a cogent and illuminating explanation . . . by their own standards of why their own intellectual tradition had been unable to solve its problems.[13]

In developing this point, MacIntyre argues valiantly that commitment to perspectivism, the view that all standards are embedded in particular cultural, intellectual, or social perspectives and traditions, does not need to entail either skepticism or relativism. For even though standards are not universal, it does not follow that they are all equally good. Some traditions respond to intellectual crises better than others. If successful, MacIntyre's defense allows perspectivists to make justified evaluative judgments. In making this point, however, MacIntyre may smuggle in universal criteria of evaluation, and thereby reject a robust perspectivism. This point has curricular implications and is worth exploring further.

Indeed, it is far from clear that MacIntyre himself holds a full fledged form of perspectivism. For one thing, he insists that the criteria of objectivity, rationality, and justice of different traditions are mutually intelligible. Members of one tradition can learn to understand other traditions. Indeed, his own analysis of different traditions would be impossible if it were not possible to understand traditions different from our own. This leads to a broader interpretation of MacIntyre in which we can reach an overarching or encompassing perspective from which different traditions can not only be understood but evaluated by criteria that apply to both. Thus, the statement "Tradition A has responded to intellectual crisis better than tradition B, even when each is evaluated on their own terms" seems to be made from a perspective that, if not entirely independent of A and B, seems vastly different and more encompassing than that of an isolated adherent of either one. That is, the evaluator must be able not only to understand the different traditions involved but also to make a comparative judgment about which tradition has done better in meeting the intellectual crisis it has faced.

What are the implications of these comments for the debate over the curriculum? They suggest, at least to me, that even if some curricular revisionists and some curricular traditionalists approach the curriculum

13. MacIntyre, *Whose Justice? Whose Rationality?*, p. 364.

from different perspectives or from within different traditions, a rational evaluation of both outlooks by common criteria of evaluation, or at least from a common perspective, is far from impossible. In this broader conception of perspectivism, then, it does not follow that all curricular discussion is unavoidably political in the sense that no independent perspective for making justified claims can be found.

On the other hand, if we interpret MacIntyre as being a robust perspectivist, no commitment to universal principles of evaluation or even to a common transperspectival point of view is implied. Suppose, for example, that we accept the assumption (an oversimplification of MacIntyre's view) that the traditional curriculum is based on a "Western" world-view, which contains its own internal standards of rationality, truth, and objectivity.[14] In this interpretation, external criticism of the traditional "Western" perspective is impossible, as all criticism, on the narrow interpretation of MacIntyre's view, can only be internal, made from within the perspective being examined.

Our discussion suggests, then, that the argument that the curriculum is unavoidably political because it expresses the limited perspectives of dominant groups is a defective one. Either such an argument embraces the narrow kind of perspectivism that makes objective curricular criticism impossible, or it acknowledges the possibility of acceptable standards of curricular evaluation and transperspectival points of view that are not partisan or applicable only within the limited perspectives or particular groups. The belief in such independent standards or viewpoints is compatible with both the broader form of perspectivism I have attributed to MacIntyre and with a rejection of perspectivism in favor of more explicitly non-perpectival epistemologies.

This is not to deny that what counts as justification, impartiality, or objectivity is often controversial. Radically different theoretical accounts of these notions exist in the field. Neither do I mean to deny that conceptions of rationality and objectivity can at times function ideologically as rationalizations for partisan political agendas. However, I do suggest that any account that regards all such notions as merely representative of a limited point of view makes rational debate over the curriculum impossible.

Thus far we have examined three conceptions of what might be meant by the claim that the curriculum is unavoidably political. According to the first, the curriculum is unavoidably political because it

14. Of course, MacIntrye himself seems to regard "Western thought" as itself made up of diverse and sometimes conflicting traditions.

is unavoidably value-laden. According to the second, the curriculum is unavoidably political because it is unrepresentative, giving too much weight to the values and standards of dominant groups. According to the third, the curriculum is inevitably politicized because the very standards of evaluation it contains – notions of rationality, objectivity, truth, and impartiality – reflect the limited points of view of particular cultures, groups, or perspectives.

While we have not considered all possible conceptions of the politicization of the curriculum, perhaps enough has been said to show not only that the concept of politicization is complex, but that the charge that politicization is unavoidable is a questionable one. What are the implications of this for discussion about the curriculum in higher education?

III. Non-Partisanship and Curricular Discussion

One implication, I suggest, is that it is counterproductive for revisionists to embrace the more extreme forms of normative or epistemological relativism and skepticism. After all, the revisionists themselves are making claims that are critical not only of more traditional forms of the curriculum but sometimes of the broader social and political order as well. And because these claims are presented as justified, those who make them are committed to some sort of criteria for evaluating claims over and above those that simply happen to be accepted by a particular group at a particular time. At a minimum, such standards include renunciation of coercion and manipulation, as the goal of the debate is not simply to win but to find which of the contesting views is more reasonable or more justified.

Of course, there is considerable room for debate over how we should conceive of such criteria. Recent attempts to "naturalize" epistemology differ radically, for example, from the classical forms of rationalism and empiricism, as well as from such contemporary approaches as reliablism and various forms of coherence theory. In ethics, communitarian approaches differ from more individualistic ones. Contractarianism, utilitarianism, pragmatism, and an emerging ethic of care are in apparent conflict over fundamental matters of substance.[15] Nonetheless, debate

15. In fact, these sorts of controversies among different conceptions of epistemic and moral justification call into question the overdrawn picture of a monolithic "Western culture" that underlies some of the criticism of the traditional curriculum. The study of Plato, Nietzsche, Hume, Mill, Kant, Marx, Rawls, and MacIntyre surely is the study of an extraordinarily diverse group of theorists.

and meta-debate about the standards that ought to govern rational discourse and inquiry is not only acceptable but highly desirable, so long as it is realized that all such standards cannot be up for revision all at once, and, most important, that all need not be at stake at once in each debate about particular issues.

This suggests a second implication of our discussion; namely, that the notion of an "academic ethic" or ethic of inquiry should be a major component of our approach to the curriculum. Much of the discussion about multiculturalism has expressed concern over the lack of social and intellectual unity that overemphasis on pluralism might promote. Perhaps part of a common core of any curriculum might be an emphasis on critical standards of inquiry, including not only non-coercion, but respect for evidence, obligations to consider criticisms, and willingness to test one's views against those of others. These are surely values, but they strike me as core values that should be acceptable to all views claiming to be open to reasoned examination. As such, they are normative but non-partisan, and thus can form the core of an approach to a non-politicized curriculum. In a sense, they supply part of an academic "overlapping consensus" in that they are not only part of the overall perspective of those groups committed to rational inquiry within the university but because they have normative force as presuppositions of such inquiry as well.

If a commitment to standards of rational discourse and critical inquiry ought to be common to defensible forms of both revisionism and traditionalism, the idea that the university itself ought to be *politically neutral* deserves consideration from both perspectives.[16] Neutrality should be understood here to mean neither total value neutrality nor consequential neutrality – that is, that the decisions of the university ought to have equal consequences for different sides to curricular debates. Rather, neutrality ought to be understood on the model of the basketball referee who impartially enforces rules that for the most part are acceptable to all competitors. Similarly, the kind of neutrality appropriate to the university might be called critical neutrality. Ideally, the university exists to provide and protect a climate of intellectual inquiry and rational discussion that is mutually acceptable to all parties devoted to the process of justification and evaluation as a major activity of the institution.[17]

16. For a fuller discussion of institutional neutrality, see Robert L. Simon, "A Defense of the Neutral University," *op. cit.*

17. As in the basketball example, conflict about the rules themselves is to be examined in meta-debate about the issues in question.

One reason for favoring critical neutrality, of course, is pragmatic. To a large extent, colleges and universities attract support and wield influence and prestige precisely because they are viewed not as being partisan agents of particular causes but as centers of critical discussion, scholarship, and examination. Once they are viewed instead as being partisan in highly sectarian debates, particularly if the espouse positions unpopular with the general population, it is likely that they will lose not only support but even end up the special target of partisan attacks from powerful political and social opponents. Indeed, even those critics who raise critical questions about the logic of neutrality often accept that what they regard as the myth of neutrality can be highly useful in shielding the university from political opponents.[18]

However, in addition to pragmatic reasons favoring neutrality, two moral reasons have special weight. While neither is in my view a "knockdown argument," they may have considerable force when each is regarded as reinforcing the other.

The first rests on concern for individual autonomy. It is far more likely, in this view, that students and faculty will feel free to make their own decisions on controversial issues if their home institution has not already staked out a partisan position of its own. The second rests on a concern for intellectual diversity. It is far more likely the university will attract an intellectually diverse faculty and student body the more it resists stating official positions on controversial issues of the day. The more partisan the university, the less likely it will be to attract those who dissent from the official point of view. And the less intellectually diverse the faculty and student body, the less fruitful critical inquiry and rational discussion is likely to be in many areas.

Accordingly, rather than dismiss the doctrine of institutional neutrality as being just another guise for imposing a traditional educational perspective on the university, revisionists as well as traditionalists would have good reason for supporting it. At the very least, if they reject institutional neutrality they need to show how they are not rejecting a concern for autonomy and intellectual diversity along with it.

The third implication I will mention concerns how disputes over the curriculum might be handled within the curriculum itself. Few traditionalists would disagree with the proposition that in the course of a university education, students should become (or even be *required* to become) familiar with a culture other than their own. Instead, disputes break out

---

18. See, for example, Robert Paul Wolff, *The Ideal of the University* (Boston: Beacon Press, 1969) pp. 75-76.

between traditionalists and revisionists over matters such as what counts as another culture, whether traditional studies of Western Civilization should be given any special priority, and what traditionalists see as a political slant or bias in much revisionist teaching. Many revisionists, on the other hand, would reply that they are merely countering the political slant in the teaching of traditionalists, and that it is a political move to give special priority to traditional courses.

One model for resolving this kind of dispute might be called the feudal model, in that each side is given its own fiefdom over which it has control. In this model feudalism at times can be combined in an uneasy alliance with free markets – as when students are given the choice of which fiefdoms they will enter. For example, students might be told that they must take a certain amount of credits in traditional areas and a certain amount in study of a culture other than their own. They might then be given the choice of just which departments they enter to fulfill each requirement. For example, courses in Asian studies *or* Africana studies *or* Islamic Studies *or* Feminist studies may be among those that satisfy the requirement for knowledge of a culture other than one's own for many students.

Although this approach has considerable merit, there are three reasons for thinking it might not be the best curricular resolution to the debate between traditionalists and revisionists. First, it leaves unclear not only what is to count as culture, and what is to count as a culture other than one's own, but also just which cultures "other than one's own" are to be represented on the list of courses satisfying the requirement. For example, can courses in Feminist Studies – as well as those in, say, Africana, Islamic, or Asian Studies – be used to satisfy requirements of learning about another culture? Second, because in the feudal model the proponents of radically different approaches to issues of methodology and justification never have to engage one another, there is a risk of generating a kind of uncritical relativism about such issues. Students learn to think by using one kind of framework in one area and another somewhere else, yet never attempt to reconcile conflicts between the two. As a result, a quite understandable but also unexamined tendency to relativize standards or ways of thought in different areas of study can be expected to develop.[19] Finally, and most importantly, direct debate over the deeper methodological, ethical, and epistemological issues dividing different

19. Here, I draw heavily on the discussion by Nalini Bhushan in "The Real Challenge of Culture Diversity: Clarifying the Boundaries of Legitimate Philosophical Practice," *Teaching Philosophy*, vol. 14, No. 2 (June 1991) pp. 169-70.

approaches would end up compartmentalized with little hope of direct engagement between the parties. Not only would this deprive students of appropriate models of scholarly disagreement on fundamental issues, it is unlikely to make any debate an intellectually profitable one either.

An alternate approach, which need not be incompatible with the feudal one, is to incorporate the dispute between revisionists and traditionalists into the curriculum at appropriate points. Thus, as Nalini Bhushan has recommended, "We can expose our students to some problems of confrontation that commitment to cultural diversity brings so they can wrestle with the difficulties themselves and come to realize that a serious accommodation of another culture is hard work and involves conflicts that are not clearly resolvable to everyone's satisfaction."[20] Philosophy, as a discipline, might be especially well-suited to examining such intellectual disputes, just as a course in ethical theory might attempt to adjudicate between the impartiality and caring approaches to our moral life. In other areas, institutional criteria could be developed to insure that at some point during their education students would be exposed to persons of different viewpoints who examined fundamental questions underlying curricular debate in some depth.

By placing the emphasis on process rather than on trying to "save" students from bad ideas, we would stand a better chance of avoiding both the preaching to the already converted that is a pitfall facing the feudal approach and the sniping and name-calling that too often replaces real debate within the academy. Of course, genuine debate also carries real risks, for if debate is to be genuine it will always be unclear which views will ultimately emerge as the most successful. Thus, one avowed aim of many multiculturalists – to have the curriculum teach appreciation and respect for different cultures – might suffer because critical inquiry might well lead to greater moral and intellectual criticism of some cultures than others. For example, treatment of women in many non-Western cultures may come to be regarded as morally deficient when compared to recent changes in many Western societies.

To conclude, nothing said here is meant to determine whether traditionalists or revisionists have the better case in curricular debate. Rather, my claim has been that to deny that curricular argument is possible, and to regard rational discussion itself as a purely persuasive practice ideologically inseparable from specific partisan traditions, is to abandon the very framework of inquiry in which curricular proposals can be justified in the first place.

20. Bhushan, "The Real Challenge of Cultural Diversity," p. 175.

Debate about the curriculum, then, is an entirely legitimate and often educationally valuable contribution to critical inquiry. However, it is important at least to attempt to distinguish between arguments that appeal to educational benefits of curricular issues and those that are more partisan or narrowly ideological in character. This distinction may often be difficult to make in practice, for partisanship is not the exclusive property of one side of the political spectrum. However, to insist that all debates about the curriculum are actually only ideological rationalizations, that all curricula are political in some partisan sense, and that rational evaluation of curricular proposals is a myth, would be to pay a heavy price. To avoid even the attempt to distinguish the partisan from the non-partisan in the mistaken belief that all education is intrinsically politicized, and hence all curricular debates are only over power, is to fail to do justice to the values of critical inquiry that should be at the heart of the educational enterprise itself.[21]

21. Although his treatment of politicization differs from our own, I have learned from and been influenced by John Agresto's "The Politicization of Liberal Education," *Academic Questions* (Fall, 1990) pp. 69-73, particularly his insistence that the liberal arts presuppose "the prospect that there can be knowledge over opinion" (p. 73).

6
Undergraduate Assessment as Pedagogical and Political Control[1]

Arthur Brown

In the early 1970s a movement in education grew around the concept of performance or behavioral objectives, discrete and measurable manifestations of academic achievement. In brief, proponents of the movement took the position that performance objectives would systematize the educational process, would make teaching more assessable and teachers more accountable, and, as a consequence, test scores would rise as would – eventually – the economic status of the underclass. The fact that none of this came true is apparently not regarded as being sufficient reason for giving up on the concept. Since the publication of *A Nation at Risk* (1983), the testing movement in the public schools has become more powerful than ever.[2] Tracking test scores is now a national pastime, and the comparison of test results with those of students in other countries has become a constant cause for breastbeating and an inexhaustible source of grist for political mills.

Although a drop in Graduate Record Examination scores has been reported,[3] the recent surge in the popularity of assessment programs at

1. This is a revision of a paper presented before a small group at the Eighth International Human Science Research Conference, August 18-22, 1989, held at the University of Aarhus, Denmark. I should like to express my gratitude to my doctoral student, Della Goodwin, for her assistance.

2. In this connection, of significance is the highly publicized report of the National Council on Education Standards and Testing recently submitted to Congress and the Education Department. The report calls for the establishment of national standards and national tests in English, geography, history, mathematics, and science and the possible use of the results of these tests in determining who graduates from high school, who is admitted to college, or who is certified for certain types of employment.

The National Council on Education Standards and Testing serves as an advisory panel to the National Education Goals Panel "which is charged with overseeing the national effort to achieve the six education goals that President Bush and the governors established in 1990." See Thomas J. DeLoughry, "National Standards for Schools Backed in Report to Government Leaders," *The Chronicle of Higher Education*, February 5, 1992, p. A35.

3. "The Governors' Report on Education: Text of the Section on College Quality," *The Chronicle of Higher Education*, September 7, 1986, p. 79.

107

the undergraduate level does not derive,[4] as is the case with the public schools, from unhappiness with test scores. Rather, undergraduate assessment has become popular for a number of other reasons. Foremost among them is the growing economic importance of higher education. Higher education is now generally considered the primary gateway to personal financial success and social status. Schools, colleges, and universities have come to be regarded by business and government officials as necessary instruments for success in domestic and international economic competition.

Other factors that probably play a role in or contribute to the demand for the assessment of undergraduate academic achievement are soaring tuition, the rising cost of state support, a perception that the education of undergraduates is being sacrificed for research activities, excessive reliance on graduate teaching assistants and part-timers, the trend toward centralization in institutional governance, and the political and public relations value of assessment. But there is more to the matter – much more. Certain values associated with higher education, i.e., professional autonomy, academic freedom, free and open inquiry, and pluralism, do not sit well with many conservatives, a number of whom are ardent advocates of assessment. By channeling the curriculum and/or establishing a system of accountability for educational outcomes, many conservatives hope to gain control over those values. I shall elaborate on this later. But first I should like to put my views into historical perspective. In 1968, I gave a talk entitled, "Education and the New Morality," in which I made the observation that

> . . . the New Morality represents a reaction to one or another of the various kinds of established authority and traditional moral codes on the assumption that they fail to achieve for individuals their fullest human potential and limit excessively the opportunity for self-direction, [and that] the New Morality is the historical and logical extension of a long-standing quest to expand individual freedom.[5]

---

4. In 1991, 81 percent of colleges had assessment activities underway as compared to 55 percent in 1988. Much of the increase is no doubt attributable to state mandates (in about 40 states) or newly established requirements of regional accrediting associations. See Theodore J. Marchese, "Introduction," and other sections of the *NCA Quarterly*, Fall, 1990. (The *Quarterly* is a publication of the North Central Association of Colleges and Schools.) Also see Education Commission of the States, *Assessing College Outcomes: What State Leaders Need to Know*, November, 1991.

5. "Education and the New Morality," in Fisher and Smith, *Schools in An Age of Crisis* (Van Nostrand Co.), 1969.

True, much of what went on in the name of the New Morality was irrational and destructive. Yet the late 1960s were euphoric days of experimentation at a number of schools and colleges. Although in my 1968 speech I correctly predicted a reaction to the New Morality, including calls for "constitutionalism" and "back to the basics" in education, I did not anticipate the force and pervasiveness of that reaction. And so, sixteen years later, in 1984, in another talk, "Pluralism – with Intelligence: A Challenge to Education and Society," I observed that:

> . . . the liberal and humane spirit of the New Morality, predicated on faith in human intelligence to control events, has given way to a pervasive conservatism which values instead accommodation to presumed independent realities. Thus, we are witnessing once again the rise of absolutism and determinism, exemplified by . . . religious fundamentalism and its intrusion into politics and education; renewed faith in the "invisible hand" for resolving economic problems; the revival of social darwinism as a rationale for legitimizing hierarchical social arrangements; and confidence that studies of our genes, such as those done by ethologists and sociobiologists, will be able to inform our ethics and our politics.
>
> It is not diversity, then, it is not cultural pluralism or ethnic differences or divergent thinking which, in my view, pose a major threat to democratic community in America. Rather it is conformity – the conformity generated by bureaucratized social institutions, entrenched economic and political interests, monopolized sources of information, and moral majoritarianism.[6]

I see assessment in higher education as an extension of this new conservatism in American society, as a move toward conformity. Though rationalized as a means for heightening institutional efficiency[7] and improving the educational experiences of students, in the final analysis assessment is driven by a philosophic orthodoxy that promises to undermine the values that higher education represents.

Before pursuing the matter further, I want to inquire briefly into what assessment is and what it is supposed to accomplish. According to one expert,

6. "Pluralism – with Intelligence: A Challenge to Education and Society," ERIC, vol. 22, No. 1 (January, 1987). For an elaboration of this thesis, see Donna Kerr, *Barriers to Integrity: Modern Modes of Knowledge Utilization* (Boulder, CO: Westview Press), 1983. Also see Steven Tozer, "Elite Power and Democratic Ideals" in Kenneth Benne and Steven Tozer (eds.), *Society As Educator in an Age of Transition*, 88th Yearbook of the National Society for the Study of Education (Chicago: University of Chicago Press), 1987.

7. Proponents of assessment at the higher level would do well to study the history of efficiency movements in the public schools. The most frequently cited work is Raymond E. Callahan, *Education and the Cult of Efficiency* (Chicago: The University of Chicago Press), 1962.

> . . . assessment is a method for the psychological evaluation of individuals that involves testing and observing individuals in a group setting, with a multiplicity of tests and procedures, by a number of staff members. Through a pooling of test scores and subjective impressions, the assessors formulate psychodynamic descriptions of the assessed subjects which, hopefully, will permit prediction of certain kinds of behavior in certain kinds of roles and situations.[8]

If one can cut through the Kafkaesque imagery in this definition, at least we have a starting point in examining how assessment in undergraduate education might be conducted and what might be expected of it. For that purpose, I thought it would be helpful to examine how well assessment programs used in some other parts of the academy predict "certain kinds of behavior in certain kinds of roles and situations." The research I have looked at is, to say the least, not encouraging.

In a 1987 study of 247 people who had taken the Iowa licensing exam in social work, Johnson and Huff concluded:

> The written test, used for social work licensures, falls short in measuring knowledge unique to the profession; furthermore, there is not a demonstrated relationship between a written exam and practice competence.[9]

Johnson and Huff added that the "major issue raised by the . . . study is the validity of the examination. . . . [I]t does not appear to measure an applicant's knowledge of social work practice."

Although in this instance the issue was the validity of the social work licensing exam, Johnson and Huff do make the assumption that knowledge of the criteria of practice competence for social workers exists. This seems *not* to be the case for medical clinical competence, according to Forsythe and his associates. In a 1986 study, they observed that there is a need for further development of a theory of medical competence, one that:

(a) explicitly defines the attributes comprising medical clinical competence and their indicative behaviors,

(b) specifies relationships between the attributes, and

---

8. Donald Mackinnon cited in Terry W. Hartle, "The Growing Interest in Measuring the Educational Achievement of College Students," *Assessment in American Higher Education: Issues and Concepts* (U.S. Department of Education, Office of Educational Research and Improvement), n.d.

9. David Johnson and Dan Huff, "Licensing Exams: How Valid are They?," *Social Work*, vol. 32, No. 2, pp. 159–61.

(c) explicitly considers attributes in the context of methods of measurement.[10]

Because it is obvious that the first prerequisite for having confidence in an assessment program is knowledge about what constitutes professional or occupational competence, Leonard Baird's conclusions should be especially disquieting to advocates of assessment. In a very comprehensive review of studies on the subject of prediction, published in 1985, Baird points out that: "In general, the studies demonstrated low positive relationship between academic aptitude and/or grades and accomplishments."[11] And one of the reasons for the low positive relationships, Baird adds, "is the statistical inadequacy and unreliability of criteria [for accomplishment]."[12]

This creates an obvious dilemma. If we accept Baird's conclusion, assessment is chimerical. Hence, we should stop any further discussion about it until we can uncover the criteria for successful accomplishment in the several occupations and professions. But if the criteria for successful accomplishment in the occupations and professions are hard to come by, what shall we say about the criteria for assessing undergraduate education, whose primary purposes, such as enabling students to live "successful" lives in a democratic society, are even more vague and less well-defined?

Regardless of the questionable ethical foundation on which it rests, assessment will no doubt continue to play a major role in academic life. We may not be able to predict "adult accomplishment," but at least we can do some legal sorting and screening as well as satisfy, to some extent, the public demand for accountability. With the advent of assessment activities designed to evaluate the education of undergraduates, the problem that must be addressed is how to employ them so that they do as little harm as possible, and perhaps some good.

For that purpose I turn to a brief review of what has happened at my own institution. For several years, Wayne State University has been in the process of developing a program of assessment, but – unlike many other institutions – without a specific mandate from the state to do so. Assessment of students in the major field as a condition for graduation

10. George D. Forsythe, William C. McGaghie, and Charles R. Friedman, "Construct Validity of Medical Clinical Competence Measures: A Multitract-Multimethod Matrix Study Using Confirmatory Factor Analysis," *American Educational Research Journal*, Summer, 1986, vol. 22, No. 2, pp. 315-36.

11. Leonard L. Baird, "Do Grades and Tests Predict Adult Accomplishment?," *Research in Higher Education*, vol. 23, No. 1, p. 3.

12. *Ibid.*, p. 7.

was first proposed some years earlier by the president of the university. After much delay, the matter was subsequently studied by the Curriculum and Instruction Committee of the University Council.

Following a year of study, in April 1987 the committee submitted a report titled, "The Program Evaluation Plan," as distinguished from a prior administration draft policy that was titled, "Assessment of Comprehensive Knowledge in Major Fields for Undergraduate Programs." What distinguished the plan put forward by the Curriculum and Instruction Committee from that of the administration draft policy was that it called for *program evaluation* and rejected *assessment* of individual students.

In studying the problem, the committee came to the realization that the assessment of student knowledge as a condition for graduation was a hazardous enterprise that would encounter a minefield of unreliable and invalid tests as well as heavy resistance from faculty and students. Hence, C&I cautioned: "Faculty, students, and administrators must work together in the decision-making process," and:

> The program must move forward carefully and deliberately, in order to gain the respect of faculty and students, and to avoid policies and procedures that will alienate faculty and be detrimental to the goals of the University.

At one forum or another, the C&I committee made plain its belief that assessment does not have to include testing; that tests are the most controversial part of assessment; that valid, reliable tests are not available; that they are by far the aspect of assessment most threatening to students and faculty; that program evaluation must be the focus, not assessment of individual students; that program evaluation can be effectively made through the use of such techniques as surveys of student and alumni satisfaction, interviews, performance reviews, and seminars; and, finally, that it can be carried out with only a sample of students, rather than the total population. All in all, the Program Evaluation Plan, which I shall call "soft assessment," would seem to be a reasonable approach toward improving undergraduate education without risking the alienation of students and faculty or doing too much damage in other ways.

When it approved the plan proposed by the Curriculum and Instruction Committee, in order to ensure no misunderstanding on the part of the administration, the University Council added an amendment: ". . . the Program Evaluation Plan *shall not* [italics mine] contain a provision for mandatory universal testing as one of the instruments to be used for evaluation."

112

Notwithstanding the position of the council, the administration expressed its intention to push ahead full speed toward an assessment program that *would* examine the knowledge of *all* students in both general education and in their major field. With respect to testing in general education, the provost pointed out that the "administration does not necessarily agree . . . that the mandatory testing of general education skills and knowledge should be precluded in the development of an assessment plan."[13] And with respect to the assessment of students in their major field and the role of testing in such a program, the provost said:

> . . . This issue is a clear and focussed one. It asks this question: does a student who receives his/her degree in economics (anthropology, mathematics, education, accounting, etc.) have a mastery of the core subject matter and the intellectual method of that field? This question can presumably be answered only by assessing the specific knowledge that each student has in his/her subject area. Answering this question especially lends itself to testing, although that is not the only method for addressing it.

Moreover, the provost added:

> The University administration remains strongly committed to a policy of systematic assessment of students' knowledge in the major field. This would assure that students are properly prepared in fields in which the University certifies their knowledge by awarding them a degree. It would serve students by advising them of the level of their competence in their field, thus guiding them toward further education if necessary. As a secondary effect, such assessment would serve academic units well by informing them whether their curriculum is properly focussed and whether teaching is effectively conveying the subject matter to students. It would also permit evaluation of grading systems by allowing academic units to compare student grade point averages in courses with student performance on assessment devices representing core knowledge in the field.[14]

As for the position of the president of the university on testing students in their major field, although not yet fully committed to that procedure, the president observed that a "vast number" of departments in the university do use the Graduate Record Exam as a condition for admitting students into their graduate programs. And every department, he said, does require qualifying exams for doctoral students prior to the

13. Sanford Cohen, "Assessment of Student Knowledge: Information Report," *Academic Affairs Committee Agenda*, July 15 and September 9, 1987.
14. *Ibid.*

writing of the thesis. "So, assessment of knowledge is not completely unknown to the University."[15] (The president, no doubt, meant testing rather than assessment.)

To sum up, the views of the administration are in conflict with those of the University Council on two major points. First, the administration expressed itself as committed to assessing *each* student in the major field as a condition for graduation; the council, on the other hand, recommended that the emphasis be on the evaluation of programs and, therefore, for that purpose, assessment could be confined to only a sample of students. Second, the administration is at least open to, if not positively in favor of, testing as part of an assessment program; the council categorically opposes testing.

One may wonder why it is that the recommendations of academics who are by tradition responsible for certifying students for graduation and who had made a reasonably comprehensive study of the problem were not readily accepted, especially in a situation where the state had not mandated an assessment program. I offer a few explanations that, while they do not exhaust the possibilities, may serve as a basis for a more comprehensive analysis of a very difficult and important problem confronting higher education.

First, institutions of higher education have become highly politicized; the loftier values that higher education represents are becoming increasingly subordinate to political and economic considerations. As a result, presidents have been rendered especially sensitive to public demands. Along with other criteria commonly perceived as signs of success – such as research grants and contracts – assessment, including testing of individual students, can be used to demonstrate to its several constituencies that the institution is concerned about the quality of its undergraduate educational programs.

Second, the competition for students, money, and prestige has accelerated and encouraged the view that tighter controls are needed. As a consequence, the decision-making process in institutions of higher education has become more centralized, more bureaucratized.[16] Insofar as the curriculum contributes to a college's competitive posture, some find it reasonable to assume that its effectiveness, like that of other institutional activities, would be enhanced by greater centralization of authority.

15. Minutes of the September 9, 1987 meeting of the Academic Affairs Committee of the Board of Governors.

16. See Ernst Benjamin, "Democracy in the University," *Thresholds in Education*, February, 1989, vol. XV, No. 1, pp. 19-20. Benjamin is the General Secretary of the American Association of University Professors.

What follows is inevitable. Centralized control of the curriculum will ultimately mean control of the faculty (a possibility that might not be especially distasteful to some administrators; faculty, after all, can be an unruly lot). Consider in this regard the implications of the aforementioned statement by the provost that assessment of each student in the major field would serve to determine "whether [the] curriculum is properly focussed and whether teaching is effectively conveying the subject matter to students," and "would permit evaluation of grading systems by allowing academic units to compare student grade point averages in courses with student performance in assessment devices. . . ." Under such circumstances, contract renewals, tenure, promotion, and merit pay could well depend on the scores on uniform and externally constructed examinations made by students of a particular professor in particular courses.

Third, college and university presidents are generally not well read in educational theory or knowledgeable about pedagogical research. (Some are, in fact, disdainful of such matters.) Moreover, because they have climbed the ladder of the system by passing tests and being evaluated at every turn, the idea of assessment and the use of standardized, external examinations pose for them no philosophic problem. Indeed, I would venture to say that very few chief executive officers in higher education would not feel favorably disposed toward E.D. Hirsch's best selling book, *Cultural Literacy: What Every American Should Know*, with it conservative values, political orientation, and traditional pedagogical views. Nor, I might add, would they look to Dewey or Buber or to contemporary educational theorists such as Maxine Greene or Henry Giroux for guidance in educational matters.

My concluding remarks should come as no surprise. However desirable tight control may be for certain functions in a university, such as the financial accounting system, it is not desirable for the academic function, especially at the pre-professional level. In fact, it is likely to be educationally destructive. This is not to say there should be no controls; some may be of pedagogical value (program reviews, for instance). But the academy thrives on a certain amount of untidiness. It needs freedom to experiment and to deal with unconventional ideas, particularly "dangerous" ones. Professional autonomy constitutes the heart of education. As Bertrand Russell put it:

> The teacher, like the artist, the philosopher, and the man of letters can only perform adequately if he feels himself an individual directed by an inner creative impulse, not dominated and festered by authority.

Furthermore, professional autonomy and academic freedom are indivisible. Insofar as an assessment program constricts professional autonomy, it also constricts academic freedom and, as a consequence, undermines the essential values of higher education so vital to a democratic society.

And it is not only professional autonomy and academic freedom that are endangered. The educational process itself – what goes on between teachers and students, inseparable as it is from the essential nature of the academy – will be compromised. If outcomes at the undergraduate level are to be measured using standardized tests or externally constructed examinations – and this seems to be the core of most assessment programs – and an accountability system is instituted, the same kind of corruption of the educational process, such as teaching to the test and the trivialization of the subject matter, can be expected at the higher level as has occurred in the schools, to say nothing about the plight of students who pass courses but fail assessment tests.[17] Moreover, the most competent teachers will either not want to enter the profession or, if already in it, will leave. Dr. Eleanor Friedman may show the way. I cite a *New York Times* article entitled, "The System Wins Over a Dedicated Teacher."

> Dr. Eleanor Friedman, an outstanding New York English teacher and department chair, described as a woman in perpetual motion in the classroom who proffers William Faulkner's words as if they were a gift, who takes enormous pleasure in finally teaching her slower students that they must bring a pencil with them each day, has retired at age 54. "I really thought," she said, "when I was 70 years old somebody would say 'You cannot teach any more' and pull me out the school kicking and screaming. I thought that was how it would end."
>
> And why is Dr. Friedman retiring? Not because of the kids. . . . "It is the system that I hate. There is less and less interest in what is. They are interested in what it says on paper is." And she is tired of having to draw up lesson plans when she is most comfortable with a few leading questions scrawled on a slip of paper. And she is tired of producing pages of goals and objectives for the coming school year when her goals are quite simply to have the teacher teach and the students learn. "I am out of sync with the system. We are here for the kids. We are not here to make paper for 110 Livingston Street. And that is why I am retiring."[18]

17. For some years, students at Wayne State have had to pass proficiency examinations in English, math, and speech prior to graduation. Failure on the English exam (at least) has aroused considerable unhappiness among students who had earlier passed their English courses.

18. *New York Times*, June 15, 1983, Section 2, p. 5.

7
Ethical Implications of Curricular Reform

Kathryn Mohrman

The curriculum is the practical manifestation of our ideals about the university. If we truly want to determine what an institution stands for in educational terms, we should look not only at the mission statement or the lofty rhetoric at the front of the catalog but also at the beliefs put into place through curricular choices made by faculty. This paper focuses upon the intersection of the curriculum with broader issues of the increasing cultural diversity of American society. What responsibilities does a university have to engage these larger societal trends? What are the requirements for scholarship as well as for students? What are the ethical implications of curricular decisions?

I approach these questions not only as interesting intellectual queries, but as pragmatic matters to be wrestled with on campuses today. My interest in public policy implementation, combined with my role as a university administrator, has focused my attention on getting things done. In this paper I discuss our historical attention to diversity as a matter of compensatory justice; while this line of reasoning continues to be valid, it is an insufficient basis for institutional action. In Part 2, I present an argument for a concept of shared responsibility that would allow for an increased inclusiveness based on the scholarly and educational missions of colleges and universities. I end by appealing to the self-interest of both faculty and administrators.

I. The Traditional View: Equal Opportunity for Disadvantaged Students

In 1960, colleges and universities in the United States enrolled 3.6 million undergraduates.[1] Some institutions in the southern and border states

1. Charles V. Anderson et. al, *1989-90 Fact Book on Higher Education* (American Council on Education, 1990), Table 48, p. 75.

117

were still segregated or had only recently opened their doors to students other than whites. Although the democratization of American higher education was already well underway with the influx of new students encouraged by the G.I. Bill, the policy arguments at both campus and national levels during the 1950s were framed less in terms of race than in terms of access. For example, the National Defense Education Act, passed in 1958 in response to Sputnik, authorized a program of student loans promising that "no student of ability will be denied an opportunity for higher education."

The civil rights movement and the Great Society programs of the 1960s focused attention on the inequalities in American society – the disparities between rich and poor, and in particular the systematic disadvantages faced by persons of color in this nation. Education was harnessed in the War on Poverty to reduce the barriers posed by race and income. Lyndon Johnson said it at its hyperbolic best: "The answer for all our national problems, the answer for all the problems of the world, comes down, when your really analyze it, to one single word – education."[2]

Policy prescriptions were focused on helping the disadvantaged gain equal access to educational opportunities. At the federal level, such initiatives as Head Start, Upward Bound, and need-based financial aid helped poor (and often minority) children gain academic skills and the financial means for success in school. These polices implied that smart, ambitious students would take advantage of these new opportunities, lift themselves up by the bootstraps, and enter mainstream society. Even when critics noted that a college degree could be seen more as a credential than an inherently valuable experience, few questions were raised about the curriculum or other fundamentals of higher education.

At the institutional level, the implementation of policies based on compensatory justice has had several interesting implications. By and large, campus efforts are focused on recruitment and admissions of larger numbers of students from under-represented groups, extra-curricular programs addressing the cultural interests of these new members of the campus community, and academic strategies that are largely remedial either by design or by implication. Tutoring and special programs often implicitly say to low income and Latino and older women students that they are less able, that they need special help, that they must adapt themselves to the status quo. All too often, these students remain on the periphery of a largely unchanged university.

2. Lyndon B. Johnson, "Remarks in Providence at the 200th Anniversary Convocation of Brown University," quoted in Lawrence E. Gladieux and Thomas R. Wolanin, *Congress and the Colleges: The National Politics of Higher Education* (Lexington Books, 1976), p. 17.

Thirty years of educational policies based on a concept of compensatory justice have not achieved what their original proponents had envisioned. By 1990, the total number of undergraduate students in the United States had grown to 11.9 million (a 300 percent increase since 1960), with 2.4 million of those students being students of color, or 12.1 percent of the total. Participation in higher education has risen dramatically; between 1980 and 1990, the increase in African-American enrollment was 10 percent, while the comparable figure for Hispanic Americans was 60 percent, for Native Americans 20 percent, and for Asian Americans 92 percent.[3] Perhaps the biggest change has been in the proportion of women in higher education, rising from 38 percent in 1960 to 62 percent in 1990.[4]

But as encouraging as these numbers may look, they must be tempered with statistics showing a continued gap in educational achievement by race. In 1990, the proportion of high school graduates aged 25 to 29 who had four or more years of college was 28.1 percent for whites, 16.4 percent for African-Americans, and 14.4 percent for Hispanic Americans.[5] If equal opportunity is designed to produce a more even distribution of educational benefits across American society, we have not yet achieved that objective.

I believe that we can do better as a nation and as individual colleges and universities. We should not abandon our concern for justice, because the dream of equal opportunity has still not yet been realized. I will argue that we must marry our goal of justice to a larger conception of shared responsibility for the intellectual directions of the future.

II. A Broader View: Shared Responsibility

Almost all institutions of higher education share two fundamental priorities: a desire to focus intellectual energies on the most important questions of the times, and a desire to prepare students to be productive professionals and effective citizens. In both scholarship and education, questions of diversity are moving from the periphery to the center of the university, not from a sense of noblesse oblige or political correctness,

3. *Chronicle of Higher Education*, March 18, 1992, p. A-35.

4. *Digest of Education Statistics 1991* (U.S. Department of Education, National Center for Education Statistics, 1991), Table 172, p. 179.

5. Nabeel Alasalam and Gayle Thompson Rogers, *The Condition of Education 1991: Volume 2, Postsecondary Education* (U.S. Department of Education, National Center for Education Statistics, 1991), Table 2:7-5, p. 130.

but because attention to diversity is increasingly linked to academic excellence in research and teaching.

Scholars in many disciplines are broadening their intellectual interests. Economists no longer study only the U.S. Gross National Product; they must understand international economic interdependence. Literature specialists interested in the human condition are reading texts from many cultural groups in addition to the classics of the Western tradition. Psychologists are identifying the physical and cultural foundations of behavior in male and females. Political scientists are debating whether the United States has become a second-rate power, while sociologists are studying the causes of the underclass. In many fields, faculty must be fluent in more than one culture in order to be good scholars.

All across the university, professors are studying new topics, listening to new voices, developing new analytical techniques – not because someone is forcing them to do so but because their intellectual development demands that they do so. Increasingly, faculty are adopting multiple perspectives and comparative methodologies because such strategies are essential for their intellectual work. As they seek to understand our world in all its complexity, scholars are quite naturally bringing questions of diversity from the periphery to the center of the university.

Thus, the first aspect of shared responsibility is to focus on the role of scholars, exploring new avenues in which questions of culture and gender and race are critical factors. Because few of us have the background to do such work as thoroughly as we would like, we need to develop collaborative relationships with scholars from different disciplines, from different cultures, and from different perspectives. The diversity of the faculty becomes increasingly important, then, because of the intellectual contributions that scholars from various cultural groups can bring to the discourse.

Attention to diversity is also assuming greater importance in our educational mission. Preparing students to be productive professionals and effective citizens calls for a liberal education of the highest order – an array of skills and knowledge that students can apply in the short-term in their current jobs, along with a reservoir of attributes providing them with the flexibility to adapt, to learn, and to continue advancing long after the specific facts they have learned in college have become obsolete. This combination of immediate usefulness and long-term value is essential whether students envision careers in engineering or the arts, whether they are recent high-school graduates or middle-aged returning students, whether they come from affluent African-American families or poor white broken homes.

120

The future that we and our students share is a world that will be ethnically and culturally richer than society today. As our students prepare for careers as business executives, teachers, government officials, doctors, scientists, social workers, and musicians, they must prepare for a future in which the people with whom they will work are likely to be very different from themselves.

The demographic realities of the future provide an imperative for curricular change. Our responsibility is to educate students for a world in which everyone will be a minority, and fulfilling this responsibility means assisting *all* of our students in acquiring the knowledge and skills necessary for effective living in an increasingly diverse world. This means that *all* of our students need foreign language ability, they *all* need facts about cultural groups other than their own, they *all* need knowledge about international relations, they *all* need intercultural communications skills, they *all* need practice in comparative cultural analysis, and they *all* need sophisticated and critical judgment. As educators, we have a responsibility to offer a curriculum that prepares all of them well for the future.

In this view of education, courses in African-American literature or Chinese language or American ethnic groups are not exotic studies of "The Other"; they are basic building blocks of liberal learning. In this view of education, students of color are not admitted merely to compensate for past injustice; they come to the university as full participants, often better prepared than many mono-cultural white students. In this kind of university, we do not demand conformity to a single cultural norm; instead we accept the challenge of learning from one another. Frank Wong, vice president for academic affairs at the University of Redlands, describes such a campus:

> We need to create an academic community where people with different cultural backgrounds view each other as having similar needs, similar aspirations, and similar problems but with different ways of manifesting them. In this kind of community, different clothes, different accents, different music, different habits, different skin color, and different self-presentation are viewed with interest and curiosity rather than hostility and suspicion. In such a community, cultural differences are regarded not as a dehumanizing stereotype but as an intriguing variation that we seek to understand. In so doing we enlarge both our understanding and our humanity.[6]

6. Frank E. Wong, "Diversity and Community: Right Objectives and Wrong Arguments," *Change*, July/August 1991, p. 53.

In addition, then, to our shared responsibility for diversity in scholarship, we have a second level of common concern for academic quality that focuses on our role as educators. As we anticipate the future and the skills our students will need, the imperatives of diversity become clear. In fact, we would be irresponsible if we were to ignore these needs of the professionals and citizens of the future. And the joint nature of this shared responsibility is manifold – shared among faculty who recreate the curriculum, between faculty and administrators who reexamine institutional policies, and with students who draw upon all of the varied human resources of our campuses.

How is this vision of shared responsibility different from simple cultural relativism? It would be easy to fall into the trap of "the more the merrier," to seek ever larger proportions of students and faculty from different ethnic, cultural, and age groups, to declare victory once no one group represents 50 percent of the campus population. But mere counting does not address the intellectual and educational missions of the university. As Pat Cross recently stated, "The quality of life and the enrichment of society that is the end goal of social transformation cannot be measured by percentages and pie charts alone."[7]

Simplistic relativism can be avoided by focusing on what we have in common as well by as acknowledging our differences. In a university, the shared values are those of the intellectual search for truth. Regardless of our cultural backgrounds, disciplinary specializations, or political persuasions, we choose to reside in academic communities devoted to the expansion of knowledge about the physical world and the human condition. We all value critical thinking, creativity, intellectual honesty, self-criticism, reason, interpretation, and the exchange of ideas. Faculty and students alike share a commitment to continual learning.

And yet the common goal of truth-seeking does not imply either a fixed definition of truth or a consensus of how to go about the search. Rather, it is an agreement to participate in the process as openly and as honestly as possible. Joan Scott, professor of social science at the Institute for Advanced Study at Princeton, reminds us of both our opportunities and our limitations:

> But the university is the best place from which to search for a different understanding of what a community might be. First of all, universities can be seen to already exemplify an alternative. They are, after all, places where sep-

7. K. Patricia Cross, "Reflections, Predictions, and Paradigm Shifts," remarks at the 1991 National Conference on Higher Education, printed in *AAHE Bulletin*, v. 43, n. 9, May 1991, p. 11.

arate and contingent, contradictory and heterogeneous spheres of thought have long coexisted; the grounds for that coexistence are mutual respect for difference and an aversion to orthodoxy.[8]

In fact, the current controversy over diversity and multiculturalism is an example of the yeasty but contentious process of truth-seeking. Suddenly we are faced with new voices, new perspectives, new discoveries, new insights that force us to make new decisions about what is to be incorporated as the closest approximation to the truth. More than ever before, we recognize the partiality of any one viewpoint in our work as scholars and teachers.

An intriguing description of the work of a multicultural university comes from Edgar Beckham of the Ford Foundation. In drawing an analogy with international trade, Beckham asserts that "the contours and borders of cultures are an asset that enriches global society, that the borders should and will remain, and that the world should concern itself less with their definition and fixity, and more with directing the increasingly rich traffic that crosses them." In such a university, says Beckham,

> cultural borders would be construed as the locus of valuable intercultural transactions, and one would need to know the location of the borders in order to confirm that they had been traversed, that a transaction had indeed occurred. The impulse to defend borders would give way to the need to study them, understand them, and manage them; and their integrity – and thus their quality – would be assessed in terms of their capacity to sustain fruitful commerce. The educational objective would be to foster deeper understanding and subtler appreciation of the multiple borders that simultaneously define human difference and mediate the transactions on which human community is built.[9]

This approach to education emphasizes critical inquiry and intercultural – not multicultural – thinking. In Beckham's view, the discourse itself is the source of commonality among members of different cultural groups, as for the foreseeable future we will all be engaged in transactions across seemingly irreducible lines of difference. These skills of communication are essential for persons of all ages, all ethnic groups, all nationalities, and both genders.

8. Joan Wallach Scott, "The Campaign against Political Correctness: What's Really at Stake?" *Change*, v. 23, n. 6, November/December 1991, p. 43.
9. Edgar Beckham, "Cultural Transactions and the Changing Requirements for Educational Quality," presentation at the annual meeting of the Association of American Colleges, January 11, 1992.

The vision of an *inter*cultural world also reminds us of the difficulties inherent in a society with multiple cultures and multiple borders. This is uncharted territory for a nation that has traditionally viewed itself as a melting pot. Even the "tossed salad" metaphor is different from Beckham's society, for in a salad each ingredient remains separate and distinct, linked only by a thin coating of salad dressing. In contrast, Beckham calls for both a celebration of difference as well as constructive interaction – a challenge that no nation has yet to meet. Both the riskiness and the potential of an intercultural society reinforce the seriousness with which we must embrace diversity in both scholarship and teaching.

The challenge of diversity is not only something that must be met by higher education but by our entire society, for the difficulties inherent in creating a new form of civil existence are not unique to colleges and universities. We in the academy do have a special responsibility, however, to exercise our roles as critics and intellectual leaders in society; there is no contemporary issue in greater need of constructive criticism and leadership than effective living in an increasingly diverse nation. Any day's newspapers provides ample evidence of the distance we still must travel together as Americans before we have achieved anything approaching Beckham's vision of a society with cultural borders sustaining fruitful commerce. We in higher education are faced with applying our scholarly and educational talents to the task of grappling with one of the most risky, exciting, and difficult issues facing our nation.

The vision of shared responsibility presented in this paper puts equal emphasis on all members of the academic community. In addition to a concern for justice (something that compels us to include in the academy members of all groups in American society), we all have a shared responsibility for academic quality in both scholarship and teaching and the greater attention to diversity this demands. If the goal is intellectual discourse embracing the cultural richness of all participants represented in the university, then the larger social responsibility is to make a positive contribution to the enormous task of rethinking the nature of American society. In the desire for continual learning, students, faculty, and administrators alike must, in Beckham's words, conduct intercultural transactions as they engage in their common search for new knowledge and understanding.

III. Policy into Practice

In this paper, I contrast the 1960s' sense of compensatory justice with a larger vision of shared responsibility for attention to diversity based on institutional missions of research and teaching. These two strands come together in a concern for the social role of the university. Education is a public good in this nation and colleges have non-profit status that allows virtually every campus in the nation to receive significant benefits in the form of research grants, tax-exempt charitable contributions, federal student aid, and public institutional underwriting. Whether state-supported or independent, institutions of higher education address the public policy goal of developing a well-educated citizenry capable of exercising professional, civic, and personal duties effectively. This is the primary reason for public support of both students and institutions.

If as a nation we declare that all citizens have a right of access to education based on interest and ability, then we cannot extend educational benefits more fully to some segments of society than to others. This is the traditional argument based on justice. But a concern for fairness also requires a curriculum of quality. A colleague recently argued as follows: If an English department were to decide that it was unnecessary to teach feminist theory, it would reveal itself as a bastion both of male egos and of intellectual mediocrity. No English department today could claim to be doing its educational and scholarly job without taking feminist perspectives on literature into account. A decision to ignore feminist theory would suggest a level of professional incompetence that raised questions of whether the institution, and the governments that support it, have failed in their obligation to provide a satisfactory level of education for the citizenry. Is the institution truly delivering the public good for which it is granted special status in our society?[10] Or to put it another way, the question is not merely access, but access to what?

Until this nation achieves the goal of equal opportunity, it cannot abandon its concern for compensatory justice. But, as noted in Part 1 above, the policies associated with this conceptualization present either implicit or explicit assumptions of deficit – student diversity is a problem to be solved through remedial programs.[11] At worst, the diversity issue becomes marginalized, ghetto-ized on the periphery of university life.

In contrast, the concept of shared responsibility places diversity at the center of academic life, a source of vitality for both scholarship and teaching. While the answers to questions about diversity are not obvious or easy, they are fundamental to academic life: What is worth knowing? What, in fact, is knowledge? How do different individuals perceive

---

10. Thanks to James Lesher for suggesting this line of argument.
11. J. Herman Blake, Ronald W. Saufley, Oscar F. Porter, and Annamarie Melodia, "The Challenge of Diversity," unpublished manuscript, October 1989.

truth? How do we in the university agree to disagree? What is the meaning of a community that celebrates its differences? What are our obligations to the public good? In fields from anthropology to zoology, we share the responsibility to grapple with such questions.

The curriculum is one location for the implementation of answers to these educational and ethical inquiries. We struggle to include in the curriculum the best that has been thought and known by the giants of both Western civilization and other cultures. On some campuses the response is a course requirement in something outside the dominant tradition; on other campuses, a "diversity across the curriculum" ethos prevails. On no campus is there complete consensus about either content or process because the search for truth is a continually evolving endeavor. Certainly, there is plenty of evidence from universities across the nation attesting to the difficulty of this process.

Students and faculty of varying cultural backgrounds are better seen as assets in a university of intercultural transactions rather than persons with deficits to be overcome. If one of our goals is a fuller understanding of the human condition in all its richness, then having women and older students and persons of color as colleagues in the search for understanding enhances everyone's ability to achieve this goal. For on this point lies the intersection of our concern for justice and our shared responsibility for intellectual excellence in scholarship and teaching.

The argument for attention to diversity can be made on the basis of educational quality, intellectual trends, public policy goals, market demand, ethical imperatives – or simple self-interest. Faculty and administrators need to be serious about diversity, not because of political correctness or noblesse oblige, but out of concern for the future success of our colleges and universities.

In contrast to the traditional ways of thinking about diversity as remediation or special programming to be handled by student affairs staff, the concept of shared responsibility concerns itself with the intellectual directions of the future, a concern that lies at the heart of what we do as academics. Particularly in public universities (but in fact in all institutions of higher education), our responsibilities to the taxpayers to provide programs of high quality compel us to rethink what we do as teachers and as scholars. Our responsibilities as critics and intellectual leaders in society should lead us to focus on questions of culture and difference and community. Thus, while we continue to give attention to matters of justice for persons from groups historically under-represented in higher education, the larger concerns of inclusiveness are grounded in the fundamental purposes of the university.

Therefore diversity is not just about *them* – it is about all of us.

8
Speech Acts and Hate Speech

Andrew Altman

I.

Responding to a recent rash of racist, sexist, and homophobic incidents, a number of colleges and universities have enacted rules against hate speech.[1] These rules have triggered wide public controversy. Some have defended the rules as essential for affirming the equal dignity of all members of the academic community. But others have condemned them as efforts to impose the ideological conformity of "political correctness" on the academy. These disagreements have pitted old political allies against one another and have created new and unexpected alliances:[2] liberals have attacked other liberals, while conservatives have allied themselves with liberals.

---

1. The most notorious of the recent hate-speech incidents occurred at the University of Pennsylvania, where white students shouted epithets from their dorm rooms at a group of black women who were outside making noise. One of the whites admitted to yelling the term "water-buffalo," which he said was a rough translation of a Yiddish term referring to an inconsiderate person. He said the term had no racial connotations in Yiddish and that he had not used it with any such connotation. Other students had reportedly shouted racial epithets at the women during the incident. Other hate-speech incidents covered by the press have occurred at University of Michigan, Brown University, Stanford University, University of Wisconsin, Memphis State University, Purdue University, and Dartmouth College. Hate-speech regulations have been adopted at University of California, University of Michigan, University of Connecticut, University of Texas, and University of Pennsylvania, among other schools. See Charles Lawrence III, "If He Hollers Let Him Go: Regulating Racist Speech on Campus," *Duke Law Journal* 1990 (1990), 431-33 and 436n.

2. The hate-speech issue has driven a wedge between two traditional allies on the liberal side of the political spectrum, civil rights activists and civil libertarians. The former tend to support the regulation of hate speech and the latter tend to reject it. See Nat Hentoff, "Look Beyond a Burning Cross," *Washington Post* February 1, 1992, A23; and Thomas Grey, "Civil Rights v. Civil Liberties: The Case of Discriminatory Verbal Harassment," *Social Philosophy and Policy* 8: 2 (1991), 81-107. Conservatives generally oppose campus hate-speech regulations on the grounds that they are a manifestation of the sin of "political correctness." President Bush prominently expressed this conservative view in his commencement speech at the University of Michigan in 1991.

In this paper I examine the controversies surrounding the regulation of campus hate speech. I argue that narrowly drawn regulations of hate speech can be defended as a reasonable part of a university's effort to ensure equal educational opportunities for all its students. My argument begins with an account of the nature and meaning of hate speech. I employ some of the basic ideas of speech-act theory, as developed by J.L. Austin, in order to show how some forms of hate speech involve acts that subordinate people.[3] I then argue that the standard justifications for hate-speech regulations are not successful. However, a successful justification *can* be developed, I argue, using the ideas and distinctions developed in the account of how hate speech subordinates persons.

II.

The philosopher J.L. Austin launched speech-act theory by noticing that we do many more things with words than simply make statements or ask questions.[4] We advise, promise, threaten, warn, intimidate, persuade, thank, greet, congratulate, assess, explain, describe, apologize, commend, condemn and so on. In order to introduce some order into the consideration of what we do with words, Austin distinguished between three general categories of linguistic act: locutionary, illocutionary, and perlocutionary. For Austin, these three categories do not represent distinct classes of utterances, as any meaningful utterance would typically be an example of all three types. Rather, they represent three types of description under which any given utterance falls. We are dealing here with actions under a description.

The locutionary act is a linguistic utterance, or locution, described in the most abstract way that still manages to convey its sense and reference. "Mary said, 'I have a gun'" would be a locutionary-act description of Mary's utterance. One could describe the same utterance in a way that abstracted entirely from its meaning-content, for example, in terms of the purely physical characteristics of the sounds constituting it: pitch, loudness, etc. But that would not be a locutionary description, for it would not describe the words uttered as words and so would fail to convey the sense or reference of the utterance.

The illocutionary act is a linguistic utterance described in terms of the

---

3. My arguments here elaborate and in some cases modify the analysis I first gave in "Liberalism and Campus Hate Speech: A Philosophical Analysis," *Ethics* 103 (January 1993), 302-17.

4. J.L. Austin, *How To Do Things With Words* (New York: Oxford U.P., 1962).

kind of action the speaker uses the locution to perform in the specific context of utterance. "Mary warned him that she had a gun" would be an illocutionary-act description of her utterance. This sort of description conveys more of the meaning of the utterance than does a locutionary description; it is a "thicker" meaning-description because it tells us what the performance of the utterance amounts to doing in the given context.

The perlocutionary act is a linguistic utterance described in terms of its effects on the hearer. "Mary persuaded him that she had a gun" would be an example. This sort of description conveys the effects on the listener's mind or conduct that ensue from his or her recognition of the locutionary and illocutionary meanings of the utterance.

In order to understand the full meaning of hate speech, it is especially important to grasp the idea of an illocutionary act. The paradigmatic performance of a specific kind of illocutionary act involves the corresponding kind of intention on the part of the speaker. The paradigmatic issuing of a command involves the speaker's intention to order someone to do something., But there are many ways in which such intentions can misfire, and much of Austin's account of illocutionary acts consists of examining misfires.

An important way in which an intended illocutionary act can misfire is if the listener fails to recognize the illocutionary intention of the speaker. Austin describes this as a failure of "uptake." If an inappropriate locution is used, for example, then it is unlikely the listener will be able to recognize the illocutionary intention. Suppose my intention is to warn you that there is a woman carrying a gun behind you. In such a case, the locution "A man in front of you is wearing a hat" will generally not do. It has the wrong sense and reference.

Sometimes locutions need to be uttered in the right way for the illocutionary intent to be recognized. Suppose I intend to insult you for what I regard as a stupid remark on your part. The locution "You're a genius" will do, if uttered in a sarcastic tone of voice, but if uttered in an apparently sincere tone of voice the illocutionary intent could well go unrecognized. Similarly, a command might be mistaken for a suggestion unless it is uttered in a certain, authoritative way.

Another way in which an intended illocutionary act can misfire is if the speaker lacks the authority to perform the kind of act he intends to perform.[5]

5. For an excellent and very pertinent discussion of the role of authority in the performance of speech acts, see Rae Langton, "Speech Acts and Unspeakable Acts," *Philosophy and Public Affairs* 22: 4 (Fall 1993), 304 ff. Langton's piece, along with criticisms of an earlier version of this paper by Ted Cohen, convinced me that Austin's account of speech acts provides a better framework for understanding hate speech than John Searle's more comprehensive account. Whether Austin's account is better tout court is another question. See Searle, *Speech Acts* (New York: Cambridge U.P., 1969).

Such authority is conferred by the rules or conventions that apply within the domain in which the speaker is operating. Thus, a jury foreman is empowered by legal rules to deliver a verdict of guilty or not guilty in the case on which he sits, but an individual seated in the spectator's gallery is not. Imagine that when a judge asks for the verdict, such an individual stands up and yells "Guilty," intending to deliver the verdict. His illocutionary act has misfired for lack of authority. Of course, most people who are vaguely familiar with the rules of our legal system would not even attempt to perform such an illocutionary act unless they had been appointed to head a jury. But one can imagine, for example, an individual from a very different legal culture failing to understand our legal conventions and thus mistakenly believing that he had the authority to deliver a verdict simply by virtue of having attended the trial. Yet while such a person might try to deliver a verdict, the relevant rules make it impossible for him to do so.

The successful performance of an illocutionary act thus typically involves three elements.[6] First is the illocutionary intention, the intention to use a certain locution to perform a specific kind of act. Second is the recognition of the illocutionary intention, its uptake by the listener. Uptake typically requires the speaker to have chosen a locution that carries the appropriate sense and reference and to have uttered the locution in an appropriate manner. Third is the authority of the speaker to perform her intended illocutionary act. There must be relevant rules or conventions that empower the speaker to use locutions to accomplish the illocutionary act in question. In the next section, I employ these ideas of speech-act theory to analyze the meaning of hate speech.

III.

A principal contention of this paper is that some – but not all – forms of hate speech involve the performance of a certain species of illocutionary act, i.e., the act of treating someone as a moral subordinate. Such illocutionary acts must be distinguished from acts of stating, recommending, or arguing that someone should be treated as a moral subordinate. The latter kinds of acts belong to hate speech as well. But the speech act of treating someone as a moral subordinate is doing something essentially different from stating, arguing, or recommending that they should be so

---

6. In this summary, I borrow from Langton's analysis of Austin's work. See "Speech Acts and Unspeakable Acts," 300-5.

treated; its illocutionary intention is different: to treat someone as being on a lower level of the moral universe, rather than simply to make a statement about him.

In the sense in which I am using "moral subordinate," treating people as moral subordinates is treating them as though their lives are inherently less valuable, and their interests less important, than the lives and interests of some reference group. Admittedly, this is a very thin explanation of what treating someone as a moral subordinate involves, yet a thin account is what is needed in order to remain neutral among the major approaches to ethical theory. Different kinds of ethical theory will fill out the account in differing ways, and the thin definition of "moral subordinate" seeks a formulation on which the adherents to these different approaches can agree.

Acts of moral subordination, whether they are speech acts or not, communicate a message about the inferior moral status of someone's existence, and they communicate this message by being instances of the sort of treatment that the message implies is appropriate. Torturing someone or forcibly expelling a population en masse from their homes is the sort of treatment appropriate for moral subordinates and, through that fact, communicates the message that the victims are moral subordinates.

My contention is that subordination can work through speech acts as well as nonlinguistic acts. The linguistic subordination of people is one important way in which the message of inferiority can be communicated through an act held to be an instance of the sort of treatment held to be appropriate for someone who is a moral subordinate.

In addition, I would like to suggest that the slurs and epithets of hate speech are words that are typically used for the performance of just such linguistic acts of subordination. "Kike," "faggot," "nigger," "spic": these words are the conventional, verbal instruments of subordination, used to mark people as moral inferiors through the treatment of them as such. They are locutions especially appropriate for the performance of illocutionary acts of moral subordination. As such, they carry roughly the same social meaning that spitting on someone does in our culture.[7]

7. It would certainly be possible to imagine a culture in which spitting on someone was an act of honoring him. Perhaps it was believed that saliva contained certain magical properties that would be of great value to the person spat on. Our conventions are, of course, quite the reverse.

Charles Lawrence uses the example of slapping someone in the face as illustrative of an act whose social meaning is to subordinate. The example is, however, dubious in many situations. In the stereotypical scenario of a woman slapping a man as a response to some unwanted sexual contact, it is the slapper – not the slappee – who is in the subordinate position. When a parent slaps a child, on the other hand, the act does seem to be a matter of treating the child as a subordinate. See Lawrence, "If He Hollers Let Him Go," 452.

It is certainly true that these slurs and epithets are also used to express the speaker's hatred or contempt for a person or group. This is why the term "hate speech" is an appropriate one. But I think that the full social meaning of the slurs and epithets of hate speech can be missed unless one recognizes that they are also used to treat people as moral subordinates. Hate speech not only expresses hate; it subordinates.

Austin's account of speech acts repeatedly emphasizes that there is no one-to-one matching of words with specific illocutionary acts. The same words can be used to warn, suggest, advise, recommend, describe, explain and so on. It all depends on how the speaker chooses to use the words and the context in which she makes the choice. I do not wish to dispute this Austinian point – indeed, it explains why certain subordinated groups have been able to transvalue the terms traditionally used to subordinate them. Homosexuals have done this with the term "queer." By choosing to use the term as an expression of pride, homosexuals have sought to cancel out the subordinating force of the term.

Nonetheless, it does not follow from Austin's point that all words are equally suitable for all illocutionary acts. Nor does Austin's point exclude the possibility that there are certain words especially suitable for certain kinds of illocutionary acts. My hypothesis about the slurs and epithets of hate speech is that they are especially suitable for purposes of subordination. Such words are conventional instruments of subordination. The transvalued use of "queer" does not contradict this hypothesis. In fact, the use of the term as an expression of homosexual pride gets its special force from the fact that it constitutes a reversal of the traditional, subordinating use of the term.

As conventional instruments of moral subordination, the slurs and epithets of hate speech belong to the general class of terms that are used to "put people down." Moreover, this vernacular expression reveals quite clearly the sorts of illocutionary act the terms are conventionally employed to perform. However, it is important to recognize that there are different types of illocutionary put-downs. An illocutionary act of treating someone as a moral subordinate must be distinguished from other illocutionary put-downs. If you call me "Stupid," you may be treating me as inferior in intelligence, but that does not necessarily mean that you are treating me as a moral subordinate. You might acknowledge that, despite my lack of intelligence, I am still entitled to a moral standing equal to any other person's. The slurs and epithets of hate speech are often combined with the other sorts of verbal put-downs. But the kind of put-down the slurs and epithets of hate speech are conventionally used to accomplish is essentially different in that it denigrates the standing of the person in the moral universe and does not simply denigrate the person's skill or capacity in one or another respect.

IV.

Advocates of campus hate-speech regulations typically argue along two lines.[8] First, they claim that such regulations are important in fighting racial and sexual subordination that pervade society at large. Second, they insist that such regulations are needed to provide students with genuinely equal education opportunity.

The former line of argument is vulnerable to several powerful objections. First, it is not clear why universities, public or private, should be in the business of adopting codes of behavior for students that aim to counter the racial and sexual subordination in society at large. This is not to suggest that appropriate educational policies may not have the incidental and happy effect of weakening such subordination, nor that individual students should be prohibited from activities that directly target such subordination. Rather, it is to suggest that codes of behavior for students need to be justified in terms of the educational mission of the university. If they are to be justified at all, speech codes need to be justified in terms of the job of providing students with an education.[9]

Yet even if it were appropriate to justify speech codes in terms of their contribution to the fight against subordination in society at large, a major difficulty remains. Speech codes that are narrowly tailored will almost certainly do next to nothing in combating society-wide subordination, while substantially broader codes involve intolerable intrusions on freedom of expression. An example of a well-crafted, narrow speech code is Stanford's.[10] It bans only the face-to-face use of slurs and epithets uttered with the intention to degrade on the basis of such characteristics as race, religion, and sexual preference. It does not ban pseudo-scientific forms of racist, sexist, or homophobic expression; it does not ban racist, sexist, or

8. For a good anthology of essays that argue vigorously in favor of hate-speech codes, see Mari Matsuda et al., *Words That Wound: Critical Race Theory, Assaultive Speech, and the First Amendment* (Boulder: Westview, 1993). For a much more restrained endorsement of speech codes, see Joshua Cohen, "Freedom of Expression," *Philosophy and Public Affairs* 22 (Summer 1993), 207-63.

9. A university's admission criteria are another matter, since it does not concern the regulation of student behavior. The same goes for an institution's investment portfolio.

10. For the Stanford regulation, see Thomas Grey, "Civil Rights v. Civil Liberties: The Case of Discriminatory Verbal Harassment," *Social Philosophy and Policy* 8 (1991), 106-7.

homophobic speech couched in terms of theological or philosophical ideas. Henry Louis Gates has emphasized the drastic limitations of these regulations: "[W]e must be clear how inadequate that code is as a response to the powerful arguments that were marshalled to support it."[11] Even if the Stanford code were in force at many institutions, prohibiting students from calling each other "Kike," "Nigger," and "Cunt," it would do virtually nothing to eliminate or weaken subordination in society at large. It is not that speech does not contribute to subordination, in Gates's view. Rather, it is that the forms of hate speech most powerful in perpetuating subordination are not gutter slurs and epithets but precisely the pseudo-scientific, theological, and philosophical ones that the Stanford code leaves untouched.

And yet to target these more "sophisticated" forms of racist, sexist, and homophobic speech would constitute an invasion of free expression that even the public proponents of speech codes repudiate. There have been policies that banned such sophisticated hate speech – for example, a policy that was once in force at the University of Connecticut placed all members of the university under an obligation to refrain from actions or utterances that "undermine [the] security or self-esteem" of others.[12] It is reasonable to think that this policy would have prohibited pseudo-scientific or theological speech claiming the inferiority of women or Blacks. But none of the public proponents of speech codes has defended such a policy, and in response to a legal challenge the University of Connecticut gave up its sweeping policy in favor of a much narrower one similar to Stanford's. This failure to defend Connecticut's original, sweeping code can be easily explained: the code was indefensible. Any contribution such a code would have made to combating oppression in society would likely have been meager in relation to the great harm done to the free exchange of ideas and opinions. Perhaps someone will come forth to rebut this argument and defend such sweeping speech codes as Connecticut's original one. But until then, it is common ground in the debate over speech codes that sweeping regulations are unjustifiable restrictions on expression. And that leads us back to Gates's point: the narrow codes do virtually nothing to combat the societal oppression that is invoked to justify them.

There is a second line of argument in favor of speech codes that appeals to the educational mission of the university: providing equal edu-

11. Henry Louis Gates, Jr., "Let Them Talk," *New Republic* (September 20 and 27, 1993), 45.
12. The University's regulations are found in the pamphlet, "Protect Campus Pluralism." The regulations have been withdrawn in response to a lawsuit.

134

cational opportunity to all students. Advocates of such codes claim that students are unduly hampered in their pursuit of educational opportunities when subjected to hate speech on campus. This is said to result from the psychological harm that hate speech inflicts on its victims. Such harm makes it more difficult for the student to concentrate, to study, and to learn.

This second line of argument initially seems more promising than the first. The dilemma of choosing between narrow but ineffective codes and sweeping but indefensible codes does not apply. Narrowly drawn codes may do nothing to eliminate oppression in society at large, but they might make a significant contribution to creating a more comfortable learning environment for women and minorities. Nonetheless, there seems to be a mismatch between this justification and the narrowness of the codes it seeks to justify, for the proposed justification would presumably cover not simply slurs and epithets, but more sophisticated forms of hate speech as well. Just as sophisticated forms of racist and sexist speech may well be more powerful in helping to perpetuate subordination in society, they may be more powerful in their capacity to cause lasting psychological injury. And yet we have seen that even proponents of speech codes reject the prohibition of those forms of hate speech not employing slurs and epithets.

Moreover, the whole idea that universities must protect students from psychological injuries stemming from what others at the university say seems dubious. It would be absurd to suggest, for example, that professors be barred from giving failing grades to students or making critical comments on their exams and papers because it will cause them psychological distress. This remains true even if, as seems plausible, a failing grade can cause deep and lasting psychological injury. Persons simply have to learn to cope with certain kinds of injuries and harm. And given the importance of speech and the exchange of ideas to the aims of the university, the only reasonable course seems to be for universities to require their students to learn to cope with the psychological harm caused by what others at the institution say.

And yet there are imaginable circumstances in which what is said (or otherwise expressed) would create such a pervasively hostile environment toward women or minorities that it would be reasonable for a university to impose some sort of restrictions on the kind of expression creating that environment. Suppose, for example, that women were subjected on a daily basis to a slew of posters, signs, and speakers denouncing their presence on campus and calling for a male-only institution on the ground that a college education interferes with a woman's natural role in society. Suppose, further, that some significant portion of the university community supported such a view of women. It would not be difficult to imagine that, in such circumstances, the pervasive hostility would cause psychological distress making it difficult or impossible for many women to take advantage of their educational opportunities. If faced with such a hypothetical scenario, I would be forced to conclude that the university would be justified in taking strong measures to counteract the hostile environment, including the adoption of a speech code regulating sexist speech. A commitment to equal educational opportunity for women would demand such measures.

Some proponents of speech codes seem to be suggesting that the actual situation on numerous campuses is as bad as the one I have imagined in the hypothetical scenario above. But such a suggestion is a gross exaggeration. My hypothetical is much more extreme than any existing situation. Moreover, the hypothetical could occur only in a society whose fight against sexism and racism is at a much more primitive stage than our own.[13] The question of whether women (or minorities) should have fair access to higher education is one that has been settled in this society. It simply is not a significant issue at any college or university or in any other forum. This is not to say that everyone agrees on what counts as fair access, for the affirmative action controversy clearly reveals the existence of disagreement on that score. Nonetheless, that controversy is a far cry from a dispute over whether women (or minorities) should have any access to higher education. The latter is a dispute that characterizes my hypothetical scenario and is an essential part of what would make the institutional environment so hostile as to justify regulations on sexist speech. My conclusion, then, is that the "hostile environment" argument is not successful in justifying speech codes, given existing conditions.

V.

To this point, my argument can be summarized as saying that an adequate justification for hate-speech codes in the contemporary context cannot be developed by invoking the perlocutionary effects of such speech. Yet if we shift our focus from the perlocutionary effects of hate speech to its illocutionary force, we can avoid the foregoing difficulties.

13. The fight against homophobia in our society is in a relatively primitive stage. Yet, on most campuses, there is much greater recognition than in society at large of the rights of homosexuals, and the kind of constant, public bombardment imagined in my hypothetical does not exist on any college campus with which I am familiar.

It may be unreasonable for universities to enact codes aimed at protecting students from the psychological harm caused by what others say, but it does not follow that it is unreasonable for universities to enact narrowly drawn codes aimed at protecting students from illocutionary acts that subordinate them on the basis of race, gender, or sexual orientation. It may be wrong to think that the college and university environments are so hostile to women and minorities as to justify speech codes, but it does not follow that it unreasonable for universities to prohibit the face-to-face use of slurs and epithets that subordinate individuals on account of their race, gender, or sexual orientation.

Let us assume that universities stand under an obligation to provide their students with equal educational opportunities without regard to their race, gender, or sexual orientation. Of course, some might deny the existence of such an obligation, but none of the public opponents of speech codes is willing to make her stand on that basis. So we can take it as common ground that universities have such an obligation.

Two questions about such an obligation can be distinguished: What must a university do in order to satisfy the obligation? And what is it reasonable for a university to do in its efforts to satisfy the obligation? The answer to the first question would specify policies or actions without which an institution would be unable to reasonably claim it took seriously its obligation to provide equal educational opportunities. For example, a university that excluded blacks from the library and from certain classroom spaces could not reasonably claim to be providing them with equal educational opportunities. There must be equal access to educational facilities, regardless of race.

There are other policies that may not be mandatory for meeting the principle of equal educational opportunity but are nonetheless reasonable ones to adopt in light of that principle. Speech codes that target the face-to-face use of slurs and epithets that degrade on the basis of such characteristics as race, gender, and sexual preference fall into the latter category. They are not required by the demands of equal educational opportunity, and yet they are among the policies that may reasonably be adopted in light of the equal opportunity principle.

Imagine a university that has adopted the policies required by the equal opportunity principle: all students have equal access to the school's educational resources, regardless of their race, gender, sexual preference and so on. There is a moral commitment implicit in such policies: the university must treat its students with equal respect, regardless of their racial, religious, or sexual characteristics. This takes us to the crucial issue: Is the enactment of a code regulating hate speech a reasonable way of honoring that commitment?

The arguments against all codes targeting hate speech do not quarrel with this commitment but instead aim to show that such codes are not a reasonable way of honoring it. These arguments point out that universities have obligations and responsibilities to their members and to society that require the free expression and interchange of ideas and opinions. The university is a major social forum for the advancement and communication of knowledge and for the understanding of human experience. Hate-speech codes unreasonably threaten the ability of the university to meet these responsibilities. Or so these arguments go.

These arguments are persuasive when applied to sweeping codes, such as the one originally in force at the University of Connecticut, and this is why the public proponents of speech codes have refused to enforce sweeping codes. But these arguments are not persuasive when applied to narrowly drawn codes, such as the one in force at Stanford. Narrow codes pose no unreasonable threat to the university and its ability to meet its responsibilities. The philosophical problem is to develop a justification for such narrowly drawn codes that does not, simultaneously, justify sweeping ones.

This is where the idea that some – but not all – forms of hate speech consist of speech acts of subordination comes in. For it is this idea, as I have developed it, that provides a justification of narrow codes that simultaneously avoids justifying sweeping ones.

Narrowly drawn speech codes target the face-to-face use of epithets and slurs that degrade on the basis or race, gender, or other personal features. Such speech subordinates. It is primarily aimed at treating its target as a moral inferior and is typically received that way by the listener. It is not primarily aimed at asserting a proposition or arguing for a conclusion or making a statement.

In contrast, the forms of hate speech left untouched by narrowly drawn regulations – pseudo-scientific, theological and so on – are primarily used to assert, argue, and state. It is true that such assertions and arguments are used in justifying the treatment of women or minorities as subordinates. But to justify subordination, or to make assertions that are part of its justification, is distinct from performing an act of subordination. And while it is reasonable for a university to target hate speech that subordinates, it goes too far when it targets hate speech that states, claims, argues and the like.

It might be said that my proposed justification for narrow hate-speech codes still ends up sweeping too broadly. For even if the distinction between subordinating and nonsubordinating hate speech were clear, there seems to be an overbreadth problem relating to nonspeech conduct. Suppose that a group of white students intentionally excludes a black student from its social activities on account of her race. Such an exclusion can plausibly be interpreted as an act of racial subordination – after all, such exclusion is at the heart of racial apartheid – and thus would seem to be suitable for prohibition under my justification. Yet it would be difficult to argue that a university may reasonably dictate to students with whom they must socialize. Moreover, the original code at the University of Connecticut – which I have condemned as excessively sweeping – contained a provision that barred among other actions, "conspicuous exclusions from conversations."[14] This provision seems no less objectionable than the one I have already rejected.

Exclusion from social activities on grounds of race can certainly count as an act of subordination, but a policy that demands that students socialize in a "politically correct" way constitutes an unwarranted intrusion into their private lives. It would accomplish virtually nothing toward providing students with equal educational opportunities, and yet it would license a sweeping invasion by university authorities into the private lives of students. Indeed, the policy rests on the misguided notion that students can be effectively forced into socializing harmoniously with those whom they intensely dislike or hate.

In contrast, a code regulating the face-to-face use of hate-speech slurs and epithets involves no effort to regulate with whom students socialize. It simply aims to prevent students from degrading one another through the use of subordinating hate speech. This is certainly a feasible aim, involving no draconian invasions of the private lives of students.

Narrowly drawn speech codes would likely be underinclusive, as it seems possible to treat someone as a moral subordinate through one's speech without the use of a slur or epithet. However, there are precious few regulations that have a perfect match with the evil they seek to control, and it is difficult to see how the regulations could be broadened in a way that would meet the need for fair warning yet avoid serious overinclusiveness. When it comes to the regulation of speech by institutions devoted to free inquiry and discussion, it is more reasonable to err on the side of underinclusiveness than on the side of overinclusivenes. Some individuals may well be wronged by subordinating hate-speakers who will escape the sanction of the rules. But that is a price that should be paid.

The arguments I have given thus far in favor of narrowly drawn speech codes have not addressed certain dangers and problems attendant

14. See "Protect Campus Pluralism," University of Connecticut.

to the adoption of such codes. Opponents of codes exaggerate these dangers and problems, yet they cannot be entirely dismissed for that reason.

One danger is that the codes will be enforced in a biased manner, to the detriment of the very minorities whom the proponents of the codes wish most to protect.[15] Blacks might be singled out for speech that is regarded as expressing anti-white racism. Women might be singled out for speech that is regarded as expressing anti-male hatred.

Although such a danger is real, university communities are not powerless to counteract it. The enforcement of speech codes can be monitored. If it appears that there is biased enforcement, then university authorities can be challenged to rebut the appearance of bias. If the appearance cannot be cogently rebutted, then the codes can be rescinded.[16] Perhaps this is all easier said than done, but it is by no means impossible to do, and it does show that advocates of speech codes need not stand idly by if the codes are being abused by those in power.

The most commonly cited danger is that the adoption of narrowly drawn speech codes could open the door to more sweeping ones down the line. This, of course, is the old slippery slope argument. In making the argument, opponents of speech codes claim that there is likely to be significant pressure to broaden the scope of a narrow code when its supporters realize that it is ineffective at combating racism, sexism, and homophobia on campus. The narrow codes will thus be mere preludes to sweeping ones.

Yet persons committed to the vigorous protection of free expression need not and will not stand idly by as freedom of expression is unduly restricted. Substantial protests have made it difficult to enact even narrow codes, and there is every reason to believe that sweeping ones would be much more difficult to enact. Moreover, the federal courts have been a powerful ally on the side of those who reject sweeping speech codes.[17] It is exceedingly unlikely that the courts will let stand any code that goes much farther than Stanford's narrowly targeted regulation of hate speech.

15. See, e.g., Nadine Strossen, "Regulating Racist Speech on Campus: A Modest Proposal?," *Duke Law Journal* 1990, 557-58, and Gates, "Let Them Talk, 44.

16. Another way to block the biased enforcement of a speech code is to write it so that it only protects the members of historically oppressed groups. Blacks would be able to call on the code if they were targets of subordinating hate speech uttered by whites, but whites would not be able to call on the code in the reverse situation. I oppose such "one-way" codes on the ground that subordination based on race (or other morally irrelevant characteristics) is a violation of the equal respect to which every individual is entitled, even if the individual does not belong to an historically oppressed group.

17. For example, the federal district court in *Doe v. University of Michigan* 721 *F.Supp.* 852 (E.D. Mich. 1989) struck down as unconstitutionally overbroad the university's regulations on discriminatory harassment.

VI.

I have argued that subordination is at the heart of the hate-speech issue. Words are not mere words; they can be as powerful in their own way as sticks and stones, and perhaps even more so. Ralph Waldo Emerson referred to this power one hundred and fifty years ago when writing about his society's debates over slavery. He wrote in his journals: "What argument, what eloquence can avail against the power of that one word *niggers*? The man of the world annihilates the whole combined force of all the antislavery societies of the world by pronouncing it."[18]

If my analysis of hate speech is accurate, we can explain the power of that one word. It is a word by virtue of which speech acts of subordination are performed. It is a word through which a race is spat upon, or, more precisely, through which speech acts are performed whose social meaning is the equivalent of spitting upon someone because of her race. Argument and eloquence cannot counteract it in any direct way because argument and eloquence have an entirely different kind of illocutionary point. When you are spat upon, even the most eloquent words cannot erase or nullify the fact that you have been treated as a moral subordinate.

18. Joel Porte, ed., *Emerson in His Journals* (Cambridge: Harvard U.P., 1982) p. 338. Cited in Cornel West, *The American Evasion of Philosophy* (Madison: U. of Wisconsin, 1989), p. 25.

9

Free Speech and the Aims of the University: Some Modest Proposals

K. Anthony Appiah

I. Interpreting the University's Mission

We have often been told that the mission of the university in our day is threefold: we are called, it is said, to the tasks of teaching, research, and the dissemination of learning. This obviously rather formal conception of the university – formal, both in the sense that it says nothing about the content of our teaching or the areas of research and learning that we recognize, and in the sense that it says nothing about the many ways in which the university is more than a community of teachers and scholars – this formal conception is obviously not one that would, by itself, make the university intelligible to someone who knew nothing of our culture and its traditions. If the triple mission captures conditions essential to our mission, it does not explain how certain kinds of teaching and certain areas of research have come to be seen as central, others more peripheral, and some to have no place at all in our work. The history of the university is a history in which conflict over these questions has been central to the politics – in the broadest sense – of culture. The debates over the role of religious instruction in the nineteenth century and the contested rise of what Trilling taught us to see as the secular clerisy of the English department, should remind us always that the consensus about what we do is hard-won and, of course, always provisional. As our culture and politics change, these debates over the content of our work are sure to continue. And because attention to these issues has a generational cycle these facts will seem less evident at some times than at others. But I think it is fair to say that the cycle has come round once more in America. Former Education Secretary Bennett's call for a return to a classical Western canon (a canon that for him, for reasons some of which are quite narrowly political, is centered on the Judaeo-Christian rather than on the Hellenic strain of Western culture), is only a symptom of our rediscovery that the content of our project is essentially a matter of contest.

These facts are important because it is important, especially in such times of contest, that we make our choices clear-headedly and with a firm grasp of the wide range both of the options available to us and of the views – both possible and actual – about what our purposes can be. And this is especially so in deciding questions of freedom of expression. For such questions should, I think, be answered in the light of a view about the purposes of the university. Because the nature of the university is a matter not for discovery but for decision, you cannot appeal simply to a shared understanding of our purposes, or to an uninterpreted tradition. Of course, we must build on the past: but an uncritical traditionalism will only leave us governed forever by the dead hands of dead people. If one thing stands out from a critical view of the tradition of the Western university, it is that it is a history of changing self-conceptions.

II. Isolating Alethic Considerations

Nevertheless, it seems right to start with our current consensus. And I think a good starting point would be recognizing that what is implicit in the current interpretation of our triple mission *in practice* is a view of the university as a moral community. In one sense, of course, this is obvious. The university seeks to avoid sexism and racism in the selection of students and faculty not because we know that discrimination is illegal but because we believe that it is wrong. Our moral ideas extend into the classroom. There are constraints within which teaching on moral and political questions must fall, constraints more substantial than the claim that you should not teach students what competent people know to be false. Even though many in the university believe that moral claims are not straightforwardly truth-valued – and would claim, as a result, that moral error is not simply a matter of believing falsehoods – we do agree for the most part, for example, that the profession by teachers in class of racist ideas would be unacceptable, and could legitimately be barred, even if those ideas did not entail errors in biology. We will hire racists, perhaps, in fields where their racism does not undermine their claim to competence; but we will not hire them to teach racism.

What is less obvious is that our teaching and research – in the sciences as in the arts – is governed by notions of method that are, in the end, rooted in an ethical demand. We all accept, of course, the uncontroversial claim that, where the notion clearly applies, truth is what we should

144

seek and teach and disseminate. But we share, as I say, a less obvious idea; and it is one that I believe we should continue in the future to respect. It is the idea that rational discourse and the development of a community that seeks rationally to assess evidence and reasons, with the minimum of partiality and prejudice, are the proper modes of pursuing that truth. Despite the limitations that we place *for ethical reasons* on the content of our research and teaching, we also largely share a sense that, where we are confronted, individually, with people whose views fall outside our consensus we should try to persuade them to our view through reasoning. What lies the other way is the Inquisition or the Gulag.

I mention this agreeable consensus, in order to distinguish reasons of this substantially moral kind from what appears often to be regarded as the *major* reason why the university has an interest in freedom of expression; a reason that is essentially practical. That practical reason – one that has been made into a philosophy of science by Karl Popper – is that we can only learn the truth by testing it against contrary views. The history of the arts and of learning has shown that the pursuit of truth requires us to allow for the expression of positions far remote from the current consensus; and that, where evidence and reasons are offered for those positions, counter-evidence and counter-argument are not only the proper but also the productive responses. This view is too familiar to need elaborating.

As teachers and students, researchers and writers, we can only be at home in a place that cares deeply about the free interplay of ideas . . . because the free discourse of free people is a tested way to the truth; because, as Locke wrote in the *Essay on Human Understanding*, "all men are liable to error; and most men are, in many points, by passion or interest, under temptation to it." To learn the truth and live by it, we need the test of contrary opinion to protect us from the temptations of passion and interest.

This kind of consideration in favor of freedom of expression I shall call an *alethic* – that is, a truth-directed – consideration.

III. Libertarian Considerations

Alethic considerations provide a powerfully important, familiar, and *prudential* argument for allowing for the widest diversity of rationally defended opinion. Moreover, because our canons of rationality are not unchanging, it is a reason for a broad understanding of what constitutes a reason and counts as evidence. It is an ethical reason to the extent that we view the pursuit of knowledge and understanding as we should view it: as something of intrinsic and not merely of instrumental value. But in this society there is another reason for allowing for the free expression of ideas: a reason that has nothing to do with the productive consequences of that freedom, and that makes our conception of the university in yet one more respect expressive of a moral vision.

This reason is our right to bar the actions of others only – this is the official liberal view that I am inclined to endorse myself – where they infringe on rights or otherwise do harm; or – and this is a view that I believe has more widespread fundamental support, even among self-described "liberals" – where those actions are, in themselves, morally repugnant in ways about which there is the broadest community consensus.[1]

Something like these principles is at the core of American pluralism: through the notion that the state will not enforce the mores of particular communities the United States has sought to live as a community of communities, each entitled to its own form of life. I shall call the first principle, for this reason, the "principle of pluralism." It says that *the state may bar the actions of others only where they infringe on rights or otherwise do harm*. Respect for this principle of pluralism has a special importance because legal restraints on freedom of action are enforced with the coercive power of the state; a coercive power whose exercise should always be capable of rational justification to the citizen.

It is this principle that grounds, in my view, the distinction between freedom of expression in public and the justified limitation of that freedom in private. If we had no such distinction, then the general right not to be interfered with unless you cause harm, would obviously risk being either impractically burdensome or quite insubstantial. For if we construed "harm" so narrowly as to include only physical damage, then we would be obliged to allow behavior that is deeply offensive to some; and anyone who was so offended would risk being upset at any time. Surely,

---

1. The difference between these two views is very sharp in the most contested recent cases of freedom of expression, which center on what its opponents usually call "pornography." In the United States there is, I think, "the broadest community consensus" in most places that the infringement of rights and the infliction of (substantial) harm (upon the innocent) are, in themselves, morally repugnant. But there is also, in many places, a broad consensus that the representation of sexual acts and organs is morally repugnant, even if it infringes on no rights and causes no harm. The appeal of grounding opposition to pornography in what I called the "official liberal view" is clear, however, in the attempts of those who advocate its censorship to represent pornography as harmful. See, e.g., Jillian Ridington, *Freedom from harm or freedom of speech? : a feminist perspective on the regulation of pornography* (Ottawa, Ont.: National Association of Women and the Law, 1983).

146

that would be too burdensome. If, on the other hand, we construed "harm" so widely as to include, say, the mild irritation of others, then practically no act that could be observed by others would be permitted. That would make this right purely theoretical. In defining private spheres in which people may, within broad limits, set their own standards, we minimize intervention by the state in both public and private behavior.

In our society, people have the right to come together in free associations that restrict both the form and the content of expression: in a Catholic church you may not curse, and you may not express contempt for God. But in the public arena we mostly – and, in my view, rightly – believe that both "vulgarity" of expression and blasphemy can be prohibited only for certain limited reasons (reasons to which I shall later return). Outrage is not, I suspect, something that can intelligibly be regarded as having an inter-subjective measure. Nonetheless, my outrage at the invocation of the divinity in public for certain political purposes that I regard as abhorrent, would count *by itself* no more as a reason for limiting that invocation than the outrage of the devout Catholic on hearing an atheist, a Protestant, a Jew, or a Muslim expressing contempt for the Holy Father, even if it made sense to try and compare them.

This sort of consideration in favor of freedom of expression on the basis that we have a *prima facie* right to freedom of action I shall call a *libertarian*[2] consideration.[3]

IV. The University as a Public Institution

Libertarian considerations reflect a view about public life and I think it should be part of our understanding of the university that it is, in this respect, a public institution, despite the fact that in the United States universities are sometimes legally private institutions. Though it does not have the coercive power of the state – and though, in my view, it should

2. I use this term conscious of the risk that it may have unfortunate associations for some. It is important to bear in mind that I use this as a term of art.

3. I shall not take up the issues raised in the literature that explores the claim that freedom of expression – that is freedom from government interference in expression – has special value because expression is central to moral personhood in the liberal tradition; see, e.g., T.M. Scanlon Jr. "Freedom of Expression and Categories of Expression," *University of Pittsburgh Law Review* vol. 40 No. 4 (Summer 1979), "A Theory of Freedom of Expression," *Philosophy and Public Affairs* vol. 1 (1972). Such considerations, while important, do not, in my view, operate to any special effect in the university. But I should point out that if the liberty to express one's views (or, as we say, one's self) is a special good, then deprivation of that good represents one of the harms that requires consideration in managing expression at a university, as it does in industry and other spheres.

not seek to invoke that power, as many universities unfortunately have done – the powers of even private universities over students and faculty, in determining both their life-chances and their ability to pursue teaching and learning, are substantial. The use and the abuse of that power raise issues of justification almost as fundamental as the use of force, fines, and incarceration against citizens generally. For although the university is, in this respect, intermediate between a small private group and the state, it is much nearer to the state than to a club, a church, or even, perhaps, a political party.

It is plain enough, however, that even someone who denies this must respect the very powerful alethic considerations in favor of freedom of expression in the university ... at least, if they share the consensus of Americans generally, and university academics in particular, about the vocation of tertiary education. This consensus is reflected in the widespread acceptance of academic freedom as the basis for the extraordinary rights associated with tenure; and those of us who have that protection should surely have a special interest in respect for the logic of academic freedom.

V. The Basic Goal of Policy

I believe it follows, once we pursue these ideas more thoroughly, that, subject to caveats I shall mention below, the university should allow the expression of opinions in public gatherings by any member of the university and anyone invited by a member of the university – and I take this to include staff, students, and faculty – quite independently of the contents of their views.

VI. Limitation of the Policy to the Public Sphere

There are, as I have already suggested, other principles by which this basic respect for unfettered freedom of expression in public discourse may be limited; I shall return to some of these below. But it is important that the reasons I have given are reasons for freedom of expression in a *public sphere*, for I have already said that I do not think the same arguments can be made for unfettered freedom of expression in private gatherings. This distinction has two important consequences that I should like to draw to your attention.

First, it is crucial when applying this principle to determine whether any particular gathering is, in the relevant sense, a private one. I see no reason, for example, why the university should permit private meetings of non-university members of the American Nazi Party or other racist groups in its rooms, even though I should argue strongly for the right of the American Nazi Party to be allowed, if invited, to express its views on any campus in public; even though, indeed, if they wished to come and there was any reason to think that their meeting would be attended by members of the university community, I am not sure that an invitation should be a *sine qua non*. I should, of course, also argue (see section 7 below) for my right to question, heckle reasonably, and bear denunciatory placards; my right to treat them with discourtesy or even with contempt (see section 12).

Though private meetings of groups from outside the university whose views are far beyond its pale can, in my view, reasonably be barred, I do not see why, if students or faculty wish to meet as members of the American Nazi party, they should be prohibited. I see three reasons for this:

A. First, such a prohibition would have to flow from a general rule, and that rule would inevitably risk being applied in cases where the views of the group were less obviously objectionable. A university administration might think, for example, that a divestment group should be banned under this rubric because its purposes threatened the finances, and thus the life, of the university.

B. Second, freedom of association, even on the basis of principles that are morally repugnant, should be protected for the same sorts of reasons as is freedom of expression. Private meetings to develop ideas provide as much scope for alethic considerations in favor of freedom of association as do public meetings for freedom of public expression. Furthermore, libertarian considerations generally favor freedom of association, except in a restricted class of cases that involve conspiracy . . . and criminal conspiracy is already governed (in my view too widely!) by law.

C. Third (and, probably, least significantly), it is always unwise to make rules whose application would be impracticable. There would be no way to stop, for example, university members who were in fact members of the Nazi Party from pretending to meet for the purposes of discussing, say, algebra, football, or ornithology.

VII. The Privacy of the Classroom

The second important corollary of the limitation of freedom of expression to public meetings follows from the fact that the classroom is not properly regarded, in the required sense, as a public place. A class is a meeting for those special purposes gathered together under the rubric of teaching. In a class, teachers must surely be supposed to have the requisite cognitive authority entitling them to know how to guide the discourse appropriately toward the overall goal of rational pedagogy. Teaching requires an atmosphere in which understanding – both factual and moral – is deepened through rational discourse. This does not require an abandonment of passion; someone who spoke of the abuses of human rights around the world without passion would risk failing as a teacher just as surely as someone who falsely claimed that such abuses were committed only on the left or the right. But teaching does require respect for the central purposes of pedagogy: the inculcation of habits of disciplined reasoning and evaluation of evidence, and the transfer of current knowledge and techniques – each of which would be hard to pursue with the distractions of heckling.

Someone who thinks a teacher does not have the requisite knowledge or skill has available to her or him the remedy of not taking the class, and the right to complain to the university that she or he is not being properly taught. Heckling and placards are not suitable methods for raising these issues in the classroom; but provided they do not make it impossible for someone to be seen or heard, they do have their place in the rough-and-tumble of public debate.

Outside the classroom it should, of course, be permitted to organize meetings explaining opposition to ideas expressed in classes. Yet a class itself is a place where students choose to be taught – they have the right to be taught in circumstances suited to that purpose and, as I say, dissent may rightly be constrained for the purposes of pedagogy.

I should say, in passing, that it is an argument of this sort that explains why most sane people do not regard prohibitions on speeches in library reading rooms as an impermissible infringement of freedom of expression: speeches in reading rooms would seriously interfere with the function of libraries. Reading rooms are, thus, for these purposes, private places.

Public meetings, by contrast, are aimed at informing of the university community – and because the speaker does not speak with the authority of a teacher, this requires that there be the possibility of rebuttal and the expression of opposing views – something that includes, as I have already indicated, allowing placards and reasonable heckling. People should be permitted to organize private meetings at which loyal disciples gather to hear the word; those who oppose should be allowed to organize outside to deny that word. But a public platform in the university is not a pulpit.

Some might want to extend my argument here somewhat further. They might say that, granted that the university as a whole is governed by the purposes of education, and granted, too, that an atmosphere hostile to women or to gay and lesbian people or to people of some particular racial or ethnic group undermines their ability to learn, constraints on offensive speech that make such learning impossible are permissible generally in and around a campus, not merely in its classrooms. I have three thoughts about this argument. First, evidence for its empirical presuppositions would be necessary to convince me that this was not simply a pretext for banning speech that was (in my view quite understandably) upsetting to historically disadvantaged groups and those who support the extension to them of full equality. Second, it would have to be shown that the end of providing an atmosphere conducive to learning for these groups could not be achieved in other ways that preserved freedom of expression. Third, if it were shown that offensive speech outside the classroom, but on the campus, really did seriously undermine learning in ways that would not persist if it were banned, there would still be an argument, flowing from the purposes of the university for banning it, for defining dormitories and dining halls as well as classrooms as private places. (I say, "in ways which would not persist if it was banned," because if the undermining effects derive from a general hostility to these groups in the society as a whole, cleaning up the university would probably do little by itself to help.)

VIII. Defining the Public Sphere

Because the distinction between public and private space has turned out to have such considerable consequences, it is a reasonable question to ask how we should seek to define a public meeting. And the answer is simple enough in theory, even if, like all of the distinctions that are required in this area, it may raise difficulties in practice. A meeting is public if it is open to any member of the university (and, therefore, of course, if it is open to the world). Therefore, it follows I believe that anyone invited to talk at a meeting at a university that is, in this sense, public, should be allowed to do so whether their views are true or false, moral or immoral, repugnant to or consonant with the views of any or all of us, subject to content-independent constraints I will now discuss. Content-independence is an important ideal in the regulation of expression on our campus. Apart from the reasons I have already given, there is one further reason that should appeal to a prudent administration: only if the university strictly maintains this principle can it be seen as not endorsing the views of those it *does* allow to speak.

This public-private distinction, then, has to do simply with the purposes for which the gathering is held: if it is held for a discussion that is open to any who choose to come, it is public; otherwise it is private. And full freedom of expression is guaranteed only in the public sphere: elsewhere it may be limited by the further purposes that define the group's governing purposes[4] and explain why it is closed to a specific sub-community.

IX. Limitations

On what other basis, besides content, may expression in public reasonably be limited?

One might think that *everything that can be said in favor of freedom of speech in the university can be said of it because speech is the expression of ideas.* And yet this, so it seems to me now, is actually a mistake, for it ignores what I have called the libertarian considerations.

Let me begin, however, by stressing in which respect I believe this doctrine to be right. In the triple mission of the university, linguistic acts have a special status because it is largely – but not, as I shall argue, solely – through them that we transmit, discuss, criticize and, thus, develop those beliefs and values that constitute the learning that is the product of our researches, and that we teach our students and disseminate to the wider world. And, so far as the alethic considerations are concerned, it is *qua* expression of ideas that we seek to permit in public speech, however repulsive or irrational or false, quite independently of content.

But the libertarian argument explicitly treats speech as a species of action that is legitimately regulated by the state and the university as – and only as – action in general. Recent philosophy has rightly stressed the consequences of the fact that speaking and writing are actions; in speaking, as in other action, we causally bring about changes in the world. Because speech and writing are actions, their significant effects may, in certain cases, go far beyond their role as the expression of our beliefs and desires. To take a philosopher's example – one, that is, illumi-

4. If the governing purpose of a group is inconsistent with the universities purposes and norms, it may be quite proper for the university to deny them space to meet on campus. When universities deny recognition to gay and lesbian groups, the objection, I think, is to their normative opposition to the group, not to their claiming the right to decide who shall be a "recognized" private group.

nating a general point while raising what is no doubt a rare occurrence! – someone whose speaking will trigger a bomb may reasonably be stopped from speaking because it would constitute a "clear and present danger" of harm to persons (including the speakers themselves) or, perhaps, to property (see section 13 below).

It is because speech may sometimes have significant causal consequences other than its expressive ones that freedom of speech may sometimes be rightfully limited. For these consequences may bring about results that infringe on the rights and liberties of others, or which, as in this case, simply and straightforwardly do them obvious harm. It is wrong, therefore, to say that freedom of speech is important because speech is solely the expression of ideas. It is wrong theoretically because the libertarian argument treats speech as action, not merely as expression; and wrong practically because it is clear, I think, that in many and perhaps most cases that are likely to be important to us, other standard kinds of non-linguistic expression will often have causal consequences more troubling than those that usually flow from speech and writing.

There are many reasons for this, among them the banal fact that speech involves very much less physical energy than, say – to pick an example not entirely at random – the erection of a shanty in a divestment demonstration, and thus often has fewer enduring detectable physical effects. It takes a moment for a spoken sentence to fly away on the wind, but may take substantial labor to tidy up after a shanty.

It follows, in my view, that though any act expressing ideas deserves the same protection *in principle* as speech and writing, other expressive acts are more often likely to have consequences beyond their expressive consequences, and these other consequences will more often in practice raise conflicts with other rights. These other acts will also more often involve higher financial costs. With all expressive acts, so it seems to me, what we need to do is to balance the very strong interest the university has in allowing freedom of expression independently of content, against other interests and purposes. In the case of speech, these other consequences will rarely matter; in other cases it will matter more often.

X. Symbolic Speech

It will be clear that what I have said relates to the question of what has been called "symbolic speech." I take the phrase "symbolic speech," as it has recently been used,[5] to mean the public performance of an act whose primary purpose is the expression of ideas or values. There seems to me a general principle here that needs to be kept clearly in mind: namely, that in any case where the form of a non-linguistic act is reasonably viewed by those who carry it out as especially appropriate to the ideas expressed, it is especially important that the acts not be banned without good reason. For to ban an act in these circumstances is, in an intelligible sense, to limit the *content* of what is being expressed.

The application of this principle to shanties built to support divestment in recent years makes the attempts to ban them particularly troubling. For the shanty-building was plainly – and for reasons too obvious to need spelling out – a particularly appropriate method of expressing the ideas of those who built them. Someone who built a shanty to dramatize a claim about the sexism of the university in its handling of acquaintance-rape, for example, would have a weaker claim to this mode of expression and a stronger claim to installing images that might, in other contexts, be banned in public as sexually obscene, even if the graphic nature of the acts portrayed was likely to raise the costs of policing. (I shall deal with some of the issues raised by obscenity in discussing the notion of *offense* in section 12 below.) Someone who painted graffiti on the walls of a university art museum because they held that its refusal to install an exhibition of subway-painting reflected ethnic prejudice against the largely black and Chicano painters who have mostly produced it, for example, would have a better claim to protection than someone who did so in order to dramatize a claim about raised tuition, even though removing graffiti might, in these circumstances, be expensive.

I shall now deal with a number of kinds of causal consequence of expression that are raised especially by non-linguistic acts.

XI. Financial Consequences

Symbolic speech can sometimes damage or alter the university's property in ways that have financial costs. Where it does so, it should be clear that the university has a right to limit it, to the extent that those costs are avoidable, while maintaining freedom through other modes of expression. (I repeat, here, the important claim made at the beginning of section 10 above, that sometimes prohibiting symbolic speech amounts to prohibiting the *content* expressed, and that where the actor reasonably

---

5. For example in discussion of shanties built to support divestment at Cornell.

thinks this to be so, great care should be taken that this is borne in mind.) But it should also be clear that, given the strong reasons, both alethic and libertarian, for freedom of expression, these costs should be counted in a way that meets two conditions:

A. that costs should be considered independently of the expressive content of the acts – content-independence once more; and

B. that the negotiation of a reduction in those costs to the university – by gaining an agreement that those who build shanties, for example, will clear them up themselves – should always be considered *first* as a means of avoiding the banning of the expressive act.

In case it should be thought that these two constraints are undemanding, two consequences should immediately be pointed out.

First, it follows from content-independence that, because the marginal[6] cost of policing (and heating and maintaining) public rooms is part of the cost of allowing any public meeting, it is not an automatic argument against shanty-building that it raises the costs of policing. A commitment to *some* costs of this kind is what gives force to the idea that the university *supports* freedom of expression, independently of the content of the views expressed.

Second, in the cases of shanty-building that I have witnessed, there was no reason to believe that the financial costs of tidying up either were or should have been foremost in the minds of those who sought, to varying degrees, to oppose that shanty-building.

XII. Offense

The question whether an act should be banned because it is offensive has been raised in a number of recent cases. It has been alleged, for instance, that some people find shanties "aesthetically" offensive, and that this provides a basis for limiting them. It has also been alleged by – predictably different – others that the views of Leonard Jeffries or David Duke are offensive to members of the university community, and that this might provide a basis for banning them. I think neither of these arguments is persuasive.

A. So far as "aesthetic" assaults are concerned, regarding shanties (or, in a more common case, posters) as an aesthetic assault strikes me as involving both a confusion and a bizarre conception of the weight of the

---

6. I mean "marginal cost" in the economist's sense: some heating and policing costs are no doubt far from marginal, in the colloquial sense.

aesthetic. The confusion is between being offended by the content of the expressive act – because, for example, you take it to be wrong to divest—and being upset by the effect of a structure on your aesthetic sensibilities. It seems plain to me that most of those who have raised objections of this sort to shanties were plainly offended in the former way: an issue to which I shall return. Such offense is not helpfully described as aesthetic.

Anyone who has truly been offended in the other, genuinely aesthetic, way should ask herself how much this sort of offense should count. Is it a reason, for example, for constructing barriers to hide building works on campus? Is it a reason for prohibiting public sculpture?

I am in some doubt as to whether any of us has the *right* to be protected from aesthetic assault, even where issues of freedom of expression are not at stake. (If there were such a right against aesthetic assault, it would surely be one of the most frequently violated!) But the general point about genuinely aesthetic offense is that we rightly hold that moral considerations generally override aesthetic ones, and the libertarian arguments for freedom of expression are in any view – like the alethic arguments, on *most* views – in the relevant sense, obviously moral ones. This is why it strikes many of us as bizarre to raise the question of "aesthetics" in such cases.

B. So far as the offensiveness of the views expressed is concerned, there are two ways in which this might be held to matter. In one view, to describe an act of expression as "offensive" is not so much a matter of considering the consequences of the utterance – not, that is, a matter of worrying about the hurt caused to the people offended – but simply a matter of having deep objections to the view expressed. Offense of this sort cannot be the basis for prohibiting expression without violating the principle of content-independence.

In the second view, however, to raise the question of the offensiveness of an expressive act is to ask that the unpleasant feelings felt by some of those witnessing the act should be taken into account. If it is true that both:

C. the offense caused by the mode of expression – by someone's choosing to address an audience with their clothes off, for example – is not essential to the expressive act, and

D. that it is an offense from which people have a right to be protected,[7]

---

7. Indeed, merely being upset shouldn't count as being *offended* in this sense unless you are to some degree entitled not to be so upset.

K. Anthony Appiah

then it is plain that there is no problem from the point of view of freedom of expression about prohibiting it.

But these conditions are rarely met together by any expressive acts that are contemplated on campus. Because some people in this society are offended by nudity, there is reason (and there may be a legal requirement) for the university to prohibit it in places where people may come upon it unprepared. There are some such constraints of decency that the university may maintain without its being regarded as an illegitimate disregard of the alethic arguments for freedom of expression, even in cases where the alleged indecency is, as it might be in a play, essential to the expressive act. The right way to respect the alethic considerations in such cases – within the limits set by law – is to prohibit these acts in any place where those who witness them have not had fair warning that material that is in this sense offensive is to be presented; and to do this is to protect us from offense from which we have a right to be protected.

Yet meeting the libertarian arguments for freedom of expression in these cases is not so easy. Why should the fact that you will be offended if I do something be a reason for my not being allowed to do it? Racists will be offended by inter-racial couples walking hand-in-hand through the campus; some old-fashioned sexists may still be upset by women in trousers . . . or women in classes, for that matter. In such cases where the offense is caused not by the ideas expressed but by the brute fact of someone's action, a university has the moral responsibility (and, in some cases, the legal duty) to make the same sort of complex trade-off as communities generally do between freedom of action on the one hand, and a conception of public decency on the other. But where the basis of the offense is the *idea* expressed, alethic considerations argue for allowing the expressive act in places where people are suitably warned in advance. Moreover, *libertarian* considerations argue for freedom of action – and thus of expressive action – in general in places where the rights of others will not be infringed upon.

For these reasons the stress on the issue of *civility* in many discussions of free speech on campus seems to me misguided. No considerations of courtesy or civility in discussions of controversial issues should outweigh our interest in freedom of expression. If the content of expression will hurt the feelings or upset the sensibilities of its audience, even if it is *intended* to do so, that may be a reason for warning those who attend that they risk this. David Duke and many members of his scant campus audiences usually know that they are likely to say things that will offend others; and neither has a right to be protected from this sort of offense from the other. If David Duke wishes to avoid being offended, he can arrange private meetings of the faithful: if those who are offended by his views do not wish to hear them, they have no obligation to come. Policing of the outraged is, where possible, preferable to banning expressions that are outrageous; on the rare occasions when it is not possible, the principles I discuss (under the heading of "clear and present danger" in section 13 below) should be operative.

There is an important reason why the fact that the expression of views that will cause offense should not be considered a reason to bar their expression: the application of this idea would involve a violation of the principle of content-independence. For we cannot allow *any* offense at all to count because we should then have to bar the expression of any views that people found offensive, even if their response was quite unreasonable; and to enquire as to whether offense is reasonable is to have to examine the content of the views expressed.

It is important, however, in cases where speakers are unable to express views because members of the audience make them inaudible, that those who make the speech inaudible should be able to invoke, in their defense, the idea of provocation. If a speaker makes statements in a public place that are outrageous and provocative to reasonable people, those responses may be blamed on the speaker. It should always be possible for people who heckle a speaker "out of court" to give reasons defending their response. Speech has a better chance than many other expressive acts of raising such problems because speech can (and can be intended to) incite passions, and those passions may lead people to act in ways that lead them to ignore the rights of expression of others. But here it seems to me that the general principle is clear. Wherever possible, within reasonable constraints of cost, it is better to provide protection against this harm than to prohibit the speech that risks causing it. And in punishing those who offend against the freedom of expression of others, it should always be borne in mind that where a person is unreasonably provoked it is the provocation, not its victim, that is to blame.

This last remark has the effect of making some content-dependent judgments necessary in the policing – though not, as I have repeatedly argued, in the licensing – of freedom of expression. It cannot be right, in considering whether to punish someone who has been intentionally provoked to indignation, to take no account of whether her response was a reasonable response in the circumstances (and this means not only a *predictable* response but one that is to some degree warranted).

XIII. Clear And Present Danger

It is plain that acts of expression, whether symbolic in the present sense, or linguistic, may have consequences that raise questions of harm and of the infringement of the rights of others. I have already said that some kinds of offense – those caused by expressive acts in public places – infringe on the rights of people to choose whether they will expose themselves to the offense caused by indecency; and I have already suggested that these problems can usually be handled by warning those who attend such a meeting that they risk being offended. Yet speech raises problems of this kind because, as I have said, it can inflame passions, and those passions may lead people to act in ways that threaten harm.

To prohibit a speaker on the grounds that what he or she says will provoke such passions may seem to be straightforwardly consistent with a content-independent respect for freedom of expression. Such a ban is not a prohibition based on the content of the speech but on its consequences: so why may we not prohibit them from speaking at all if they do not agree to avoid language that will predictably inflame passions? The reason is simple, of course: to do this is to give to those who oppose a view the power to prevent its expression by threatening to riot. As I have said earlier: "Policing of the outraged is, where possible, preferable to banning expressions that are outrageous. . . ."

But once a speaker is on campus, it is always possible that even the most prudent administration may find itself in circumstances where a gathering gets out of hand. It will always be right to order someone to cease from speaking for the moment where not doing so would involve a clear and present danger of harm to persons or property; moreover, this will always be right whether the danger is the result of their intended provocation or of the unreasonable response of others.

XIV. Rationing

The erection of enduring structures may raise problems of rationing of a kind not normally raised by public meetings. The competition for space for meetings on campus is not so great as to make it likely that allowing one speaker will ever *ipso facto* force the university to disallow another. But it is, I suppose, a more real – though, in my view, still frankly an unlikely – possibility that permitting enduring structures in public spaces for reasonable periods in places where they will have any effect could lead to problems of over-crowding.

In such cases, the university should deal with rationing in the way that it should deal with all questions of scarce resources where each group has an equal – meaning in this case, a content-independent – claim on resources: namely, by allotting them according to such fair and previously announced procedures as "first come, first served" or a lottery.

(It is for the same reason that public meetings where speech is the mode of expression should also be governed by a rule, such as currently obtains at most universities, requiring that speakers who take questions take them from anyone who raises them, allocating reasonable time to people insofar as is practicable in the order in which they express a desire to speak. For we should be a community of equals, so far as expression is concerned; principles of selection based on race, ethnicity, gender, politics, religion and so on, are inconsistent with the idea that scarce resources should be allocated fairly. The selection of respondents on the basis of opinion, on the other hand, may well undermine the alethic function of public debate – protecting speakers from questions that they would find difficult to answer reduces the chance that weaknesses in their positions will be uncovered.)

XV.

I have already mentioned some principles that I believe should govern the policing of freedom of expression. By what procedures should they be encoded? Some principles are obvious. As I have said:

A. It will always be right to order someone to cease from speaking where not doing so would involve a clear and present danger of physical harm to persons or of serious damage to property. . . .

It is also clear that:

B. A code should guarantee content-independence in the administration's licensing of public meetings, and that the administration should have the duty, where harm to persons or property is anticipated, to arrange, where possible, suitable policing of them.

C. All speakers should be informed that the bearing of placards and reasonable amounts of "heckling" will be permitted; and that if speakers do take questions, they must take them from any who raise them, allocating reasonable time to people insofar as is practicable and calling on them in the order in which they express a desire to speak.

But how should the university respond in cases where members of the university fail to respect the rights of others to express their views, either by refusing to take certain questions, by shouting down a speaker, or by shouting down his or her questioners? Once again, it seems clear that:

D. The first response to a breach of the university's policy on freedom of expression should be to repeat the substance of that policy and then to seek, by prudent policing, to remove those (and this could include the announced speaker) who fail to respect it. Only where this fails should a meeting be brought compulsorily to a close.

So far as acts of "symbolic speech" are concerned:

E. The university should seek to license all acts of symbolic speech that do not involve unreasonable costs, especially where the mode of expression is an important element in the expressive content of the act. And it should seek to negotiate with those who seek to perform such acts both a reduction in their costs, should it deem them excessive, and the avoidance of conflicts with such reasonable demands as that people should not for long periods restrict the free passage of others.

As for expression in a public place that would reasonably offend others by prevailing standards of decency:

F. The administration should seek to arrange suitably restricted places that can be avoided by persons reasonably entitled to avoid public offense and outside which fair warning should be given.

All of these suggestions should be read along with the glosses entailed by my earlier remarks.

XVI.

It has not been clear everywhere and always that the university is a place valuing the expression of diverse opinions: the College in the University of Cambridge at which I was an undergraduate, graduate, and Fellow, required in my great-grandfather's day that its dons should be members of the Church of England and commit themselves to the "thirty-nine articles" of its creed. The government of Ghana, where I first taught, has not always allowed the free expression of opinion on campuses, even by teachers in classes. I believe that there are some in this country, even in the university, who recognize neither the fragility of free expression nor its crucial importance in the life of humane reason. For while, as I have tried to show, the presumptions in favor of freedom of expression can be overridden, my impression, for what it is worth, is that many on both the right and the left are currently *too* keen to override them.

10
Reinventing the First Amendment in the University

Randy E. Barnett

Introduction

Speech can hurt and hurt badly. For this reason, discussions of offensive speech put defenders of free speech in the difficult position of seeming to favor a kind of conduct that they personally find morally objectionable and even disgusting. Such was the position of those who, for example, defended the constitutional right of American Nazis to march in the predominantly Jewish town of Skokie, Illinois a few years ago.

Defending free speech in the setting of a private university is made more difficult by the fact that the First Amendment protects free speech only against governmental interference. Private actors and institutions are free to restrict speech. You are not violating a person's constitutional rights when you ask him to leave your home after he has made an offensive remark. For this reason, no constitutional barrier prevents a private university from regulating and punishing speech deemed to be offensive.

For some, the fact that the First Amendment is limited to state action makes the issue easier because it means that private institutions are unencumbered in their ability to root out speech that deeply offends most members of the university community. However, removing the protective legal barrier of the First Amendment poses a most difficult challenge, by putting the persons governing a private university in the position of those who framed the United States Constitution. They must decide whether the regulation of speech by a private university more closely resembles censorship by the government, with all its dangers, or the free exercise of the private rights of individuals to shape their own community free of governmental interference. In other words, in the absence of First Amendment protection, we cannot avoid the theoretical question of why speech deserves protection from the state. Only by answering this question will we be able to conclude that something like a First Amendment should or should not exist within a private university.

I will offer examples of two different kinds of arguments concerning the dangers of restrictions on speech. The first kind of argument explains why free speech is a good thing – even when the ideas being expressed are wrong and even when they are offensive. The second kind of argument explains why coercive regulation of speech is a bad thing – why it is dangerous to create an institutionalized and hierarchical power to control speech. I will then discuss how this analysis may apply to the problem of offensive speech in the university.

I. Arguments for Free Speech

A powerful argument in favor of the right of free speech was presented by John Stuart Mill in his nineteenth-century work, *On Liberty*, but it is a mistake to think that this argument originated with Mill. It can be traced to the fight against religious persecution and in favor of tolerance – a long and bloody struggle in England and Europe that greatly influenced the framers of the United States Constitution. The argument is that the general good is served by protecting the freedom to express one's religious and other convictions, whether these convictions are true and therefore good, or false and therefore evil.

The argument begins by stressing the undeniable fact of human fallibility. The erroneous suppression of an unpopular but true idea may deprive society of the benefits of knowing the truth. This is no mere theoretical possibility. Authorities charged with policing ideas as well as the general public can be and often are mistaken – even when they are very certain in their convictions – and great harm is done to the members of any society in which truth is suppressed. Mill offered two examples of what he believed were such errors: the execution of Socrates for the crime of teaching immorality and corrupting youth, and the crucifixion of Jesus.

Even when an expressed idea is false, Mill maintains, society pays a high price for its suppression. Although a person can believe the right things, he argues, persons cannot fully understand and appreciate their own beliefs unless confronted with those who persuasively express disagreement. Only when they are effectively challenged will most people examine the views they unthinkingly hold and strive to fully comprehend why their beliefs are true. Thomas Aquinas, for example, defended the right of the clergy to read heretical writings on the grounds that only by confronting these untrue arguments can their own reason and faith be improved.

Moreover, dispassionate or polite "academic" disagreement is not enough to make people come to grips with their most basic beliefs. Most people need to be emotionally as well as intellectually provoked before they are willing to set aside their day-to-day pursuits in order to consider the basic truths they have been raised to accept. In this way dissent – even hateful dissent – serves to temper and strengthen the received wisdom and the resolve of people to continue accepting this wisdom as true.

Paradoxically, then, the open expression of hateful ideas can play a more constructive role in improving the general moral climate than when such sentiments are driven underground only to fester in secret as well as be ignored by those who complacently believe the surface appearance of moral behavior. Perhaps it is no coincidence that hateful speech becomes an acute problem when the hard-won moral truths of one generation have become mere bloodless pieties to the next. In this regard, hate speech can be viewed as a vaccine that can provoke an immune response from the social body in which it is injected. We inject polio viruses into an otherwise health body precisely to strengthen it – because we want to prevent, not contract, polio.

II. Arguments Against Regulation

Let me now turn my attention to arguments against the regulation of speech. These arguments begin with the assumption of human fallibility and add to it the increased harm created by institutionalized coercion. In particular, they focus on the twin problems of enforcement error and enforcement abuse.

By drastically increasing the severity of a sanction, the use of coercion increases the harm done to the innocent by mistake. This is the problem of enforcement error. The existence of this serious problem provides a powerful argument against the death penalty and, at a minimum, favors elaborate procedures to protect the innocent from wrongful punishment. The problem of enforcement error is one reason why we place the burden of proof on the government and require prosecutors to prove a defendant guilty beyond a reasonable doubt.

The problem of enforcement error is acute in the area of speech. If history demonstrates nothing else, it shows that mistakes are likely to be made when authorities are given the power to regulate speech and their use of coercion will drastically increase the harm inflicted upon the innocent by these mistakes.

The problem of enforcement error assumes that those charged with doing the enforcing are acting in good faith although mistakenly. Unfortunately, we know all too well that those entrusted with the powers to coerce are susceptible to abusing these powers and persecuting dissenters merely for disagreeing with the prevailing view or even for other more self-interested reasons. This is the problem of enforcement abuse.

The political philosophy known as Liberalism has attempted to address the twin problems of enforcement error and abuse incident to legal coercion by adopting procedural and formal standards associated with what is called the Rule of Law. The use of coercion by government is to be regulated by law – meaning, at a minimum, publicized general standards of conduct that people are able to understand and adhere to before they act. This formal requirement of "legality" serves at least two purposes: first, understandable rules announced in advance enable people to avoid punishment by following the rules. Second, general rules that are publicized in advance of a dispute permit outsiders to judge whether those doing the enforcement are either mistaken or abusing their powers.

III. Free Speech in the University

With this analysis in mind, we must now ask whether a private university is subject to the same dangers when it attempts to regulate speech that have long been recognized as attaching to government. Or is the university more like the family or a private association where the mother and father can regulate the conduct – including the speech – of the children in their charge? I don't think there is a simple answer to this question. In my view, the university shares aspects of both types of institutions and therein lies the seeds of the current controversies over the regulation of so-called hate speech.

Universities are inherently different from government in that the cost of exit is quite low. The university does not claim a monopoly jurisdiction over large tracts of land as does the government of the United States. Choosing one's university or transferring out of one is a much lower cost transaction than leaving one's country. Private universities also lack the power to tax. These differences argue against extending the reach of the actual First Amendment to protect speakers on campus from regulation from the private university. Moreover, the dangers of permitting government intrusions into the operation of the university are manifest. Indeed, because the integrity of the university is easily threatened by the state, the First Amendment has been interpreted, properly in my view, as protecting the rights of the university from interference by government.

On the other hand, there are several important similarities between the university and the state – similarities that argue in favor of reinventing the First Amendment within the university. First, a university is unavoidably bureaucratic and hierarchical. Those responsible for its administration are necessarily distanced from those who are subject to its regulation. Like a legal system and unlike a parent, an administration lacks any direct knowledge of the actions of its constituents and for this reason is vulnerable to making mistakes. Second, the university can be as political as any state institution. This makes it vulnerable to enormous temptations to abuse its powers in pursuit of a political agenda. Third, the sanctions imposed by a university can be extremely painful. The stigma of being expelled from a university often exceeds that of being convicted of a criminal misdemeanor and, perhaps, even some felonies. For this reason, the injuries imposed by enforcement error and abuse are great.

Moreover, the university's two-fold mission of education and research places a tremendous premium on the value of free speech. Its educational mission means that people must be exposed to erroneous beliefs in order to be better able to appreciate correct beliefs. The university is the paradigm of a community that benefits from the robust debate about ideas that Mill so eloquently defended. Hateful ideas cannot be either ignored or simply condemned. They must be forcefully presented to challenge and provoke students into not merely understanding that they are wrong, but why they are wrong. Moreover, the research mission of those in the university is to pursue truth, especially truths that run counter to the common opinion of both intellectuals and the general public. Many of the ideas pursued by academics might seem hateful to a majority who believe otherwise.

Finally, I am highly skeptical that we can effectively combat the dangers of regulating speech by resorting to procedural protections of the sort associated with the rule of law for at least two reasons. First, it has proven impossible to define offensive speech with sufficient precision to put people on notice that they are acting illegally and to enable us to detect enforcement error and abuse. In the absence of clear-cut guidelines, the robust exchange of opinion inside and outside of the classroom is certain to be jeopardized.

Second, procedural protections are most effective when there is an overwhelming consensus that a certain type of conduct – such as murder or rape – is wrong, and when we must determine whether or not a particular person has performed the wrongful act. With speech, however, in addition to the problem of ascertaining the facts, there is the problem of determining whether the type of conduct engaged in is or is not the sort of action that ought to be regulated.

IV. Alternatives to Regulation

These then are some reasons why a private university ought to reinvent its own version of the First Amendment. If we reject the formal and bureaucratic regulation of offensive speech, is a community powerless to respond to incidents of hate speech? I think not. If the university community is truly a community, then it has other means at its disposal. People who engage in offensive conduct can and should be publicly condemned as well as shunned. Where a consensus exists that a person has acted in a grossly immoral manner, there are many ways to make such a person's life miserable.

But this requires that people take it upon themselves to act as a community. Forcing people to take personal responsibility for sanctioning offensive conduct – rather than simply letting an administrative bureaucracy do the dirty work – is essential for the development of a true community. Where an institution is so large or so heterogeneous that a bottom-up approach is impractical, there is reason to doubt that such an institution can be a true community, and in these cases the top-down regulation of speech will usually lead to the sorts of error and abuse that only the right of free speech can prevent.

Moreover, when hate speech takes the form of conduct that is generally prohibited by the university regardless of content, such as the defacement of property or the disruption of classes or meetings, such conduct can be formally sanctioned by university procedures without many of the risks associated with policing speech for offensiveness. Personal harassment, such as abusive or threatening phone calls and notes, may also fall into this category.

Finally, I wish to mention one further danger of regulating speech in the university. A general acceptance of such regulation in this sort of private but still impersonal, hierarchical, and bureaucratic setting, is quite likely to lead to acceptance of regulating speech in the public sphere. There is, in short, both a "legality" and a "morality" of free speech. We may well find that preserving the legality of free speech against abuses by government requires the preservation of an underlying morality of free speech in such private institutions as the university. For once the morality of free speech is sufficiently eroded there, the legality of free speech will not last long elsewhere.

Eroding the morality of free speech in, of all places, the institution where free speech is central to intellectual inquiry poses a grave risk to the legality of free speech outside the university. By underestimating the connection between legal and moral norms, the assumption that free speech in the university – and especially in a law school – is completely unrelated to the First Amendment protection of free speech is perhaps too simple after all.

11
Fighting Racism: Hate Speech Detours[1]

Thomas W. Simon

I. Introduction

A white male student shouts to a black woman student, "My parents own you people." Fliers are distributed declaring "open season on blacks" in which blacks are referred to as "saucer lips, porch monkeys, and jigaboos." White students spit on and taunt Asian American students. A letter is addressed to a black student dormitory that discusses "wip[ing] all g.d. niggers off the face of the earth."[2]

Over 100 colleges and universities have enacted hate-speech codes[3] in response to numerous racial and related incidents on college campuses. The National Institute Against Prejudice and Violence has documented the dramatic increase in ethnoviolence, affecting literally hundreds of thousands of students on hundreds of campuses.[4] Universities have garnered praise from some for taking a stand against racism, and condemnation from others for intruding upon free speech.

The analysis below puts forth the claim that hate speech represents the wrong issue if countering racism is the primary goal. Legalistic and free-speech nets trap the unwary, creating diversions from more important anti-racism efforts. The nets come complete with untenable distinctions between crude and sophisticated hate speech, along with other insuperable problems of drawing boundaries about an intractable pool of categories.

---

1. This chapter was previously printed in 26 *Indiana Law Journal* (1993) and is reprinted here with the permission of the Indiana Law Journal.

2. As quoted in Note, "The Power of Words: The Power of Advocacy Challenging the Power of Hate Speech, 52 *University of Pittsburgh Law Review*, 955, at 960 (1991).

3. Depalma, "Battling Bias: Campuses Face Speech Fight," *New York Times*, February 20, 1991, at 9, Col. 1.

4. Erlich, "Campus Ethnoviolence and Public Opinion," 4 *National Institute Against Prejudice & Violence* 4 (1990).

Deflating the importance of hate-speech regulation does not thereby entail abandoning a full acceptance of either the impact of hate speech on victimized individuals or the connection between hate speech and racism. It means that instead of expending energies in countering the deplorable incidents of hate speech, it would be more fruitful to use the incidents as a means of addressing the more fundamental problems of racism. Words can hurt, but the sticks and stones of racism harm in even greater ways.

Instead of taking free speech as the framework for rejecting hate-speech regulation, I take anti-racism as the point within which to evaluate hate-speech regulation. From the perspective of an anti-racism policy, hate-speech regulation creates a detour. The first detour along this road consists of the search for a legal pigeonhole for making hate speech an actionable offense. The lack of a consensus over the correct legal analysis indicates that something is wrong with the search.

II. The Search for a Legal Pigeonhole

The following represent the various legal pigeonholes within which regulators have attempted to restrict hate speech:

1. Free Speech-Fighting Words [5]
2. Hostile Work Environment[6]

5. In Chaplinsky v. New Hampshire, 315 U.S. 568 (1942), the Supreme Court first articulated the fighting words test and refused to give First Amendment protection to words that were likely to provoke violent responses. In Cohen v. California, 403 U.S. 15 (1971), the court refused to extend the fighting words doctrine to an inscription on the back of a jacket that was not intentionally directed at any specific individual or individuals. The fighting words approach to hate speech is embodied in a number of university codes including the University of Connecticut (Students Handbook, 1990-1991 at p. 61), the University of Wisconsin (Wisconsin Administrative Code Section 17.06, August 1989), and Stanford University. For a defense of the fighting words approach to hate speech, see Charles R. Lawrence III, "If He Hollers Let Him Go: Regulating Racist Speech on Campus," *Duke Law Journal* 431 (1990).

6. In Meritor Savings Bank v. Vinson, 477 U.S. 57 (1986), the Supreme Court ratified the common law extension of Title VII's prohibitions against quid pro quo sexual harassment to a hostile work environment. A number of universities have adopted the hostile work environment approach to hate speech: Emory University, Campus Life 112 (1990-1991); Kent State University, University Life, Digest of Rules and Regulations 12-13 (1988); University of North Carolina at Chapel Hill, The Instrument of Student Judicial Governance 5-7 (1991). To prove a hostile work environment, the complainant must show a series of repeated incidents and not simply a single event.

3. Group Libel [7]
4. Tort[8]
5. International Human Rights (International Convention on the Elimination of All Forms of Racial Discrimination)[9]

I shall confine my analysis to the attempts to deal with hate speech within the free speech category. The reason for placing an emphasis on the speech aspects of hate speech are obvious and subtle. After all, hate speech by its very nature is about speech. Yet, on a more subtle level, the speech component of hate speech places the issues within a set of categories that doom hate-speech regulation as a relatively ineffective means of combating racism. While the other legal categories listed above differ markedly in their analyses, they all nonetheless focus on the speech element. Working within the confines of speech actually serves to divert opponents of racism from more important issues. As discussed below, a key indicator that hate-speech regulation diverges from a policy of anti-racism is found in the policy goals articulated by various universities.

III. Universities Goals

Although universities differ as to the type of regulations adopted to regulate hate speech, the following serves as a fairly typical example:

7. In Beauharnais v. Illinois 343 U.S. 250 (1952), the Supreme Court adopted a group libel analysis. However, many claim that Beauharnais is no longer good law. Nevertheless, a number of commentators have attempted to revive the group libel approach. Arkes, "Civility and the Restriction of Speech: Rediscovering the Defamation of Groups," 1974 *Sup. Ct. Rev.* 281 (advocating a group libel approach); Kretzmer, "Freedom of Speech and Racism," 8 *Cardozo Law Review* 445 (1987); Lasson, "Racial Defamation as Free Speech: Abusing the First Amendment," 17 *Columbia Human Rights Law Review* 11 (1985); Lasson, "In Defense of Group-Libel Laws or Why the First Amendment Should Not Protect Nazis," *New York Law School Human Rights Annual* 298 (Spring 1985); Note, "A Communitarian Defense of Group Libel Laws," 101 *Harvard Law Review* 682 (1988); Riesman, "Democracy and Defamation: Control of Group Libel," 42 *Columbia Law Review* 727 (1942). The University of Kansas has adopted a group libel approach to hate speech *University of Kansas Student Handbook*.

8. Richard Delgado, "Words that Wound: A Tort Action for Racial Insults, Epithets, and Name-Calling," 17 *Harv. C.R.-C.L.L. Rev.* 133 (1982) (proposing a tort cause of action against racial hate speech). The University of Texas has modeled part of its hate speech code on the common law tort of intentional infliction of emotional distress (University of Texas at Austin, General Information 1990-1991, Institutional Rules of Student Services and Activities 174, Appendix C).

9. Mari J. Matsuda, "Public Response to Racist Speech: Considering the Victim's Story," 87 *Michigan Law Review* 2320 (1989).

Arizona State University ("A.S.U." or "the University") is committed to maintaining hospitable educational, residential, and working environments that permit students and employees to pursue their goals without substantial interference from harassment. Additionally, diversity of views, cultures, and experiences is critical to the academic mission of higher education. Such diversity enriches the intellectual lives of all, and it increases the capacity of a university to serve the educational needs of its community.

A.S.U. is also strongly committed to academic freedom and free speech. Respect for these rights requires that it tolerate expressions of opinions that differ from its own or that it may find abhorrent.

These values of free expression justify protection of speech that is critical of diversity and other principles central to the University's academic mission. However, values of free expression are not supported but are undermined by acts of intolerance that suppress alternative views through intimidation or injury. As members of an institution of higher education, we must stand against any assault upon the dignity and value of any individual through harassment that substantially interferes with his or her educational opportunities, peaceful enjoyment of residence, physical security, or terms or conditions of employment.[10]

This policy statement typifies those of universities that have drawn up guidelines for the regulation of hate speech. This and similar statements contain the following policy goals:

1. Maintain civility and decorum
2. Instill citizenship and virtue in its students.[11]
3. Protect students from harm.[12]
4. Foster diversity.
5. Protect academic freedom.
6. Protect freedom of speech.

The positions on the hate-speech issue roughly divide according to

---

10. Policy Statement Supporting Diversity and Free Speech at Arizona State University, p.1.

11. Sherry has collected some illustrations of hate-speech regulations that invoke a virtue rationale, as, for example, the Ohio State preamble, which states that "acceptance, appreciation of diversity, and respect for the rights of others must be institutional values for a major public university and are values that it must impart to its students and to society as a whole." As quoted in Sherry, "Speaking of Virtue: A Republican Approach to University Regulation of Hate Speech," 75 *Minnesota Law Review* 907 at 940.

12. Protecting students from harm is the doctrine underlying in loco parentis. See, e.g., M. Olivas, *The Law and Higher Education*, pp. 599-615 (1989). For an analysis that extends the protective function to the hate-speech context, see Charles H. Jones, "Equality, Dignity and Harm: The Constitutionality of Regulating American Campus Ethnoviolence," 37 *Wayne Law Review* 1383, at 1418 (1991).

which policies the proponents choose to adopt. Those advocating a strong form of regulation (the Strong Regulators) accept policy goals 1,2,3, and 4. In contrast, those proposing a weaker form of regulation (the Weak Regulators) accept the four policy goals of the Strong Regulators but add goal 5, which weakens the scope of the regulations by making the classroom immune from regulating what the Strong Regulators think qualifies as hate speech. The Weak Regulators, who make up the dominant group among the regulators, draw a sharp distinction between crude hate speech, governed by policy goals 1,2,3, and 4 and sophisticated hate speech, immunized from regulation through adherence to policy goal 5. The Anti-Regulators draw most of their arguments from within a strong commitment to policy goal 6, freedom of speech. However noble the Anti-Regulators regard the other policy goals, they find them insufficient to justify restrictions on hate speech.

Notice that I have not invoked any policies that proclaim a university's commitment to the eradication of racism, sexism, ethnocentricism, and homophobia[13] For the sake of completion, let us formulate this policy goal as:

7. Eradication of group subjugation in the form of racism, sexism, ethnocentrism, and homophobia.

Universities usually do not articulate their policy goals in the bold form of goal 7. In spelling out the rationales for hate-speech regulation, universities do announce their condemnation of subjugation but generally confine their condemnation to subjugating speech. Public universities seem to have good reason for avoiding the adoption of goal 7, for to issue a wholesale condemnation of subjugation would present problems. For one thing, the policy constitutes a political stance favoring certain groups, and thereby violating the university's claims to neutrality.

Nonetheless, wholesale condemnation is exactly what universities should do, even if it violates some sense of neutrality. Universities need to develop an overall plan of action to combat subjugation, and hate-speech regulation may or may not be part of that overall plan. In any case, hate-speech regulation should play at most a minor role instead of occupying center stage as it does now.

Universities that do give priority to policy goal 7, thereby abandoning pretenses to neutrality, have a stronger position than the Strong or Weak

13. For the sake of brevity I shall incorporate sexism, homophobia, and ethnocentricism under the rubric of racism.

Regulators. The regulators, no matter what their allegiance, find themselves entangled in a legalistic, free-speech web that poses insuperable problems. For one thing, the Weak Regulators draw a questionable distinction between crude and sophisticated hate speech, while the Strong Regulators open the door to academic censorship. Both Strong and Weak regulators find themselves mired in what I call the Boundary Problem, that is, where to draw the line between protected and unprotected speech. Nonetheless, these problems do not have to lead to the adoption of an Anti-Regulation stand, for that is not the only alternative. Nor does it need to simply serve as a challenge for the Regulators to become more sophisticated in mapping out their position. Rather, it shows the need to abandon the regulation debate and instead give priority to positive programs that begin to address the serious problems of subjugation facing colleges in particular and society at large.

IV. Crude Versus Sophisticated Hate Speech

(1) "Run, niggers, run."[14]

(2) "Black children in the United States have a mean IQ score of about 85 as compared with 100 for the white population, on which the test was standardized."[15]

According to some proponents of hate-speech regulations, particularly the Weak Regulators, the first of these statements illustrates the type of crude hate speech that calls for regulation. The second statement may seem to simply state a fact, although context can change a supposedly simple factual statement into a controversial one. Let us assume that claim 2 is made in the context of a lecture designed to demonstrate the inheritability of IQ. In the course of the lecture, the lecturer says nothing whatsoever about the intellectual inferiority of blacks.

The added contextual features make this a prime example of what Professor Matsuda has called the case of the "Dead-Wrong Social

14. "Ugly Racial Melee Shakes Students, Official at Small Michigan College," *Washington Post*, April 12, 1992, A3, Col 1-6.

15. Steven Rose, Leon J. Kamin, and R.C. Lewontin, *Not in Our Genes: Biology, Ideology, and Human Nature* (New York: Penguin, 1984), p. 118. (I purposely cite a leftist critique of the race/IQ debate to highlight an instance of mention as opposed to use). See Jensen, "How Much Can We Boost IQ and Scholastic Achievements?," 5 *Harvard Education Review* 1 (1969). Cf. S. Gould, *The Mismeasure of Man* (1981).

Scientist."[16] On the Weak Regulation analysis adopted by Matsuda, this represents a sophisticated version of hate speech that, while admittedly offensive, should not be subject to prohibition because it does not have the following characteristics of crude hate speech: a persecutorial, hateful, and degrading message of racial inferiority directed against a historically oppressed group.[17]

Accordingly, universities should not be the types of places that foster racial slurs and epithets should encourage debate over controversial academic positions, even if those positions support, however indirectly, racism.

Despite Matsuda's efforts, claims such as number 2 above fall within the sphere of hate-speech regulation that she promotes because theories linking race and IQ possess the elements of crude hate speech. First of all, the racial groupings in the IQ debate deny the "personhood of target group members" in considering all members of the target group alike and inferior. Racial groupings become suspect depending upon whether or not they constitute social constructs or biological categories. If race is, as many claim, a social and not a biological construct, then its scientific status becomes questionable. Second, historically, so-called scientific theories of racial inferiority have served as powerful mechanisms of subjugation. The harm to group interests flowing from scientifically supported institutional forms of racism are of a far greater magnitude than the hurt feelings associated with incidents of racial slurs.[18] Finally, while the degrading aspects of the message may be more subtle in the scientific case than those of the more paradigmatic crude speech, sophisticated speech can have a more persecutorial and hateful intent once fully analyzed.

Those attempting to distinguish between crude and sophisticated speech resort to another argument. Face-to-face racial insults do not deserve First Amendment protection because the injury from being called "nigger" or some similar invective is instantaneous, allowing no

16. Mari J. Matsuda, "Public response to Racist Speech: Considering the Victim's Story," 87 *Michigan Law Review* 2320, (1989).

17. Matsuda "Public Response to Racist Speech: Considering the Victim's Story," 87 *Michigan Law Review* 2320.

18. For a discussion of different kinds of harm, see Joel Feinberg, *Harm To Others*, 33-36. Kretzmer narrowly confines himself to the kind of harm likely to stir up a racial group. This leads him to allow research findings showing a lower IQ for racial minorities. Kretzmer, "Free Speech and Racism," 8 *Cardozo Law Review* 445, 500 (1987). Far greater harm than audience reaction is at stake with scientific findings.

time for dialogue and rational deliberation.[19] The word mentioned in the previous sentence serves as a good example of "fighting words," which fall outside the range of constitutional protection.[20] In fact, the offensive level of slurs and epithets reaches such heights that it would be inappropriate to respond verbally to this type of abuse. Rational deliberation seems neither possible nor appropriate in the midst of crude hate speech.

However, crude speech does not neatly fall outside the gambit of rational discourse while sophisticated speech fits comfortably within the realm of debate and argumentation. Crude speech need not be immune from rational deliberation. Even in the heat of crude speech, rational dialogue can emerge, however unlikely that might be. More plausible is a situation where the crude-speech incident becomes a stimulus for later dialogue. The University of Michigan enforcement model, for example, includes a provision for informal mediation before initiation of formal procedures.[21] Thus, a crude hate-speech incident could serve as an opportunity to open dialogue over abusive speech.[22]

In parallel fashion, sophisticated hate speech does not always leave room for informed rational debate between its proponents and the representatives of vulnerable groups.[23] A presentation demonstrating the inverse relation between racial characteristics and intelligence within the classroom may leave little room for challenge, particularly from racial minority students. Students find themselves in a deferential power relationship with their professors. For example, according to one report, "at the University of Washington, a professor called in campus police to bar a student from class who had questioned her assertion that lesbians make the best parents."[24] Situations like these do not lend themselves to rational and open dialogue. Students at Arizona State University reacted to a

19. Charles R. Lawrence, "If He Hollers Let Him Go: Regulating Racism Speech on Campus," 1990 *Duke Law Journal* 431, 452.
20. Chaplinsky v. New Hampshire, 315 U.S. 568 (1942); Cohen v. California, 403 U.S. 15 (1971).
21. Doe v. University of Michigan, 721 F. Supp. 852, 866 (E.D. Mich. 1989).
22. Alan E. Brownstein, "Hate Speech at Public Universities: The Search for an Enforcement Model," 37 *Wayne State Law Review* 1451 (1991) (proposing an informal education as opposed to a formal enforcement model of hate speech regulation).
23. See Henry W. Saad, "The Case for Prohibition of Racial Epithets in the University Classroom," 37 *Wayne State Law Review* 1351 (". . . a minority who is the object of racial, sexual or ethnocentric epithets in the park may leave or engage in verbal combat. In the classroom, however, a student is victimized by racial or ethnocentric invective should not be forced to resort to such activity.") Id. at 1357. Mr. Saad represented the University of Michigan in Doe v. University of Michigan.
24. Henry Hyde and George Fishman, "The Collegiate Speech Protection Act of 1991: A Response to the New Intolerance in the Academy," 37 *Wayne Law Review* 1469 at 1472 citing Sykes and Miner, "Sense and Sensitivity," *National Review*, March 18, 1991 at 30-31.

racist flier, containing crude speech, by organizing open discussions where they could educate others about the hurt resulting from the speech.[25]

One further problem with the crude/sophisticated hate-speech distinction deserves attention. Consider the impression that one could have that the perpetrators of crude speech have not yet learned the sophisticated, polite, academic, indirect, but even more effective means of subjugation and subordination. While the crude yell epithets and racial slurs, the sophisticated bemoan diversity and collect data to show how blacks manifest their inferiority through intelligence tests or through being immersed in a culture of poverty.

While I do not regard class bias as a telling objection to the crude/sophisticated distinction, one can detect it in the attack on crude hate speech in that hate-speech regulations focus on the more vulnerable class of college students and not on the relatively less vulnerable college professors. Some of the cruder forms of hate speech, as the well-publicized case at Brown University illustrates, come from the mouths and pens of sophomoric college students in varying states of intoxication.[26] While not minimizing the hurt that can stem from these incidents, it would be equally foolish to see these incidents as at the forefront of racism.

The arguments marshalled so far against the crude/sophisticated hate-speech distinction have not succeeded in showing that the distinction is an impossible one to maintain. They do show the inadequacy of the lines drawn so far. The crude/sophisticated hate-speech distinction forces the Weak Regulator to make unpleasant choices between types of speech. The problem described in this section is part of a larger problem within hate-speech issues, namely, the Boundary Problem.

V. Boundary Problem

Regulators of hate speech must face the problem of what kinds of speech to include under the restrictions and what to exclude. The regulations have the following problems:

25. Nat Hentoff, "The Right Thing at ASU," *Washington Post*, June 25, 1991, at A19, col. 5.

26. Brown University expelled an undergraduate, Douglas Hann, for an incident involving racial epithets and alcohol abuse. "Student at Brown Is Expelled Under a Rule Barring 'Hate Speech'," *New York Times*, February 12, 1991 at 17, col. 1.

1. *Too narrow.* With respect to those regulations now in place, many regulations actually cover a small range of activities. Stanford University's hate-speech regulations states:

> 4. Speech or other expression constitutes harassment by personal vilification if it:
>
> a). is intended to insult or stigmatize an individual or a small number of individuals on the basis of their sex, race, color, handicap, religion, sexual orientation, or national and ethnic origin; and
>
> b). is addressed directly to the individual or individuals whom it insults or stigmatizes; and
>
> c). makes use of insulting or "fighting" words or non-verbal symbols.[27]

Thus, under the fighting-word model, the speech must be targeted directly against and at specific individuals or an individual, and it must be intentional. Crude, direct (individually targeted), intentional speech covers few instances. In fact, the very incident (where a white student left a black caricature on an African American student's door) that served as a stimulus to the construction of the hate-speech code at Stanford would not be covered by Stanford's regulations.

2. *Too Broad.* On the one hand, hate-speech regulations may not apply to certain cases that, at least according to the intuitions of the Weak Regulators, it should. On the other hand, the regulations can sweep far too broadly, applying to seemingly innocuous jokes, innuendoes, and derogatory remarks.[28] The effectiveness of hate-speech regulation could be measured by how effectively it chills speech. Many times prejudicial attitudes can only be brought out into the open for examination if they find expression through various speech mechanisms. Stifling the relatively more innocuous expressions of prejudice in the form of jokes may actually stimulate the manifestation of hatred in more pernicious forms.[29]

3. *Hate Speech Within and Between Protected Groups.* The classical case of crude hate speech occurs when a white male student addresses a black student in a derogatory manner. However, as the following examples

---

27. Fundamental Standard Interpretation: Free Expression and Discriminatory Harassment, adopted by Stanford University, June 1990.

28. The University of Michigan Office of Affirmative Action issued a set of later withdrawn guidelines on actionable hate speech, which included: "You tell jokes about gay men and lesbians. You laugh at a joke about someone in your class who stutters." University of Michigan v. Doe, 721 F. Supp. at 858.

29. The University of Michigan Office of Affirmative Action Guideline gave the following as an example of blatant racial harassment: "A male student makes remarks in class like 'Women just aren't as good in this field as men' thus creating a hostile learning atmosphere for female students." University of Michigan v. Doe, 721 F. Supp. at 858.

illustrate, instances of hate speech do not always fall into the classical mode:

> 1. A black male graduate student in social work states, "Homosexuality is a disease."[30]
> 2. A dental student in a course taught by a minority female professor accused the teacher of being unfair to minorities; the teacher charged that the remark jeopardized her tenure.[31]

Perhaps these cases can best be handled by treating the perpetrator's group affiliation as irrelevant to the determination of whether or not the instances qualify as actionable hate speech. Nonetheless, they demonstrate the types of entanglements within which Weak Regulators will find themselves ensnarled. Moreover, the examples help to point out that speech regulation does not constitute a very effective way to fight racism, for it may result in imposing more punishments on protected groups.

4. *Non-Paradigmatic Cases.* Many candidates for hate-speech regulation do not fit the crude speech paradigm:

> 1. "I'd had too much experience that women were only tricky, deceitful, untrustworthy flesh." – Malcolm X.[32]

The derogatory element in statement 1 may not be as blatant as the paradigmatic case, but it may be just as loathsome. Furthermore, the derogatory comment may be directed at the dominant group.

5. *Already Proscribed.* Finally, does prohibiting hate speech proscribe anything more than current prohibitions? Most incidents of hate-speech complaints occurred in conjunction with other violations. Adding the hate-speech element to an already agreed upon violation may add very little. At the University of Wisconsin, for example, all serious cases – that is, all those resulting in probation or suspension – involved some other violation of the student code of conduct, such as assault, whereas all charges involving only the use of racial epithets were resolved informally.[33]

The Boundary Problem, as exemplified by the above, may pose nothing more than a challenge to make the delineations more precise. And

---

30. At the University of Michigan a black male social work student was charge with saying in class that homosexuality was a biological disease.

31. University of Michigan v. Doe, 721 F. Supp. at 866.

32. Malcolm X, *The Autobiography of Malcolm X*, at p. 226.

33. Patricia Hodulik, "Racists Speech on Campus," 37 *Wayne State Law Review* 1433, at 1441 and 1445 (1991).

yet something more serious is amiss with the hate-speech approach to combating racism. Regulators need to meet these challenges in order to provide an adequate theory of hate speech, although following the necessary analytical path puts the regulators on a road to nowhere, as the following case study shows.

VI. An Illustrative Interlude

In a public presentation of this paper, I peppered the analysis with many illustration of hate speech. The first response from the audience came from a woman who asked why I had used these particular examples. Anticipating this kind of concern, I invoked the use/mention distinction, often made in the philosophy of language. I claimed only to have "mentioned" but not "used" hate speech. Mentioning "number" in the metalanguage about arithmetic has a far different character from using number in the object language. Similarly, I had merely mentioned hate speech for illustrative purposes and had not used it.[34] Hardly satisfied with my intellectual maneuvering, she replied that she had been unable to hear any of my substantive claims because she was so offended by my use of hate speech.

Before I could muster a more informed reply, a fellow panelist, representing the Anti-Regulator position, jumped to my defense and assured the audience that although he would not have had the audacity to do what I had done, he thought my right to do so worth defending. This incident dramatically raises a number of important issues.

1. *Hidden Sophisticated Hate Speech.* First of all, my invocation of the use/mention distinction did assume the crude/sophisticated distinction that I had, then, and have, in this paper, attacked. Mentioning examples of hate speech can have a legitimating function, although it can also sometimes have an effect no different from an unsophisticated use of hate speech. The victims could be just as offended and harmed by the persistent mention of hate speech as by the occasional blurting out of crude hate speech.[35]

---

34. For a defense of the use/mention distinction in the context of the hate-speech debate see Peter Linzer, "A White Liberal Looks at Racist Speech," 65 *St. John's Law Review* 187, 213-19 (1991).

35. ". . . a case can be made that a lecturer on crime statistics who mentions that some ethnic groups have a higher crime rate than others, uses insulting language." David Kretzmer, "Freedom of Speech and Racism," 8 *Cardozo Law Review* 445, 489 (1987).

Mentioning examples of hate speech has a subtle dynamic. Culturally, the mention of some words is more acceptable than the mention of others. Writers and editors of journal articles leave examples of hate speech intact, whereas they almost always leave it to the reader's imagination to fill in the blanks for obscene language such as "F--k you."

2. *Social Meaning.* Second, I am not the one to determine what offends and harms in these cases. Regulators and Anti-Regulators alike (at least, those who do not come from the protected classes) assume, incorrectly, that they can determine harm in these instances. The victims of hate speech and not their self-proclaimed advocates need to determine the social meanings, and those in the dominant groups must respect the victims' determination. Victims determine social meanings in these contexts.

Those of us who do not belong to the victimized classes should listen to those harmed by hate speech, taking preventative measures to assure the victims that they in fact belong to our community. For word and deed go together, arm and fist, making up the complex array of racism, sexism, and homophobia. Allowing racist speech to go unchallenged creates an opening for racism, in its manifold and more vicious forms.

The protections against hate speech are not, as previously claimed, symmetrical – for whites as for blacks, for men as for women, for straights as for gays. I challenge you to hurl hate speech my way, for "my way" includes the well-paved, sanitized roads of white, heterosexual, male privilege. The protections must encompass the vulnerable. What we need is an understanding of who makes up the vulnerable classes. We must live with celebration and despair, within the dialectical tension that praises and condemns our differences; we must encourage criticism that pushes the bounds of tolerance without sacrificing our understanding of each other and ourselves.

Above all, we must find the courage to face the despicable hatreds that envelop our everyday life and that thrive within each of us. The truly colorblind, gender-neutral test lies in whether or not we can face ourselves in the mirror and confess our deep-seated bigotry, irrespective of our own race, gender, etc.[36] Only then can we fully dismantle the structures that allow oppression and subordination to fester and thrive.

Finally, words have tremendous power. Hate-speech regulators have a powerful argument when they point to past mistakes. Anti-Semitic

---

36. A recent survey found two-thirds of white students at the University of Maryland almost totally oblivious to racial incidents that 80 percent of Afro-Americans vividly recalled.

defamation flourished for decades before the Nazis rose to power, thereby providing a supportive cultural background for the "Final Solution."[37]

Having tried to make the most forceful case against hate speech, particularly its sophisticated version, I want to now turn the tables. In short, I claim that we should condemn hate speech in no uncertain terms but that we should not regulate it.

3. *The Free Speech Takeover.* Even if the protected classes justifiably find that sophisticated, and, of course, crude, hate speech should be banned, at some point the incidents of hate speech need to be reported and mentioned in order to be evaluated. Attacking sophisticated or even crude speech as speech not only stymies the ability to bring the speech to public view,[38] it also imposes First Amendment discourse upon what is not really a free speech issue. The issue at stake is racism and not free speech. At points, anti-racism and free speech concerns dovetail; minimally, the voices condemning racism need First Amendment protections.[39] Nevertheless, giving free speech center stage imposes grave risks. The danger with First Amendment discourse is that it can swamp many other equally, if not more important concerns. A law school, for example, may do all it can to halt the proliferation of hate-speech incidents while at the same time making little or no attacks on the structural features of racism – refusing, for example, to establish clinic programs that primarily serve poor urban blacks or to fund adequately loan forgiveness programs that provide students with an incentive to seek public interest employment.

In short, the cynic sees, with some justification, hate speech as a speech issue having all the makings of an academic issue, in the double sense of "academic." Academic issues thrive when they stay largely at the level of words, and academics love to argue over words. The fight takes place over words while the structures continue to subjugate and subordi-

---

37. Charles H. Jones, "Equality, Dignity and Harm: The Constitutionality of Regulating American Campus Ethnoviolence," 37 *Wayne Law Review* 1383, at 1423-24, note 156.

38. "Racist speech can be used as a 'social thermometer' that allows us to 'register the presence of disease within the body politic.'" Henry Hyde and George M. Fishman, "The Collegiate Speech Protection Act of 1991; A Response to the New Intolerance in the Academy," 37 *Wayne Law Review* 1469, at 1489 1991).

39. Delgado captures the effect of permitting low-level racism to persist: "It prevents us from digging in too strongly, starting to think we could really belong here. It makes us a little introspective, a little unsure of ourselves; at the right low-grade level it prevents us from organizing on behalf of more important things." Address by Richard Delgado, State Historical Society, Madison, Wisconsin (April 24, 1989) as quoted in Charles Lawrence, "If He Hollers Let Him Go," *Duke Law Journal* (1990) at 476. Ironically, fighting racism within the confines of free speech has the same damping effect.

nate unabated. Controversial issues such as hate speech arouse the passions, but, like so many academic issues, the action taken on them has little practical or political impact.

The hate-speech issue fits another view of the cynic, namely a model of ideological impotency. Having lost a major war but also having won modest victories against racism and sexism, liberals and leftists finds themselves in the middle of a backlash of hatred sanctioned from sophisticated circles on high. Unable to even ruffle the sophisticated conservatives, they thrash out in anger against the most visible and easily targeted enemy-the drunken Brown University birthday fraternity boy, etc. In casebook fashion, the peculiarities of the mildly dramatic incident are blown up to form their own reality, while the more pernicious forms of racism in the streets blithely pass by unchallenged.

I am not advocating the cynic's views, but they have some merit. They help to illuminate the free-speech trap. Fighting racism on the free speech terrain will result in a victory for free speech and in a draining of political energy in the war against racism.

VII. Recommendations

I have tried to argue in the strongest possible terms for the adoption of two seemingly incompatible positions: the condemnation of hate speech in its crude and sophisticated versions, and the inadequacy of a free-speech approach to the problem. As a way of reconciling these positions, consider the following proposal. The regulation of hate speech becomes more viable the more it is tied to a more far-reaching program that attacks racism. But the more programs a university adopts in order to combat racism, the less it will need hate-speech regulations. Anti-racism should take priority over hate-speech regulations.

Universities as educational institutions quite naturally respond to racism with educational programs, requiring students to take courses in different American cultures.[40] Some universities use educational programs in place of hate-speech regulations.[41] The University of Florida

---

40. "The University of Minnesota requires that all students take at least two courses on different American cultures. Mt. Holyoke and Tufts University have a similar requirement. The University of California, Berkeley, Faculty Senate recently ruled that all undergraduates must take at least one course in American Cultures." *Carnegie Foundation for the Advancement of Teaching, Special Report: Campus Life in Search of Community* 20 (1990) at 32.

41. This is the position adopted by Nadine Strossen, "Regulating Racist Speech on Campus: A Modest Proposal?" 3 *Duke Law Journal* 484, 562-69 (1990).

cites the following examples of non-legal steps to foster good race relations and diversity: the annual affirmative action conference, the annual multicultural retreats, and special events to celebrate diversity.[42]

Neither hate-speech regulations nor educational programs should occupy the center stage of a university's anti-racism platform. The educational programs reflect a university's commitment to foster diversity (policy 4, discussed above), which, although related in some respects, is not the same thing as a commitment to fight racism. Let me suggest one litmus test for a university's fight against racism: its non-academic employment practices. Paradoxically, on many college campuses hate-speech regulations and educational measures exist next to employment practices that result in the mistreatment of African American and female secretarial staffs.

Anti-racism policies must take priority. To the extent that hate-speech regulations and educational programs help to effectuate anti-racism, they have a strong justification. Yet, as I have tried to indicate, because of the conceptual entanglements connected to hate-speech regulations, the regulations probably do not aid the fight against racism and educational measures often have relatively little impact.

Universities need to develop programs that undermine the structural supports for racism, carefully examining their employment practices, investment decisions, and community service.

VIII. Conclusion

Hate speech can rile the emotions. Racism is on the rise, and hate speech is something that cannot be condoned. Moreover, universities need to take a long hard look at less visible forms of racism and take the lead in adopting a truly anti-racism agenda.

---

42. Letter (May 4, 1992) from Pamela J. Bernard, General Counsel, University of Florida. For another example of advocating a lame response to racism, see Peter Linzer, "A White Liberal Looks at Racist Speech," 65 *St. John's Law Review* 187, 236-44 (1991).

12
Affirmative Action and the Ethics of Pedagogy

Mark Tushnet

While researching an article on political correctness, I repeatedly came across references to the disruption of a class taught by the noted Berkeley anthropologist Vincent Sarich.[1] As with many stories about political correctness, this one was badly reported, lacking details one needed to understand the events. Yet, as I pieced together what had happened, it seemed to me that the incident directed attention to important questions about pedagogy – that is, classroom teaching – in an era of affirmative action.[2]

Some preliminary definitions and observations about my perspective seem appropriate. First, by pedagogy, I mean classroom teaching primarily, and not other student-related obligations such as counselling that faculty members have.[3] Second, by affirmative action I mean policies aimed at achieving greater demographic diversity in the student population; among those policies, but not exhausting the set, are the reconsideration of traditional definitions of merit and rigor. Third, I take affirmative action to be a permanent fact of campus life in the United States. Disagreements over the proper scope of affirmative action, and over whether specific policies are appropriate forms of affirmative action, will also be permanent features of campus life. As a result, when faculties deal with demographic changes in student population, they will act in a contentious atmosphere, and there will be divisions among the faculty. These facets of the issue raise distinct problems for opponents and supporters of affirmative action taken broadly and opponents and supporters

---

1. For the result of my research, see Mark Tushnet, *Political Correctness, the Law, and the Legal Academy*, 4 YALE J. L. & HUMANITIES 127 (1992).

2. As indicated below, however, Sarich's actions themselves do not raise interesting questions; in my view, they clearly violated minimal norms of pedagogic ethics under any circumstances.

3. I include in "classroom teaching" the different forms of clinical education that some departments and schools practice.

of specific affirmative action programs.[4] Finally, I write as a faculty member, demographically representative of many majority groups[5] who entered the academy before the rise of affirmative action.

In September 1990 Sarich published an article in the Berkeley alumni magazine sharply critical of the University's affirmative action plan. Two months later 75 students entered the room in which Sarich was teaching his introductory course in anthropology, stood in the back, and "started to yell and chant," shouting, among other things, "Bullshit." Although they did not drown Sarich out, they made it impossible for him to continue his lecture.[6]

To understand these events, it would help to know exactly what Sarich had been saying. For it turns out that it may indeed have been bullshit.[7] For example, Sarich asserted in one class, "Male figure skaters are disproportionally homosexual. This is because figure skating and other kinds of activities disproportionally populated by homosexuals have one or both of two characteristics. First, you are not given very much freedom of choice as to what you do. Second, there are females making the basic decisions with respect to whether you are doing your job well or not." When asked what evidence he had for this claim, Sarich later responded, "I have to admit that there isn't a lot of foundation behind that." He added that "he does not teach the course based on 'facts,'" and that his "fundamental point was to explain that there is no genetic basis for homosexuality."[8]

Sarich also discusses in his class the relation between race and gender, brain size, and intelligence, suggesting that "women on average have

4. Members of demographic minorities who entered the academy both before and after the rise of affirmative action fall into the contending groups; consider, for example, the positions of John Hope Franklin and Stephen Carter, who both support particular types of affirmative action but do not believe that affirmative action entails substantial changes in traditional definitions of merit and rigor.

5. In light of my uneasiness about using demographic categories as surrogates for much of substance, I feel compelled to note (a) that my political perspective is definitely not widely shared in the legal academy; and (b) that I am a member of a religious group that is a substantial minority in the country and a minority in the academy.

6. Kenneth J. Cooper, "'American Cultures' at Berkeley: Requiring a Variety of Perspectives," *Washington Post*, May 27, 1991, p. A-1. In this article Sarich is quoted as saying that they did not drown him out. Jerry Adler, "Taking Offense," *Newsweek*, Dec. 24, 1990, p. 48, asserts that the students "drowned out" the lecture.

7. This is not to say that disrupting the class when the teacher utters ridiculous statements is correct. I want to focus, however, on Sarich's pedagogy, not on the students' behavior.

8. "Campus Life: Berkeley; Campus is Split Over Statements by a Professor," *New York Times*, Dec. 23, 1990, p. 28.

smaller brains than men."[9] A colleague in his department asserts that "there are many studies that discredit that," and that Sarich had "told the department that there is scientific evidence for his theories but 'has not provided any citations for us.'"[10]

Sarich's behavior, while clearly extreme, seems to me an example of a more general phenomenon. Changes in the composition of the campus population lead some teachers to lose their way. Surely one must wonder about the pedagogic reasons a professor would have for not teaching a course based on facts, or for making controversial factual assertions with no evidence to support the assertions.

I believe that Sarich's actions reflect his discomfort with the fact of affirmative action, and introduce us to the pedagogic issues affirmative action raises. I want to address those issues by considering the impact of affirmative action on the pedagogy of opponents and supporters of affirmative action. To anticipate my conclusion, teachers run two risks: they might not change their pedagogy enough, or they might change it in the wrong way. These might be called, respectively, the pathology of resistance and the pathology of intellectual collapse.

From the point of view of teachers who made fundamental pedagogic decisions before the era of affirmative action, affirmative action means that the composition of their classes has changed from what it was when they made those basic decisions. The distribution of backgrounds and abilities in the classroom has changed. On the margin, the difference is that, instead of a white student interested in opera or playing the tuba, they have an African–American student interested in jazz or Egypt. How is a teacher to respond to that change?

Consider a different change in a class's composition. Suppose I have been teaching the second, advanced course in constitutional law for many years. I structure my presentation based on my knowledge that students who enter the course have already had the introductory course. As a result, I assume that they have already been exposed to certain kinds of arguments and some basic court cases. I know, of course, that not all of them have had exactly the same prior instruction, and that many of them will have forgotten much that I believe they should have assimilated from the introductory course. I therefore offer quick reviews of important topics, and then go on to the advanced discussion. In devising the quick reviews, I understand that I will be going over ground familiar to some students and unfamiliar to others, but I know that I want to get on to the

---

9. MacNeil/Lehrer Newshour, June 17, 1991, Transcript #4056 (available on NEXIS).
10. *Id.*; "Campus Life," *supra* note 8 (both quoting Nancy Scheper-Hughes).

advanced material. Typically, then, I try to give my students enough so that they can do whatever additional thinking necessary to catch up; to do more would bore some students and would detract from my ability to move on to the advanced material.

Now suppose that the faculty, over my opposition, changes the course outline in the introductory constitutional law course. As students enter my advanced class, they no longer know some things they used to know, although – if the faculty has been responsible in changing the curriculum – they know other things they did not know before. From my point of view, students entering the class are nonetheless less well educated than before.

Still, it would be irresponsible for me to continue to teach the advanced course exactly as I had before. The common fund of knowledge students had earlier has changed. My "quick reviews" of some topics will no longer be "reviews," and their brevity will make them an inadequate foundation for the advanced work I want to do. As a result, I will have to spend more time than before on what I regard as introductory material. That, in turn, means that I will be unable to develop some aspects of the advanced course in as much detail as I have in the past.[11] Undoubtedly I will be unhappy with this change, believing that I am no longer providing as good an education to my students as I used to.

I believe that the analogy between a curricular change and affirmative action is quite close with respect to one aspect of affirmative action. Affirmative action leads to student bodies with a different distribution of backgrounds than existed before. Teachers who structured their courses based on accurate information about what students knew as they entered the class now face classes where students know other things. To be pedagogically responsible, they must change what they do in class, even if they believe at first that the quality of their instruction decreases.

Sarich's behavior, I believe, reflects one common response to the changes in background attendant on affirmative action, particularly among those not entirely comfortable with affirmative action. It is the simple refusal to change in the face of undesired change, and it leads to ineffective teaching.

Yet I think it important to stress that up to this point I have not been discussing a problem peculiar to changes in class composition due to affirmative action. My constitutional law example is hypothetical, but

11. It would be convenient if I could believe that I could compensate for this change by devoting less time to material that students now would have received from the restructured introductory course, but, because I believe the change to be pedagogically unsound, I cannot: students have lost more than they have gained from the change.

analogous changes in student backgrounds are pervasive. Every teacher draws on what he or she believes to be commonly available cultural references to make points in class. We lay out an argument about the constitutional law relating to families, for example, and try to make sure that students understand the argument by saying, "The Supreme Court's image of the family is drawn from 'Ozzie and Harriet.'" For students who have not quite gotten the argument when we laid it out explicitly, the reference to "Ozzie and Harriet" gives them an image that helps them complete the argument in their minds.

We know that not all our students get every one of the references, but we try to use enough such references so that, when coupled with the direct arguments we make, students will understand the point. Yet, as time passes, we no longer face students with the common cultural background that we used to. When we refer to "Ozzie and Harriet," the reference is puzzling, and the students we were trying to help, the ones who had not quite gotten the argument, become even more puzzled.[12]

Now, recall that we use those references to make it *easier* for students to understand our arguments, because we know that we need to offer some students assistance beyond the explicit arguments we make. What are we to do when we discover that the reference is no longer helping? An irresponsible teacher might continue to use it. A more responsible teacher might be tempted simply to drop the reference because it no longer works. That, however, means that some students will not be getting the assistance that the teacher believed necessary (and that used to be provided by the reference). To continue to be as effective as before, then, the teacher must come up with some substitute reference – something about MTV, for example.[13]

It deserves mention, though, that although students may not have available to them the same common cultural background that they used, they continue to have cultural resources on which the teacher can draw. If "Ozzie and Harriet" will not work, perhaps MTV will. Thus, the changes in the composition of classes does not mean that pedagogy necessarily becomes worse because cultural references to augment explicit arguments have become impossible. Rather, they mean that pedagogy become harder because I, an older teacher whose style was formed under different circumstances, must adapt to new ones.

12. For a discussion of the pedagogy of cultural references, see Tushnet, *supra* note 1, at 141–42.
13. In the family example, the teacher might say, "The Supreme Court hasn't got the point about changes in families that's part of the Billy Joel video 'We Didn't Start the Fire.'"

Effective pedagogy in circumstances of changing classroom composition means that we always have work to do.[14] Yet experienced teachers ought to have known that from the beginning. I suspect that we all know teachers who were superb earlier in their careers, but who have become stuck in a pedagogic rut, not realizing that what was effective ten years ago just does not work anymore. To the extent that affirmative action means only that the distribution of our students' backgrounds is different from what it was before, affirmative action's pedagogic implications are basically the same as those teachers have confronted throughout this century.

Even more, the demographic changes attendant on affirmative action may compel a responsible teacher to rethink some pedagogic decisions, but they need not compel changes after that reconsideration. Discussions of pedagogy tend to be cast in universal terms: a teacher must do everything possible to reach and engage every student. We know, however, that this is a fantasy. Teachers differ in their ability to engage students, and ordinarily we accept these differences without question. If a teacher is able, using the techniques he or she has always used, to reach the new population of students at the same rate he or she did earlier, the teacher can responsibly continue to use those techniques. And, I should emphasize, this is true even if the rate is quite low; what was a tolerable rate of success before affirmative action does not become intolerable simply because of demographic changes.[15]

But, of course, affirmative action means more than simple demographic change on campus. Affirmative action changes not only the distribution of students' backgrounds; it also changes the distribution of abilities and talents in our classes. And if changes in background may lead opponents of affirmative action to become bad teachers because they refuse to adapt to those changes, changes in the distribution of abilities and talents may, I believe, lead some supporters of affirmative action to become bad teachers for a different reason.[16]

---

14. That is another reason why opponents of affirmative action may not react properly to it: not only is it wrong on the merits, as they see it; affirmative action also makes more work for them.

15. There is a danger in not changing pedagogic techniques, however: the teacher may be perceived as having written off the new population of students, in the belief that they really did not deserve to be on campus – and that perception may be correct.

16. Not surprisingly, I have in mind primarily white male supporters of affirmative action, many of whom are, it seems to me, committed to affirmative action for reasons of social justice, but do not believe that affirmative action enhances what they regard as the fundamental "value" of the university, the disinterested pursuit of truth through rational inquiry.

Again, I believe that the best way to approach this question is by thinking about teachers who developed their pedagogy before affirmative action. They faced a student body that presented them a particular distribution of scores on standardized tests and other traditional measures of intellectual ability, traditionally conceived. Those scores did measure something about student abilities, and good teachers developed lectures and class presentations that effectively communicated what they believed to be important to students with that distribution of scores. Meaningful affirmative action leads to a student body with a different distribution of scores and the like. This implies, as before, that a teacher's pedagogy must change.

The danger then is two-fold, and I believe that supporters of affirmative action are more likely to face these dangers than opponents. One danger arises when a teacher believes that traditional measures of intellectual ability, traditionally conceived, accurately measure real intellectual ability. This teacher may believe that affirmative action is socially desirable for a variety of reasons, but he or she also believes that the student body is "less able" now, in the relevant sense, than it used to be. As a result, the teacher may make his or her classes easier – will "dumb them down," in the jargon – or may write only the affirmative action students off by refraining, for example, from insisting that they participate in class discussions when participation is otherwise the norm.

The other danger arises when the teacher believes that traditional measures of intellectual ability did not accurately measure real intellectual ability. He or she believes, therefore, that the affirmative action class is no less able intellectually than prior classes. This teacher may then not change his or her pedagogy at all. The difficulty here, I believe, is that such a teacher may not realize that affirmative action challenges not only the measures of intellectual ability, but the very conception of it.[17] If that challenge is correct, pedagogic strategies that were effective before affirmative action, given a distribution of intellectual ability traditionally conceived, may no longer be effective with classes that are indeed "equally" able, because the institution's understanding of ability has changed but the teacher's has not.

As a general matter, a teacher runs a risk in an affirmative-action era in continuing to teach exactly as before. And yet there is an argument against change that deserves mention.[18] As I have continually stressed,

17. For an extensive discussion, see Duncan Kennedy, *A Cultural Pluralist Case for Affirmative Action in Legal Academia*, 1990 DUKE L.J. 705.
18. This argument might be understood as an elaboration of the proposition that responsible pedagogy requires only that teachers make their pedagogic decisions in good faith.

teachers always face students with a distribution of abilities and backgrounds, and, as mentioned earlier, no teacher is equally effective with students from every point in the distribution. A responsible teacher might conclude that, given his or her own abilities and built-up experience, the gains from changing – the ability to reach some part of the class that he or she would not be able to reach as effectively using his or her prior methods – are not worth the losses – failing to reach a part of the distribution that the existing methods did reach. This is particularly true when, as is necessarily the case, the affirmative-action distribution overlaps with the prior distribution. The teacher then will reach some students who would not be in the class in the absence of affirmative action, though he or she will not reach all such students.

Vincent Sarich's behavior appears to represent the pathology of rigidity in the face of change. I offer another anecdote to suggest how failing to change might not be pathological. Sarich attributed his difficulties with students to "political correctness." Eugene Genovese, the historian of slavery, holds views that have been, I suspect, almost as politically incorrect as Sarich's. Genovese recounts that, when he was a visiting professor at Yale University during the late 1960s when the Black Panther Party was active in New Haven, his African-American students were so upset with what he said in class that they sat in the back taking detailed notes. After each class, Genovese says, the students parcelled out the notes and went to the library to check the accuracy of Genovese's assertions. Genovese being who he is, of course, they always found the evidence to back up what Genovese had said. I regard this as an example of successful pedagogy in an affirmative-action era, even though Genovese did nothing different.[19]

"Dumbing down" and failing to change represent the collapse of appropriate pedagogy in the face of affirmative action. Again there is nothing special about the remedy for these difficulties. Teachers in an affirmative-action era ought to appreciate that their students now have a different distribution of abilities according to traditional measures, and that the students are indeed no less able intellectually than students were earlier. Our pedagogy therefore ought to demand no less of our students than it used to. At the same time, however, it may have to become demanding in a different way, because what we understand as intellectual ability ought to have changed. As before, what is required is more work from the teacher.

19. It may be too obvious to note, but consider what would have happened had Sarich's students done the same. What, other than acquiring accurate information that the teacher ought to have provided in the first place, would they have learned from the exercise of discovering that their professor made unsupported assertions in class?

13
Understanding Affirmative Action: One Feminist's Perspective

Sharon E. Rush★

Introduction

Recently, a colleague and I co-taught a seminar on Feminist Jurisprudence. The seminar was wonderfully diverse with respect to race and sex; it included a black man, two black women, three white men, and ten white women. Admittedly, the ratios could have been better, but my experience teaches me that having some men in the class is better than having none (the typical situation) and that having more than one black in the class is better than having none or only one (again, the typical situation). Not surprisingly, having "allies" makes talking and expressing one's feelings much easier. Consequently, the discussions were rich with input from all of these different groups.

Operating in conjunction with these pleasant dynamics was another surprise: the black students played a large role in shaping the direction of our discussions. Black students often lack a forum where they can express their opinions in such an open and supportive way. Moreover, it is quite rare that white students are exposed to an intense showing of opinions and analyses by blacks,[1] especially one with the possibility of exchanging ideas and thoughts. As a result, the feminist theory was interlaced quite heavily with racial themes. In my opinion, this is consistent with feminist methodology and also quite refreshing and enlightening. Together, these particular dynamics seemed to truly enhance the quality of the class.

★Copyright 1992. Professor of Law, University of Florida.

I would like to thank my friends and colleagues for helping me with this effort: Alex Bongard, Alyson Flournoy, Jannis Goodnow, Reesha Kang, Elizabeth McCulloch, Kenneth Nunn, Juan Perea, Scott Rogers, Jane Schukoske, and Walter Weyrauch.

1. Of course, I am not suggesting that there is something like a "black" opinion, or that all blacks think alike. Rather, I think that quite often blacks are so outnumbered by white students (two blacks out of a class of 103 in Constitutional Law I, a required course) that they may be hesitant about participating. *See infra* note 3.

Nevertheless, I also was somewhat disturbed by what I saw and heard in this seminar. Often the black students expressed their anger and frustration with racism, which seemed quite natural. Correspondingly, and this also seemed quite natural to me, some of the white students expressed anger and frustration with "affirmative action."[2] They felt that efforts by various government officials to enhance opportunities for people of color is wrong when the effect of those efforts excludes whites. Echoing similar sentiments were the women and men in the class with respect to sex discrimination. Adding to the confusion was one black student who "sided" with some of the white students in condemning affirmative action because of the stigma associated with it. Ironically, their debates often were tempered with a growing concern about sounding "politically correct."[3] Not surprisingly, in their anger and frustration none of these groups seemed to be hearing what the others were saying. Often the discussion seemed to be a showdown about who was hurting more.

I am troubled by what I saw and heard in this seminar because I fear that what I witnessed may be a reflection of a showdown between outsiders and insiders[4] nationwide. A primary concern is that insiders who

2. I use "affirmative action" in this paper to mean the promotion of people of color and white women in hiring and admissions to various programs. This is its more popular meaning, although affirmative action in other guises has been around for a long time. *See infra* notes 77–79 and accompanying text. I also use the phrase "people of color and white women" to acknowledge that women of color belong to both groups.

3. For example, the University of Florida has support from its legislature to conduct a summer institute for entering black students. The impetus behind such funding was the history of race discrimination at the University's law school, evidenced by a court order to remedy the situation. *State of Fla. ex rel. Virgil Hawkins, Relator v. Board of Control et al.*, 93 So.2d 354 (Sup. Ct. Fla. 1957). Many white students, who are ineligible to attend the institute, feel that the black students receive an unfair advantage in their preparation for law school. At least one white student saw the seminar as an opportunity to learn more about the institute, so she asked. Clearly, the student who raised the question was hesitant because she apologized for needing to ask it. I think she was afraid to ask for fear she would be perceived as opposed to the institute and therefore racist. Unfortunately, the black students interpreted her question as a suggestion that the programs were "bad" so they also got defensive and essentially reinforced her fears.

4. By "insiders," generally I mean people who have characteristics that reflect dominant values or preferences. For example, whites, men, Christians, able-bodied persons, heterosexuals, and so forth are members of insider groups. Conversely, persons who possess characteristics that fall outside normative standards comprise the communities of outsiders. The dichotomy between insiders and outsiders is not always distinct, and some people have both insider and outsider characteristics. For example, depending upon the context, white gay men can be insiders or outsiders. In my opinion, much of the friction surrounding affirmative action derives from this point. Some poor white men, in particular, oppose affirmative action policies because generally they define the outsider group according to sex and race, and not wealth. *See* Jeffrey Harrison, *Confess'n the Blues: Some Thoughts on the Class Bias in Law School Hiring*, 42 J. LEGAL EDUC. 119 (1992). I explore this in more detail in *Understanding Diversity*, 42 U. FLA. L. REV. 1 (1991).

feel hurt, threatened, or excluded by affirmative action policies that prefer people of color and white women over others will react to their pain by using their power in ways that will maintain the status quo.[5] This is the impetus behind the "politically correct" movement, in my opinion. Pulling in the other direction, moreover, are outsiders who shun affirmative action because they believe it marks them as inferior.[6]

The growing anti-affirmative action sentiment is tragic because it augments the divisiveness between women and men, people of color and whites, and outsiders and insiders generally. The divide between insiders and outsiders is growing, in my opinion, primarily because of affirmative action, and because affirmative action is so misunderstood. Thus, the primary purpose of this essay is to explore affirmative action policies to better understand where the tensions and disagreements are with this concept. A major theme of this essay will be to illustrate that affirmative action policies favoring people of color and white women[7] are justifiable because they make inroads, albeit small ones, on the hegemonic power structure that itself benefits from countless unacknowledged affirmative action policies protecting the status quo.

Specifically, Part 1 briefly discusses the origin of affirmative action, examining some of the primary rationales behind the concept. Part 2 focuses upon major arguments in opposition to affirmative action. Part 3 offers a feminist critique of the anti-affirmative action movement and explores how the growing opposition to affirmative action is only one part of a growing hostility toward outsiders and outsider jurisprudence. Finally, Part 4 explores why we, as a nation, need to recommit ourselves to affirmative action and the policy goals behind it. Perhaps with a better

5. Efforts in this direction are quite evident. *See* SUSAN FALUDI, BACKLASH: THE UNDECLARED WAR AGAINST AMERICAN WOMEN (1991); DINESH D'SOUZA, ILLIBERAL EDUCATION: THE POLITICS OF RACE AND SEX ON CAMPUS (1991).

6. *See* STEPHEN CARTER, REFLECTIONS OF AN AFFIRMATIVE ACTION BABY (1991); SHELBY STEELE, THE CONTENT OF OUR CHARACTER: A NEW VISION OF RACE IN AMERICA 116-18 (1990).

7. Whether other outsiders should benefit from affirmative action policies is also debatable. For example, valid reasons exist for implementing affirmative action policies for lesbians and gay men. See Jeffrey S. Bynre, *Affirmative Action for Lesbians and Gay Men: A Proposal for True Equality of Opportunity and Workforce Diversity*, ll Yale Law & Policy Rev. 47 (1993). Moreover, it is essential that all subordinated groups attain equal citizenship status with members of the dominant culture. KENNETH KARST, BELONGING TO AMERICA: EQUAL CITIZENSHIP AND THE CONSTITUTION (1989); CASS SUNSTEIN, THE PARTIAL CONSTITUTION (1993). At present, existing affirmative action programs for white women and people of color are under attack. Thus, this paper focuses on those programs and saves for another paper an exploration of affirmative action programs for other outsiders.

understanding of affirmative action some common ground will become evident and the differences of opinion that divide us will be narrowed. In turn, policies consistent with achieving our common goals can be implemented.

I. The Origins of Affirmative Action

A. Involuntary, Voluntary, and Quasi-Voluntary Policies

Historically, affirmative action grew out of a need to remedy specific instances of race and sex discrimination in the workplace, educational environments, and housing that existed prior to and during the Civil Rights era of the 1960s and 1970s.[8] The concept first appeared in law in Title VII of the 1964 Civil Rights Act, which allowed for its use to remedy past discrimination.[9] For example, the United States Supreme Court has held that the fourteenth amendment requires public schools that intentionally adhere to racial segregation policies to use racial classifications in their efforts to desegregate.[10] Perhaps few would disagree that court-ordered remedies for specific discriminatory acts or practices are legitimate.

"Voluntary" affirmative action programs, in contrast, are quite controversial. In fact, most of the controversy surrounding affirmative action stems from efforts by employers, educators, and government officials to adopt affirmative action policies either in response to specific allegations of discrimination,[11] or even without regard to any specific showing of current discrimination against particular individuals or groups. A major example of this arose in the *Bd. of Regents of Calif. v. Bakke*, in which the United States Supreme Court held unconstitutional a voluntary racial preference admissions program adopted by U.C. Davis medical school.[12]

Finally, the third and perhaps most significant category of affirmative action policies involves some coercion, although not by court order. For example, political boycotts are one way for concerned citizens to "force"

8. *See generally*, GERTRUDE EZORSKY, RACISM AND JUSTICE: THE CASE FOR AFFIRMATIVE ACTION 28-38 (1991).

9. 42 U.S.C. 2000e-5(g) (1993) provides that judicial relief in instances in which an employer has intentionally discriminated may include "such affirmative action as may be appropriate."

10. *Swann v. Charlotte-Mecklenburg Bd. of Education*, 402 U.S. 1 (1971).

11. These were upheld by the Supreme Court in *United Steel Workers of America v. Weber*, 443 U.S. 193 (1979).

12. *Regents of the Univ. of California v. Bakke*, 438 U.S. 265 (1978).

employers to hire more people of color and white women.[13] Other "incentives" are provided directly by the government, which often makes receipt of federal funds contingent upon complying with specific policies. For example, schools that discriminate on the basis of sex or race, in addition to being subject to suit by aggrieved individuals, generally are not entitled to federal funding. I say *generally* because sometimes even the government gets away with overt discrimination, as is the case at the Virginia Military Institute where an all-male admissions policy was held not to violate women's equal protection rights.[14]

Moreover, it is important to note that government-sanctioned "quasi-voluntary" policies work both ways. With the growing opposition to affirmative action, government officials may feel pressure to stop certain policies favoring people of color and white women. For example, during the Reagan and Bush administrations, scholarships available only to students of color came under sharp criticism.[15] While President Clinton's administration supports race-based scholarships, had they been eliminated, many schools would have been forced to comtemplate receiving federal aid in other programs by foregoing promises of financial aid to students of color.[16]

---

13. *See generally* GERTRUDE EZORSKY, *supra* note 8 at 31.

14. *U.S. v. Va.*, 766 F. Supp. 1407 (W.D. Va. 1991) (as the only single-gender school in state's university system, Virginia Military Institute's males-only admissions policy served the state's interest in providing diversity in education and survived an equal protection challenge). Federal District Court Judge Jackson L. Kiser recently accepted Virginia's plan to provide a "separate but equal" leadership program at Mary Baldwin College (an all-female college) as an alternative to opening VMI to women. The Justice Department plans to appeal this decision in part because the women's leadership program would consist of a mere two to four hours of military classes per week. [No author], *Judge Endorses VMI Plan on Excluding Women*, N.Y. Times, May 2, 1994, at A12.

15. *See* Ronald Brownstein, "Beyond Quotas: A New Generation of Scholars Is Stressing Class, Not Race, In An Effort to Break the Civil Rights Impasse," L.A. Times, July 28, 1991, at 18.

16. And the recent decision in *Rust v. Sullivan*, 499 U.S. 173 (1991), is some indication of how pernicious the government can be in employing this tactic. In *Rust*, the United States Supreme Court held that it was constitutional for the government to withhold federal aid to hospitals who advise women about their abortion rights. Although a hospital has the option of ignoring *Rust* and continuing to counsel women about their abortion options, in reality, the federal aid may be crucial to a particular institution's existence such that the option is no option at all. In one of his most heralded executive orders, President Clinton lifted the ban on abortion counseling in federally funded clinics soon after he was inaugurated. Alison Carper, *Clinton's New Abortion Rules Meet Approval*, Newsday, Jan. 23, 1993, p. 77.

B. Justifications for Affirmative Action

A variety of rationales have been offered in support of affirmative action policies. Specifically, advocates of affirmative action suggest it is necessary (1) to remedy past and present race and sex discrimination against people of color and white women; (2) to promote diversity in the work or school community; and (3) to increase the number of people of color and white women in community leadership roles. For example, in *Bakke*, the U.C. Davis medical school defended its admissions policy that preferred American Indians, Asians, Blacks, and Chicanos for (at least) 16 of 100 of its seats, relying upon reasons that I will now explore in detail.[17]

1. Remedying Past and Present Societal Discrimination

Given the history of race and sex discrimination in this country,[18] it is reasonable to take this history into account in the hiring and admissions policies we adopt today. Assuming we could agree that the history of discrimination has impeded the efforts of people of color and white women to achieve equality with whites and men, then our focus as a national community should be to remedy the inequalities. Admittedly, the rele-

17. *Bakke*, 438 U.S. at 275. The Davis plan did not limit the number of minority candidates to a maximum of 16, and made clear that it was open to accepting more than that if advisable. *Id*. at 276. The distinction between goals and quotas can be elusive, and it is critical to understand the difference. In the context of affirmative action, goals are aspirational. That is, an employer or educational institution uses goals as a way of striving to *increase* the representation of people of color and women in their programs. Quotas, in contrast, suggest that only a *limited* number of outsiders are to be included. The contexts in which these terms were originally used also are significant. The use of quotas originated as a way of minimizing the inclusion of Jews in professional schools, or stated alternatively, they were used to exclude many Jews. *see* GERTRUDE EZORSKY, *supra* note 8 at 38. ("To tag such [affirmative action] measures as quotas falsely suggests that they, like yesterday's quotas, serve an immoral end.") This also should be remembered in the context of the *Bakke* case.

18. By including both people of color and white women in the debate on affirmative action, I do not mean to suggest that the histories of the two groups are the same. Moreover, I am not attempting to make a comparative analysis of the harm inflicted on these two groups. Rather, I am making a claim that people of color and white women have both been sufficiently burdened by discriminatory practices so that it is appropriate and necessary to target both groups for affirmative action relief. Finally, I think special consideration must be given to women of color, who encounter particularly severe degrees of discrimination because of their sex and race. For an analysis of the intersection between race and sex, see b. hooks, AIN'T I A WOMAN: BLACK WOMEN AND FEMINISM (1981) and Kimberle Crenshaw, *Race, Reform and Retrenchment: Transformation and Legitimation in Antidiscrimination Law*, 101 HARV. L. REV. 1331, 1369-87 (1988).

vancy of our history of race and sex discrimination could be tied into specific situations of sexism and racism, which is the position taken by the United States Supreme Court.[19]

Alternatively, racial and sexual equality could perhaps be achieved more swiftly and efficiently through affirmative action policies responding to the reality of institutional sexism and racism that often present impenetrable barriers to people of color and white women seeking admission to these institutions.[20] Thus, a primary disagreement over affirmative action stems not from what most Americans believe to be the *ultimate goal* behind affirmative action, but rather from what they perceive to be an *unfair process* used to achieve this goal.

Logically, then, the next question is whether affirmative action policies are a legitimate means of accomplishing this goal. In an ideal world, history's lesson would be learned and decision-makers would truly and voluntarily commit themselves to promoting sexual and racial equality. But experience teaches us that without some kind of incentive, most institutions will not voluntarily participate in remedial efforts to stop sexual and racial discrimination.[21] In fact, some evidence exists that in response to affirmative action policies some decision-makers have simply become more discreet about their sexism and

19. *See, e.g., City of Richmond v. J.A. Croson Co.*, 488 U.S. 469 (1989) (a city plan preferring minority-owned businesses for city contracts was held invalid because no showing plan was related to remedying discrimination in that community).

20. See generally, DERRICK BELL, AND WE ARE NOT SAVED: THE ELUSIVE QUEST FOR RACIAL JUSTICE (1987). *See also*, GERTRUDE EZORSKY, *supra* note 8 at 48-49 (demonstrating the strides blacks have made in private industry through the 1970s as a result of affirmative action; suggesting that since 1980 progress has slowed considerably because of increased resistance by the Supreme Court to affirmative action). For similar findings, see Thomas Rich and Kenneth Whitby, *Racial Inequality in Unemployment: The Effectiveness of the Civil Rights Act of 1964*, in AFFIRMATIVE ACTION: THEORY, ANALYSIS, AND PROSPECTS 66 (1986) (positive effects stopped around 1977); Lee Sigelman and N. Joseph Cayer, *Minorities, Women, and Public Sector Jobs: A Status Report, Id.* at 107 (biggest winners were white women).

21. GERTRUDE EZORSKY, *supra* note 8 at 32-33 ("Hence, as a number of government agencies and courts have recognized, increased recruitment of blacks requires that reasonable strategies be devised to reduce institutional discrimination, that is, to lessen the racist impact of employment neutrals: selection by personal connections, qualification requirements, and seniority status."). See generally Michael B. Preston, *Affirmative Action Policy: Can It Survive the Reaganites?*, in AFFIRMATIVE ACTION: THEORY, ANALYSIS, AND PROSPECTS (Michael Combs and John Gruhl, eds. 1986) ("past experience indicates that elimination of job segregation for women and minorities on a voluntary basis was meaningless until a strong enforcement program, including affirmative action and goals and timetables, provided an incentive for action") *Id.* at 174 (quoting, House Subcommittee Report, 1982 at 46).

racism, successfully masking them so that they are immune to legal challenges.[22]

2. Promoting Diversity

Similarly, few people, if any, would disagree that some workplaces and school environments reflect a de facto, if not de jure, exclusiveness. For example, it is not uncommon to see "Men Working" signs that mean exactly that: there are no women working on this crew. Many students are able to complete an entire degree program, spanning years, without studying with a professor of color or a white women professor. While including outsiders necessarily breaks down the white-male hegemony, some would argue that the inclusion of people of color and white women in various environments is also beneficial because of the diversity they bring to the community.

Affirmative action does promote diversity, but exactly what diversity means can be unclear. Elsewhere I explore three possible definitions of diversity,[23] only one of which is consistent with affirmative action as it is commonly understood. Specifically, I suggest that diversity might mean facial diversity, hardship diversity, or ideological diversity. Facial diversity is achieved by having a fair representation of women and men, people of color and whites in a particular environment. Hardship diversity focuses upon including in the insider environment people who suffer disadvantages because of hardships such as being deaf or blind, gay or lesbian, non-Christian, poor, and so forth. Finally, ideological diversity is achieved by including in the exclusive environment people who espouse views different from those of the group. In a law school environment, for example, this would include critical legal scholars, feminists, and critical race scholars.

22. Fundamentally, this is the problem with most government policies that are status quo-oriented, which started with the Reagan Administration. *see* Randall Kennedy, *Persuasion and Distrust: A Comment on the Affirmative Action Debate*, 99 HARV. L. REV. 1327, 1337-45 (1986). *See also*, Sharon Rush, *Understanding Diversity, supra* note 4 at 7-8, n.25. I try to demonstrate that the University of Florida's last presidential search, which came down to a decision between a white man and a black women, ostensibly looked free of sex and race biases, but was ultimately a sexist and racist decision in favor of the white man. Some of the comments that were made just before the final decision was announced included, "what some [alumni] most particularly do not want is a new president who is female and black," quoting *The Call of the Bull Gator*, St. Petersburg Times, Nov. 8, 1989, at 16A.

23. *see* Sharon Rush, *Understanding Diversity, supra* note 4.

In listing these categories, I do not mean to suggest that my list is exhaustive. In fact, today I would add cultural diversity to this initial list.[24] Nor do I mean to suggest that a person can diversify an environment in only one of these ways – a black lesbian feminist, for example, promotes diversity in a variety of ways. Significantly, non-traditional areas of legal scholarship, especially feminist jurisprudence and critical race theory, are of particular importance, concern, and relevance to many white women and people of color.[25]

The critical point, of course, is that regardless of how many different definitions of diversity exist, in the affirmative action context it must include facial diversity at the very least. Otherwise, it would be all too easy to "diversify" an environment by selecting the poor white man, or the white male critic. I am not suggesting that it is never appropriate to hire such candidates – for example, gay white men can diversify a heterosexual environment; Jewish white men can diversify a Christian environment. In specific contexts, then, diversity can be achieved in a variety of important ways (especially if we, as a society, are to achieve a sense of national community). Significantly, however, hegemony is primarily white and male and to continue to hire white men to the exclusion of others would do less to deconstruct hegemony than would affirmative action policies promoting people of color and white women.

3. Providing Services to Broader Community

Proponents of affirmative action also suggest that such policies further the goal of achieving equality by increasing the number of people of color and white women in various jobs and professions. For example, the U.C.

24. *see* Duncan Kennedy, *A Cultural Pluralist Case for Affirmative Action in Legal Academia*, 1990 DUKE L.J. 705 (exploring relationship between race and scholarship, without espousing essentialist view); *See also,* Neil Gotanda, *A Critique of "Our Constitution is Color-Blind"*, 44 STAN. L. REV. 1, 56-59 (1991) (suggesting that one way of defining race is by culture).

25. Professor Duncan Kennedy makes a compelling argument that this is one reason we need to hire more women and people of color. Duncan Kennedy, *supra* note 24. Many scholars interested in critical race theory also are writing convincing pieces suggesting that race-consciousness is the path we ought to be taking. For several years now, many scholars of color have been suggesting this: Derrick Bell, Kimberle Crenshaw, Richard Delgado, Charles Lawrence, Mari Matsuda, Patricia Williams, to list a few. Clearly, they and others have been convincing. More recent articles that build upon their work and the works of others include, Gary Peller, *Race-Consciousness*, 1990 DUKE L.J. 758; Duncan Kennedy, *supra* note 24; Neil Gotanda, *supra* note 24. *But see,* Randall Kennedy, *Racial Critiques of Legal Academia*, 102 HARV. L. REV. 1745 (1989) (questioning significance of critical race theory scholarship).

Davis medical school adopted a racial preference admissions policy partly upon the rationale that more doctors of color are needed to deliver medical care to their people.[26] Statistics show that certain neighborhoods, generally split along class and race lines, are inadequately served with respect to health care. The premise underlying the Davis policy is that if opportunities are given to people of color to become physicians, then the odds of increasing medical service to poorer neighborhoods will be increased. Clearly, not all doctors of color will want to pursue public interest medicine; nor should there be a presumption that this burden falls upon them because of their color. Rather, the policy merely allows for an increased likelihood by creating a possibility that without the policy, might not exist at all. In short, one goal behind a policy like Davis' is to provide health care in areas where there are shortages of doctors, and where experience demonstrates that even fewer white doctors choose to practice.[27]

A second aspect of this rationale for affirmative action is more general in its effect. Proponents argue that affirmative action provides role models for younger people in the outsider groups. Despite the Supreme Court's rejection of this rationale in support of affirmative action,[28] the role model justification is legitimate because it reinforces the idea that people of color and white women do belong in various jobs and professions that historically have excluded them. Not only does this enable young people to think about pursuing similar careers, it also reinforces the attitude among older people that, in fact, people of color and white women are competent, capable workers. As attitudes begin to change,

26. *Bakke*, 438 U.S. at 279, 310. *See also*, J. HARVIE WILKINSON III, FROM *BROWN* TO *BAKKE*: THE SUPREME COURT AND SCHOOL INTEGRATION: 1954-1978, 283-83 (1979). At the time of Bakke's suit, statistics showed that there was one black physician for every 2,779 blacks versus one white doctor for every 599 whites. The situation in the deep South was even worse: one black physician for every 15,000 to 20,000 blacks.

27. *see* WILKINSON, *supra* note 26 at 283-84. "White doctors certainly had not [returned to ghetto practice.]" Moreover, although one cannot predict with certainty that a black medical student will return to practice medicine with black patients, there is some indication that many of them do. *Id.* at 285. *see* S.N. Keith, R.M. Bell, A.G. Swanson, and A.P. Williams, *Special Article – Effects of Affirmative Action in Medical Schools: A Study of the Class of 1975*, 313 NEW ENG. J. MED. 1519 (1985) ("Physicians from each racial or ethic group served disproportionately more patients of their own racial or ethnic group . . . , but minority physicians did not serve significantly more persons from other racial or ethnic minority groups than did nonminority physicians.").

28. *See, e.g.*, *City of Richmond v. J.A. Croson Co.*, 488 U.S. 469, 497 (1989) (plurality) and *Wygant v. Jackson Bd. of Educ.*, 476 U.S. 267, 274 (1986) (plurality). *But see* T. Alexander Aleinikoff, *A Case for Race-Consciousness*, 91 COLUM. L. REV. 1060, 1108 (1991) (arguing that blacks need to be *seen* in equal roles with whites before they can truly be equal) (emphasis in original).

less discrimination will occur, the need for affirmative action will decrease, and the predominantly white-male hegemonic power structure will also begin to disappear, creating an atmosphere that comes closer to achieving sexual and racial equality.

These primary arguments in support of affirmative action do not tell the entire story and are not completely unassailable. Opponents of affirmative action have legitimate criticisms, although these criticisms also suffer from similar shortcomings. Below, I explore the major criticisms of affirmative action and then try to put the discussion into a critical framework of analysis that ultimately favors affirmative action.

II. The Opposition to Affirmative Action

Opponents of affirmative action argue that none of the proffered rationales supporting it is justifiable. Moreover, their opposition seems to run deeper, suggesting that *nothing* could support voluntary affirmative action policies because they are fundamentally unfair. Specifically, opponents seem to rest upon the arguments that affirmative action is unfair because (1) it burdens innocent victims; (2) it fails to take into account the hardships of whites and men who could also benefit from preferential treatment; and (3) it lowers standards. Interestingly, these arguments fit very neatly into the same arguments that proponents of affirmative action espouse under very different terms.

An exploration of the specific objections to affirmative action is aided by an understanding of at least two other dynamics in the debate. First, many Americans, especially white men, seem to be afraid that they are being displaced by white women and people of color through such policies. Although one could say that this growing anti-affirmative action sentiment is sexism or racism,[29] I think to dismiss the feelings of those Americans who have legitimate concerns about unemployment, for example, may be too facile an explanation.[30] Moreover, affirmative action becomes quite complex once it is understood that many insiders also suffer disadvantages in common with many outsiders. Often this aris-

29. *see* Charles Lawrence, *The Id, the Ego, and Equal Protection: Reckoning with Unconscious Racism*, 39 STAN. L. REV. 317 (1987) (analysis of how prejudice operates subconsciously). *See also*, Lani Guinier, *The Triumph of Tokenism: The Voting Rights Act and the Theory of Black Electoral Success*, 89 MICH. L. REV. 1077, 1113 (1991) (suggesting that voting patterns reflect that "whites still harbor racial prejudice").

30. *See, e.g.*, Cass Sunstein, *Three Civil Rights Fallacies*, 79 CALIF. L. REV. 751 (1991) (exploration of economic considerations that might cause one to discriminate).

es in the context of wealth and is a legitimate concern among poor whites,[31] and all of us during these difficult economic times.

Second, playing off the unfairness accusation is a tension that focuses upon individual versus group identity. Generally, individual whites, particularly men, are not viewed by decision-makers as group members, and are often evaluated and treated as individuals. In contrast, affirmative action policies are targeted at groups, although individual members of those groups are the beneficiaries. At least two negative consequences flow from this. On the one hand, many whites and men feel disadvantaged in evaluation processes because they believe they are not being compared one-on-one with individual people of color or white women. On the other hand, the presence of at least one outsider in an exclusive group can result in a sense that enough has been done to meet affirmative action goals, making it even more difficult for the next person of color or white woman to break into the group.[32] Below, I explore these dynamics in the context of specific objections to affirmative action.

A. The "Innocent Victim"

Perhaps the primary argument against affirmative action rests upon the "innocent victim" rationale.[33] Throughout *Bakke*, the Court refers to the notion that Allan Bakke is innocent because he was not responsible for the discrimination against people of color in this country. For example, the Court explicitly states that "there is a measure of inequity in forcing

31. *see* Jeffrey Harrison, *supra* note 4. White women and people of color suffer different kinds of discrimination as a result of their "outsiderness," and our laws ought to respond to those differences. *see* Sharon Rush, *Understanding Diversity, supra* note 4. *See generally*, STEPHEN CARTER, *supra* note 6 at 18-19. Richard Lempert, *The Force of Irony: On the Morality of Affirmative Action and United Steel Workers v. Weber*, 95 ETHICS 86 (1984) ("Blacks are not the only Americans who have suffered the evils of discrimination, but no other group has been disadvantaged simultaneously in so many spheres, over such a long period of time, and in such a peculiarly American way."). This is not to suggest, however, that discrimination on the basis of wealth is acceptable, but only that it is different from race and sex discrimination.

32. Professor Juan Perea described this dilemma as the token person of color or white women in the group "becoming larger than life." He also thinks that making the token outsider count for all other outsiders is "wishful thinking" on the part of the majority group members.

33. Professor Thomas Ross explores the origin of this concept in *The Rhetorical Tapestry of Race: White Innocence and Black Abstraction*, 32 WM. & MARY L. REV. 1 (1990). Essentially, he argues that white innocence has been a rhetorical device used by the Supreme Court since *Dred Scott v. Sanford* to absolve contemporary white Americans of any wrongdoing with respect to race discrimination. *Id.* at 3.

innocent persons in [Bakke's] position to bear the burdens of redressing grievances not of their making."[34] Thus, even if one were to concede that people of color (and white women) have suffered harm through discriminatory practices in this country, the problem, according to some people, including the *Bakke* Court, is that affirmative action is an unfair way to remedy past wrongs.

A fundamental concept of democracy is that the punishment of innocent people is wrong, which perhaps makes this argument appealing. From this perspective, then, it is legitimate to argue that whites and men who are not perpetrators of discrimination against people of color and white women are being "punished" through affirmative action programs that diminish opportunities for them. Furthermore, if one adopts this view the argument by proponents that affirmative action is justifiable as a means of remedying past and present societal wrongs falls by the wayside. This is exactly what happened to it in *Bakke*, for example, and this continues to be the position adopted by the Supreme Court.[35]

B. Hardships are Hardships, Regardless of Race and Sex

A second perceived unfairness is that affirmative action policies favor people of color and white women, regardless of any individual showing of hardship. Correspondingly, if hardship is what truly counts in hiring and admissions decisions, then members of the non-preferred group believe that fairness dictates that disadvantages other than sex or race should also be considered in making decisions about who gets hired or admitted to a program. For example, advocates of this view might suggest that an individual white man who lives in poverty is perhaps more deserving of preferential treatment than is a privileged black woman.

This view of affirmative action by opponents is very similar to the view by proponents that affirmative action is justified because it promotes diversity. The only difference, of course, is that opponents of affirmative action have defined "diversity" to mean hardship diversity, or at least something other than facial diversity. In their opinions, then, affirmative action policies would be less objectionable if preferences were available to all persons based upon individual hardships, and not race or sex alone.

---

34. *Bakke*, 438 U.S. at 298.

35. *See, e.g., Wygant v. Jackson Board of Education*, 476 U.S. 267, 276 (1986) (layoff provision in collective bargaining agreement that protected percentage of minority personnel held unconstitutional because burden on "innocent individuals" too high). *See also supra* note 17 and accompanying text.

Typically, this arises in the context of wealth or financial need. For example, scholarships that are available only to people of color incur the wrath of many white students who feel they are more needy than the students of color. Clearly, the perception of affirmative action opponents is that scholarships ought to be based on financial need, and not on sex or race.

Moreover, this attitude extends to almost all preferential programs and policies, suggesting that they are justified only if some special need for them exists. The suggestion that being a person of color or a white woman, that is, belonging to a group with a particular and unique history of discrimination, is insufficient to create that special need.

Interestingly, some outsiders who oppose affirmative action enter the debate here, although I am not sure they would agree with my analysis. Generally, some outsiders, most notably Professor Stephen Carter, have denounced the diversity rationale upon the theory that it suggests that all members of an outsider group think the same way. In other words, this rationale suggests that by hiring a black person, the employer is hiring a "black" view. Or by appointing a woman to a court, the president is placing a "woman's" view on the bench.

The tendency to see individual outsiders as members of a larger group has generated several controversial debates about whether there is something "essential" about being a woman, or being black, such that it would be accurate to speak of "women's experiences," or "blacks' experiences."[36] For example, when a black person tries to gain acceptance into a white community, it is not uncommon for the black person to find that he or she all of a sudden represents all black people. Similarly, many white women may have a sense that they hold jobs as token women. The black's and woman's individual identities are often hidden by their group identities. The individual is remade into "every other other." If this happens the dominant group may then decide that there is no further need to add more people of color or white women. For example, until Justice Ginsburg's appointment to the Supreme Court, it appeared that there was one spot for white women on the bench. With respect to increasing

---

36. For example, many feminists have written about gender essentialism in the struggle for equality. *See, e.g.*, ELIZABETH SPELMAN, INESSENTIAL WOMAN: PROBLEMS OF EXCLUSION IN FEMINIST THOUGHT (1988); Angela Harris, *Race and Essentialism in Feminist Legal Theory*, 42 STAN. L. REV. 581 (1990). The debate on race essentialism perhaps came to the fore with Randall Kennedy's piece, *Racial Critiques of Legal Academia*, 102 HARV. L. REV. 1745 (1989). For replies to Professor Kennedy, see *Colloquy: Responses to Randall Kennedy's Racial Critiques of Legal Academia*, 103 HARV. L. REV. 844 (1990) and Richard Delgado, *When a Story is Just a Story: Does Voice Really Matter?*, 76 VA. L. REV. 95 (1990). *See also*, Duncan Kennedy, *supra* note 24.

the number of justices of color on the bench, it still appears that there is one spot for men of color.[37] Thus, the tendency of insiders to think of individual outsiders as representatives of their groups, thereby limiting opportunities for outsiders to gain strength in numbers, is borne out by experience.[38]

Significantly, the opposite situation usually does not hold. When outsiders ask to be viewed as groups, quite frequently their requests are denied. For example, when people of color or white women ask that their group status be considered in employment discrimination cases, the insiders reject the outsiders' group status and rationalize that they need to look at the individual outsider "on the merits." For example, under current Supreme Court doctrine, systematic exclusion of blacks by various government officials generally cannot substitute for a finding of intentional discrimination against a particular individual[39] or group.[40]

Affirmative action should not be abandoned because of the difficulties inherent in the essentialism debate. The appointments of Justices O'Connor and Thomas to the Supreme Court illustrate the value in affirmative action policies even though they are controversial. At the times of their appointments, if Justice O'Connor was expected to "think like a woman," and Justice Thomas was expected to "think like a black man," whatever that might mean, it is safe to assume that they probably would not have been appointed. Both nominees appeared to be politically aligned with Presidents Reagan and Bush, who personify white-male hegemony.

37. Of course, it is too early to see a pattern here, because Justice O'Connor has not retired and Justice Ginsburg was just appointed. Moreover, the replacement of former Justice Marshall, the only black man ever to serve on the bench, with Justice Thomas, a black man, may be coincidental. *But see infra* note 87.

38. Note also how this view is consistent with a philosophy that rejects quotas or "set asides," as *Bakke* and subsequent cases have. The concern with quotas and set asides is not that they might hurt outsider groups by placing unnecessary caps on their entry into insider groups, otherwise objections to such policies ought to be heard by outsiders. Instead, the objections are coming from insider groups in the context of anti-affirmative action rhetoric. It seems logical that the objection is that quotas and set asides create too many opportunities for outsiders, or, stated alternatively, they take away too many opportunities for insiders. The 30 percent set aside in *J.A. Croson* seemed to be viewed this way. *see* PATRICIA WILLIAMS, THE ALCHEMY OF RACE AND RIGHTS 106 (1991).

39. *See., e.g., Washington v. Davis*, 426 U.S. 229, 239-46 (1976) (evidence that black applicants for police officer positions were more likely than white applicants to fail the qualifying exam is not sufficient alone to demonstrate that individual petitioners were discriminated against on the basis of race; discriminatory purpose must be shown when the law is neutral on its face).

40. *City of Richmond v. J.A. Croson Co.*, 488 U.S. 469 (1989) (discrimination against group must be found to exist within community and affirmative action policy must be tailored to remedy that discrimination).

In contrast, proponents suggest that selecting people of color or white women, regardless of their ideologies, is the best evidence that not all members of a particular group think alike. Policies that reinforce individuality and move away from stereotypes are valuable in helping to dismantle oppressive forces that keep subordinated groups on the outside. Affirmative action policies, viewed from this perspective, can be quite liberating even in situations where facial diversity is valued over ideological diversity.

C. Affirmative Action Lowers Standards

Finally, underlying much of the tension with affirmative action is the "qualifications" issue. One group of opponents of affirmative action suggests that persons selected through such programs are less qualified than members of the non-preferred group who are rejected by the hiring or admissions process. Another group of opponents argues that affirmative action policies stigmatize their beneficiaries and open them up to criticism that, in fact, they are less qualified than others. In turn, the candidates themselves often wonder where the truth lies.[41]

Opponents of affirmative action often attempt to justify this objection by relying upon the use of standardized test scores and other "objective" measurements of candidates' abilities.[42] Moreover, reliance upon such methods is constitutionally permissible unless a discriminatory purpose behind the test can be demonstrated.[43] The use of test scores often creates a dilemma for proponents of affirmative action. Let me try to explain by focusing upon law school admissions, an area in which I have some familiarity.

Admission to most law schools is dependent upon scoring above a certain level on the LSAT and achieving above a certain grade point average in undergraduate school. These scores are combined in some elaborate way to create an index score, which represents the candidate's likely grade point average after his or her first year in law school.

---

41. see CARTER, *supra* note 6 and accompanying text. *See also* STEELE, *supra* note 6 and accompanying text. *But see*, Randall Kennedy, *Persuasion and Distrust: A Comment on the Affirmative Action Debate*, 99 HARV. L. REV. 1327, 1332-33 (1986)(positing that most blacks understand the policy goals behind affirmative action and are not unduly stigmatized by it).

42. Professor Mark Kelman explores the validity of using "objective tests" as a measure of job performance in *Concept of Discrimination in "General Ability" Job Testing*, 104 HARV. L. REV. 1157 (1991).

43. *Washington v. Davis*, 426 U.S. 229 (1976).

Most schools break down the admissions process so that some applicants with "outstanding" index scores are automatically admitted, while others with index scores on the lower end are automatically rejected, and everybody else falls into a "hold" category. Only "hold" files are reviewed by committee members for special qualifications (generally left to the reviewer to decide) that might distinguish one "hold" applicant from the hundreds of others. In other words, some applicants have files that are never reviewed for qualifications beyond the index score, so that any special factors that might make an "automatic admit" applicant less attractive or an "automatic reject" applicant more attractive are considered entirely irrelevant.

In most law school classes, then, is a group of people who may have nothing especially unique to offer society as lawyers. In fact, some students may not be very good lawyers at all even though they may perform quite well in law school as predicted by their index scores. Correspondingly, absent from many law school classes may be many applicants who would make outstanding attorneys but never got reviewed because of their low index scores.

Most members of the entering class, then, are admitted because their individual files presented some characteristics that impressed a reviewing committee. Personally, I have given high scores to one applicant who was president of his undergraduate Gay Student Organization; another candidate who was the youngest of nine children from a lower-middle income class family; another candidate who had acted on Broadway, and so forth. The only check against my preferences was other committee members and their preferences. If asked to make a list of factors we considered in our decisions, we probably all would agree that we looked for candidates who were "likely to succeed" *and* who offered something unique to the class as a whole. Sometimes we succeeded in achieving this goal, and sometimes we did not.

Opponents of affirmative action generally argue that standardized tests are good predictors of success in a particular program. The Law School Admissions Council makes this claim with respect to the LSAT and law school performance. There is some validity to this with respect to white students. Operating with that assumption, opponents further suggest that relying upon test scores in the decision-making process is an efficient way to cull out the "qualified" from the "unqualified" candidates. Having served on my school's admissions committee, which has entailed my personally reviewing hundreds of files a year, I am sensitive to the amount of time it takes to review them.

As appealing as it may be to rely upon measurements of success like the LSAT and GPA index score in law school admissions, reliance upon them necessarily creates a dilemma for proponents of affirmative action. They are puzzled that so much reliance is placed upon standardized tests even though they often are biased against some test takers. For example, developers of the new version of the LSAT were concerned that the exam was biased against women and blacks.[44] Consequently, they developed a version of the exam so that the bias against women seems to have been eliminated, but blacks continue to score much lower than whites who take the exam.

Proponents of affirmative action suggest that as long as the test is designed so that blacks, as a group, score one standard deviation below whites, as a group, it will always seem that blacks are less qualified than whites. Furthermore, if steps are not taken to factor in the racial-bias effect of the exam so heavily relied upon in the admissions process, blacks, as a group, have no realistic way of competing with most of the white test takers for admission. Thus, proponents of affirmative action are in an awkward position of having to justify the use of "different" standards for evaluating people of color. Opponents of affirmative action view the use of different standards as synonymous with "lower" standards.[45]

Complicating matters is that often the dilemma does not end with the admissions process. Others have documented how traditional legal education fosters white-male hegemony to the disadvantage of white women and people of color.[46] Professor Kimberle Crenshaw uses some poignant examples that are worth sharing. For example, whether a police officer is justified in taking action against a citizen depends on whether the officer, acting as a reasonable officer, thinks there is "probable cause" to believe a crime is being committed. Professor Crenshaw suggests that it is extremely difficult, if not impossible, for students of color to take a "perspectiveless" ("objective") view of what "probable cause" means. It results in the following absurdity:

44. *see* Susan Kiles, *New LSAT Opens to Mixed Reviews*, Chicago Daily Law Bull., June 5, 1992, p. 3.

45. In fact, much of the literature on affirmative action presumes the definition includes a "lowering" of standards. *See, e.g.*, ROBERT FULLINWINDER, THE REVERSE DISCRIMINATION CONTROVERSY: A MORAL AND LEGAL ANALYSIS 17 (1980) ("a black is preferentially hired over a white when the black, because he is black, is chosen over at least one better qualified white, where being black is not a job-related qualification"). Presuming affirmative action means lower standards is a set-up to insure its failure. It totally ignores the inherent biases in the way ability is measured.

46. Karl Johnson and Ann Scales, *An Absolutely, Positively True Story: Seven Reasons Why We Sing*, 16 N.M. L. REV. 433 (1986).

It is not unusual for professors to base a hypothetical [about probable cause] on the presence of a Black person in a white neighborhood. When the instructor has not opened the dialogue to allow students to question the potentially discriminatory effects of determining reasonableness from the perspective of the arresting officer, the minority student is essentially required to look back at herself to determine whether her own presence in a white neighborhood would be sufficient cause for her to arrest herself.[47]

Other examples of people of color and white women being left out of legal analysis abound. For example, law school exams often portray stereotypes of people of color and white women.[48] In order to perform well on these exams, students are expected to gloss over the stereotypes and deal with the legal issues. Many times the harm is more direct. One semester, a female student came to me in tears because she was positive she had flunked one of her exams. The exam described in rather intimate, and unnecessary, detail a woman being raped. The professor who wrote the exam not only failed to consider the effect the exam might have on women students who had been raped, but was also insensitive to the fact that the exam exploited the reality of violence against women.[49]

At some law schools, black law students, as a group, generally do not perform as well as most of their white classmates when measured according to traditional methods. At some schools, a disproportionate number of them end up on probation. Many black students graduate with a C+ average, at best. They are woefully under-represented on most law reviews (there may have been two blacks students on law review during my seven years at Florida, for example). Generally, most black students are not getting jobs, or even interviews, with top law firms. In short, people of color and white women remain on the margins even once they are admitted to law school.

Opponents of affirmative action point to these realities and suggest that affirmative action is a failure. Moreover, I think that even proponents of affirmative action would agree that something has failed here. But the critical question, in my opinion, is whether the failure stems from the initial admissions decision or from a failure to follow through with the initial decision by allowing for the continuing effects of cultural bias against particular groups. In other words, if admissions policies rely upon standardized tests to measure performance, and the tests themselves are biased against particular groups, then it seems institutionally defeating

47. Kimberle Crenshaw, *supra* note 18 at 3.
48. PATRICIA WILLIAMS, *supra* note 38 at 80-97.
49 *Id.* at 83-85.

to expect those groups to perform in a system that perpetuates the same biases.[50]

Thus, it seems that the growing anti-affirmative action sentiment has placed us at a crossroads. I have explored the major arguments for and against it, and explore below how those positions represent only the beginning of a thorough understanding of affirmative action. The following is a critique of the *Bakke* case, which allows for an in-depth analysis of affirmative action in a specific context. *Bakke* seems an appropriate example to use because it is typical of many affirmative action programs, and also because it is the beginning of the end of affirmative action.

III. One Feminist's Analysis of Bakke and Affirmative Action

The Supreme Court held in *Bakke* that a higher educational institution accepting federal funds cannot prefer racial minority applicants over white applicants by reserving a certain number of places in the class for the minorities.[51] One immediate consequence of the *Bakke* ruling was to order the medical school to admit Allan Bakke, a white man.[52]

Allan Bakke's allegation that his rejection from U.C. Davis medical school was based upon an impermissible racial distinction raises some very fundamental constitutional questions worthy of Supreme Court review. Unfortunately, an analysis of the case suggests that the Court never explicitly transcended the individual plight of Allan Bakke to get to the "moral crux of the matter."[53] From a normative standpoint, the potential risk of harm in the *Bakke* case was not solely to Allan Bakke or

50. See Ann Scales, *supra* note 46. *see also* Anita Manning, *How Bias in Coed Classrooms Hold Girls Back*, USA TODAY, Feb. 2, 1994, p. 5D ("Girls come into school ahead of boys (on test scores) and leave behind.") (quoting David Sadker, author with Myra Sadker of HOW AMERICA'S SCHOOLS CHEAT GIRLS (1994)); Susan Chira, *Bias Against Girls Is Found Rife in Schools, with Lasting Damage*, N.Y. TIMES, Feb. 12, 1992, p. 1 ("School is still a place of unequal opportunity, where girls face discrimination from teachers, textbooks, tests, and their male classmates.").

51. *Bakke*, 438 U.S. at 309, 314. Specifically, five justices (Rehnquist, Stevens, Stewart, Chief Justice Burger, and Powell) held that the special admissions program violated Title VI of the Civil Rights Act. *Id.* at 281, and 307 n.44. Interestingly, Chief Justice Burger, and Justices Stewart and Rehnquist wrote separately to state that because their decision rested upon Title VI, they did not need to reach the equal protection issue under the Fourteenth Amendment. *Id.* Finally, Justice Powell also believed that the program violated the Constitution, but did not go so far as to say that all affirmative actions programs would be unconstitutional. *Id.* at 318.

52. *Id.* at 320.

53. Ann Scales, *The Emergence of Feminists Jurisprudence: An Essay*, 95 YALE L.J. 1373, 1387 (1986)("Feminism brings law back to its purpose – to decide the moral crux of the matter in real human situations.").

even other whites in the event he lost, but rather to people of color and white women in the event that he won.

A number of criticisms could be leveled at *Bakke*, and I want to focus upon three. Specifically, I will analyze the meaning and consequences of creating an "innocent victim" rationale; explore the tension between individual and group identity; and provide a critical analysis of the qualifications issue.

A. Who is the "Innocent Victim"?

The Court's use of the concept "innocent victim"[54] to describe Allan Bakke with respect to the racial preferences admissions policy at Davis is unfortunate. By placing its imprimatur on the belief that whites in today's society are not responsible for racial discrimination, the Court validated the growing sentiment that racial discrimination is not an acute problem of modern society but rather an historical incident that, if it is to be dealt with at all, must be dealt with in a benign way that does not disturb whites' status quo. Moreover, the effect of the "innocent victim" language in *Bakke* has carried over into subsequent decisions,[55] augmenting the growing divide between opponents and proponents of affirmative action. A better understanding of the meaning and effect of the "innocent victim" language might reduce the tension in the affirmative action debate.

First, in order to have an innocent victim there must be someone who is "guilty."[56] In turn, the concept of "guilt" implies an intentional wrongdoing on the part of the perpetrator. Because most whites and men truly do not "intentionally wrong" people of color and white women, it is difficult to think of them as "guilty" of discrimination. Logically, then, they are innocent and innocent people should not be held accountable for redressing wrongs they did not commit.

54. *Bakke*, 438 U.S. at 298. For critiques of the "innocent victim's" rationale and role in affirmative action policy, see David Chang, *Discriminatory Impact, Affirmative Action, and Innocent Victims: Judicial Conservatism or Conservative Justices*, 91 COLUM. L. REV. 790 (1991); Kathleen Sullivan, The Supreme Court, 1985 Term – Comment: *Sins of Discrimination: Last Term's Affirmative Action Cases*, 100 HARV. L. REV. 78 (1986). Professor Thomas Ross also explores "black abstraction" as the other side of the "innocent white" syndrome. *see* Thomas Ross, *The Rhetorical Tapestry of Race: White Innocence and Black Abstraction*, 32 WM. & MARY L. REV. 1 (1990).

55. For an analysis of this, see David Chang, *supra* note 54.

56. *see* Thomas Ross, *supra* note 54 at 15. *See also* Kathleen Sullivan, *The Supreme Court, 1985 Term – Comment: Sins of Discrimination: Last Term's Affirmative Action Cases*, 100 HARV. L. REV. 78 (1986). I also benefitted enormously from conversations with my colleague, Juan Perea, with respect to this point.

Unfortunately, although somewhat accurate, this analysis fails to tell a complete story. The suggestion is that if Allan Bakke is "innocent," then the minority applicant who took his spot in medical school is responsible for harming him. In other words, the rhetoric of "innocent victim" shifts the burden of fault for past and present racial and sexual discrimination onto the true victims – people of color and white women.[57] Somehow, if a person of color or a white woman gets hired or admitted into a program, it is their fault that a white or a man gets rejected. It is quite telling and significant that this phrase is used only to describes whites, so that the language in more recent Supreme Court cases is directed at "innocent white victims."[58] Ironically, the phrases "innocent black victim," and "innocent female victim" are never heard.[59]

Significantly, by creating this dichotomy between innocent and guilty persons, the Court not only pitted groups against each other but also curtailed a deeper analysis of discrimination that, if undertaken, would present a different picture. The issue is not one of "guilt" or "innocence," but rather one of power. Simply being a member of a dominant group (whites, men) gives one an advantage over non-members.[60]

The "innocent victim" rhetoric shifts the focus away from dealing with the historical and continuing subordination of people of color and white women. How should our society redress those injuries? What if the government were to give each black person and white woman a lump sum settlement?[61] An individual letter of apology? For example,

---

57. *see* Thomas Ross, *supra* note 54 at 37 ("[T]he rhetoric of innocence obscures this question: What white person is 'innocent,' if innocence is defined as the absence of advantage at the expense of others? . . . As with the first part of the rhetoric, the argument avoided is the one that derives from societal discrimination: if discrimination against people of color is pervasive, what black person is not an 'actual victim?'"); *see also* Thomas Ross, *The Richmond Narratives*, 68 TEXAS L. REV. 381, 399-405 (1989). Professor Ross provides a rich description of Justice Scalia's concurring opinion in *City of Richmond v. J.A. Croson Co.*, 488 U.S. 469 (1979). Specifically, Professor Ross cogently demonstrates how Justice Scalia is able to take his view that affirmative action will "destroy" society and use narrative to make his abstract allegation into a vivid picture in the white reader's imagination of whites suffering oppression "at the hands of black people." *Id.* at 401.

58. *See generally*, Thomas Ross, *Affirmative Action supra* note 54 at 34-40 (tracing use of "innocent white victim" concept in affirmative action cases).

59. The profoundness of this point was made clear to me by Juan Perea.

60. Cheryl Harris, *Whiteness as Property*, 106 HARV. L. REV. 1710 (1993).

61. In 1969, James Forman suggested that American churches pay blacks $500 million in reparations for past discrimination. For a fuller discussion of this, see ROBERT FULLINWIDER, *supra* note 45 at 25. Of course, I must agree with Professor Steele that no amount of money can redress the injuries suffered by white women and people of color for the history of discrimination in this country. STEELE, *supra* note 6 at 119. Nevertheless, there is symbolic significance in having the government recognize and acknowledge through such gestures that its practices were wrong.

216

this was an acceptable approach to redressing the injury suffered by Japanese Americans for their unlawful internment during WWII. Just as the government has imposed tremendous costs upon various institutions to make buildings and programs accessible and meaningful for handicapped persons,[62] it might also be persuaded or mandated to do the same for white women and people of color. As Professor Randall Kennedy stated years ago: "What is so remarkable – and ominous – about the affirmative action debate is that so modest a reform calls forth such powerful resistance."[63]

Moreover, the "innocent victim" rationale totally ignores the continuing effects of the past wrongs. Racial and sexual discrimination permeate this society, yet many Americans seem to believe that racial and sexual discrimination are no longer problems. In reality, however, it is almost impossible to separate past discrimination from its present effects.[64]

Examples of this arose very recently in the Clarence Thomas nomination hearings and the William Kennedy Smith rape trial. In both situations, many stereotypes about women were exploited to make Anita Hill and Patricia Bowman seem incredible to most Americans. Moreover, recent studies show that girls continue to be discriminated against in education, which means they begin to lag behind their male classmates at such an early age that it is almost impossible for them to catch up.[65]

Most people adhere to racial stereotypes about people of color, often making it impossible to overcome biases against them. Recall the racist campaign tactics in the Dukakis-Bush presidential election.[66] David Duke's popularity with some Americans stems from his willingness to openly express his disdain for government preferences for blacks. When he comments that he thinks that people ought to work for their welfare checks, he implies that those who do not are lazy.[67] Of course, most people on welfare are people of color and white women.

---

62. Professor Juan Perea used this example in our discussions.

63. Randall Kennedy, *Persuasion and Distrust, supra* note 41 at 1334.

64. Professor Chang suggests that one way to justify affirmative action policies that are premised upon remedying past societal discrimination is by requiring specific fact-finding that relates past discrimination to the present situation. Chang, *supra* note 54 at 836-39.

65. *see* Manning, *supra* note 50 ("By middle school, girls' test scores start to slide, and the longer they stay in school, the wider the gap grows.") (quoting David Sadker); Chira, *supra* note 50 (gap is widening between boys and girls in math and science test scores).

66. Willie Horton, a black rapist and murderer from Massachusetts, was used to imply Michael Dukakis was soft on crime. *see* Judge Mann, *The Willie Horton Riot*, The Wash. Post, May 6, 1992, p. C29.

67. This is consistent with the "lazy black" and "welfare mom" stereotypes. *see* EZORSKY, *supra* note 8 at 62-63.

Clearly, neither people of color nor white women have achieved parity with whites and men in our society, nor are they likely to achieve equality in the near future, especially if most people in power think there is no problem. For those who do "break in," I think Professor Patricia Williams is exactly right when she said that outsiders can never really become insiders.[68] Overcoming social attitudes that people of color and white women are inferior to whites and men has proven to be an impossible chore. Characterizing the people in power as victims, however, is a disingenuous twisting of reality and a gross misrepresentation of affirmative action philosophy.

B. Balancing Individual versus Group Identity

The *Bakke* court's decision to invalidate the racial preference admissions policy played into the fear that many whites, and, in particular, white men have of being displaced by people of color and white women. This fear is premised on the view held by many Americans that "but for" affirmative action, whites and men would be hired or selected in most situations where they compete with people of color and women for positions. Adopting this view in support of its holding that the medical school's racial preference admissions policy was unconstitutional, the Court focused directly on Allan Bakke's individual interest in attending U.C. Davis medical school, and focused indirectly on the interests of whites, as a group, in competing for all the enrollment spaces at the school.

Moreover, the Court's holding that Allan Bakke, an individual white man, should not be responsible for helping to remedy past discrimination against people of color illustrates the tension between individual and group identity in affirmative action programs. Unfortunately, the Court confused this point and unfairly pitted the races against each other. On

---

68. PATRICIA WILLIAMS, *supra* note 38 at 89. She states it so well that it is worth quoting:

> We could continually try to be insiders, which would have been quite frustrating, because "insider" is not an act of will but a cooperative relation, defeated as easily as the turn of a head; or we could resign ourselves to being outsiders. A few exceptionally strong people, usually reinforced by an alternative sense of community, can just ignore it and carry on, despite the lack of that part of education which flows from full participation, perhaps thus resulting in a brand of knowledge that is more abstract than relational. But most others become driven to transform the outsider status into its own excuse, either by obsessional and abstracted overachievement, or by underachievement occasioned by the loss of relation and loss of interest. Either way the outsider status is a kind of unresolved wound, driven by pain, for after all that is the seeded prophecy contained in the word and the concept of those who are designated "outsider."

one side of the equality scale it placed an individual white man and on the other side it placed all people of color.[69] It then proceeded to measure the individual white man's potential harm of being rejected from medical school against a group's potential benefit of having a member admitted. As presented, of course, the white man is portrayed as the underdog – he cannot hope to be selected over the entire world of people of color.

In reality, however, the U.C. Davis policy considered the minority applicants on an individual basis, and, as individuals, some of them were rejected.[70] As individuals, some white men were accepted. Significantly, at least five justices stated that race can be a factor in admissions policies, although Justice Powell was not willing to give it the weight that Justices Brennan, White, Marshall, and Blackmun were.[71] Thus, on an individual basis, Bakke's rejection hurt him no more than a minority applicant's rejection. Assuming, however, that the Court should have focused upon group status, the opinion still seems disingenuous. Although the Court focused on minorities, the group targeted for the special admissions program, it failed to take into account the fact that Allan Bakke is a member of the most privileged group in this country – white men. Supporters of Allan Bakke's suit suggest that to uphold the racial preference policy hurts not only Allan Bakke, but also many other whites who are the potential "victims" of affirmative action policies. In short, the racial preference scheme in *Bakke*, and affirmative action in general, threatens whites, as a group.

If insiders were to take a closer look at affirmative action, perhaps they would not feel so threatened. Careful analysis and thought demonstrate that many assumptions that continue to favor insiders underlie affirmative action. For example, the Davis school racial preference policy reserved for minority applicants only 16 out of 100 seats in the class (allowing for the possibility that even more might be admitted). Who was preferred by setting aside 84 out of 100 seats for applicants who were not American

---

69. Professor Chang makes a similar argument with respect to the black plaintiffs in *Washington v. Davis*, 426 U.S. 229 (1976), and the white plaintiff in *Wygant v. Jackson Board of Education*, 476 U.S. 267 (1986). *see* Chang, *supra* note 54 at 799.

70. Justice Brennan makes this point. *Bakke*, 438 U.S. at 377 ("Davis considers on an individual basis each applicant's personal history to determine whether he or she has likely been disadvantaged by racial discrimination.") (Brennan, J., concurring in part and dissenting in part).

71. *Bakke*, 438 U.S. at 317 n.52 ("The denial to [Bakke] of this right to individual consideration without regard to his race is the principal evil of petitioner's special admissions program. Nowhere in the opinion of Mr. Justice Brennan, Mr. Justice White, Mr. Justice Marshall, or Mr. Justice Blackmun is this denial even addressed.") (Powell, J., for the Court).

Indian, Asian, Black, or Chicano? Underlying the entire Davis scheme is an assumption that whites are entitled to *every* seat, and that correspondingly, non-whites are entitled only to those seats whites are willing to give up.[72] Thus, even if one looks at group status, the general admissions policy at Davis and most other schools certainly prefer white applicants over applicants of color.[73]

Moreover, this concern raises more fundamental questions about equality and fairness when viewed from a different perspective. The assumption that whites and men are or should be the favored groups in our society is a pervasive one.[74] The best evidence of this, of course, is the reality that they are the ones in power. Moreover, even when slight encroachments into the white-male power structure are made, efforts to maintain the status quo often are implemented. Efforts to abolish affirmative action are only one manifestation of this. The "political correctness" movement is another.[75] A more concrete example is seen in the suggestion by some people to cap the enrollment of Asian students in the University of California system because they believe Asian students are over-represented, which creates fewer spaces for other students, in particular, white students.

72. Professor Chang notes that recent cases "[reflect] an unstated premise that the displaced 'innocent white victims' have a constitutional claim to receive benefits denied them by affirmative action policies." Chang, *supra* note 54 at 810.

73. *See generally,* Richard Delgado, *Affirmative Action as a Majoritarian Device: Or, Do You Really Want To Be a Role Model?*, 89 MICH. L. REV. 1222 (1991).

74. *See generally* CATHARINE MACKINNON, TOWARD A FEMINIST THEORY OF THE STATE (1989) (on men); MARTHA MINOW, MAKING ALL THE DIFFERENCE: INCLUSION, EXCLUSION, AND AMERICAN LAW (1990) (on men and whites); PATRICIA WILLIAMS, *supra* note 38 (on men and whites); DERRICK BELL, AND WE ARE NOT SAVED: THE ELUSIVE QUEST FOR RACIAL JUSTICE (1987) (on whites).

75. I am particularly troubled when some insiders rely upon principles and rhetoric to maintain their privileged status, when the same principles and rhetoric are largely ignored when invoked by outsiders. Consider the efforts by some outsiders to regulate pornography and hate speech. They argue that such speech promotes racism, sexism, violence, and, in some instances, denies outsiders equal educational opportunities. *See generally* Catharine MacKinnon, *Pornography: On Morality and Politics*, in TOWARD A FEMINIST THEORY OF THE STATE 195 (1989) (on pornography); Charles Lawrence, *If He Hollers Let Him Go: Regulating Hate Speech on College Campus*, 1990 DUKE L.J. 431 (on hate speech); Mari Matsuda, *Public Response to Racist Speech: Considering the Victim's Story*, 87 MICH. L. REV. 2320 (1989). These scholars believe in the "correctness" of their views, even though many people disagree with them. A primary argument posed by many who disagree with regulating such speech relies upon the sanctity of academic freedom and the "absolutist appeal" of the First Amendment's guarantee of free speech. *See, e.g.,* Kenneth Karst, *Boundaries and Reasons: Freedom of Expression and The Subordination of Groups*, 1990 U. ILL. L. REV. 95, 149 ("To include all our people as equal citizens is to recognize that their views deserve to be heard, and so to come full circle to the classical expectations for the freedom of expression.").

Furthermore, another critical aspect of this debate often gets omitted or toned down. Consider specific programs or policies that have a primary beneficial effect on whites or men. Military veteran's preferences in hiring give men an advantage in competing with women in the job market, but the Supreme Court upheld this practice because veterans are a "particularly deserving group," suggesting that this is an acceptable way of "repaying" men for their service.[76] The amount of money available to young men for college athletic scholarships far surpasses that available to women.[77] The Supreme Court in *Bakke* ignored the discriminatory effect at Davis of the "Dean's Special Admissions Program" that enabled the dean to admit "white children of politically well-connected university supporters or substantial financial contributors [even though they were] less qualified than other applicants, including Bakke."[78] Scholarships that are based upon criteria such as place of residence, achievement test scores, membership on law review, or academic achievement after the first year of law school – more likely than not, are

In contrast, the "politically correct" movement exemplifies the enormous power insiders have to take an outsider's view of the world and make it look malicious, even un-American. By accusing a speaker who expresses an outsider perspective of being intolerant of any speech that is not "politically correct," the insider attempts to silence the outsider. It may be difficult for some insiders to raise issues that seem to be politically insensitive to others. For example, if I were a man, it might be hard for me to speak out and suggest that women are not equal to men. That it might be hard, however, does not mean that I cannot make sexist comments, or that I should not be prepared to "take the heat for it" if I do. (Comment made by my colleague, Elizabeth McCulloch.) This is a dilemma outsiders know so well. For example, many times I feel that as a woman in a group comprised mostly of men that my speech is not valued at all, regardless of what I might say.

Moreover, a fundamental principle of First Amendment jurisprudence is to fight disagreeable speech with more speech. *Whitney v. California*, 274 U.S. 357, 372 (1927) (Brandeis, J., concurring and referring to John Stuart Mill's theory). How wonderful that outsiders are beginning to be heard and included in the "marketplace of ideas." How ironic that some insiders are so threatened by what outsiders are saying that they disingenuously accuse outsiders who engage in politically sensitive speech of inhibiting academic freedom and violating free speech. *See, e.g.*, Tracy Thompson, *Standing Firm Against the P.C. Tide: GWU Law Students Form Group to Fight School Speech Codes*, The Wash. Post, Oct. 15, 1991, at B3 (said one student, "We see the Politically Correct movement as being the new McCarthyism."). *See supra* note 3 and accompanying text.

76. *Personnel Administrator of Mass. v. Feeney*, 442 U.S. 256, 278-80 (1979) (preference constitutionally permissible because purpose was not to exclude women).

77. "Colleges award twice as much money in athletic scholarships to men and spend more than five times as much to recruit male athletes." Joannie M. Schrof, *A Sporting Chance?*, U.S. News and World Report, April 11, 1994, at 51; Tom Maloney, *Title IX: Legislation Whose Time Has Come – Gender Equity is Changing the Face of College Athletes*, The San Diego Times Union-Tribune, Feb. 2, 1994, p. D-1.

78. J. HARVIE WILKINSON III, *supra* note 26 at 259 (footnote omitted) (quoting Charles Lawrence, *The Bakke Case: Are Racial Quotas Defensible?*, Saturday Review, Oct. 15, 1977, at 14).

awarded to white students. Many tax laws, such as capital gains provisions, benefit a group of wealthy people primarily comprised of men and whites. The government actually pays farmers not to grow certain crops. Most beneficiaries of these and similar policies are white men.[79]

My point here is not to debate the rightness or wrongness of these policies, which usually depends upon context. Rather, I do think it is disingenuous to suggest that programs or policies that are targeted expressly at helping people of color and white women are unlawful "reverse discrimination" when other programs or policies that provide tremendous benefit to whites and men survive criticism and challenge. In the context of the history of discrimination against women and people of color, in the stark reality that women and people of color continue to lag behind men and whites in job security, job procurement, economic stability, education and so forth, certainly affirmative action is as justifiable as some of these other affirmative action policies.

C. Qualifying Standards and Affirmative Action

As difficult as it may have been for Allan Bakke not to attend U.C. Davis medical school, perhaps no one would contend that he had a right to be admitted. At a minimum, the Court should have required him to prove that but for the racial preferences admissions policy, he would have been admitted. Some might suggest that it would be difficult or impossible for him to prove this, but that is my point. This is the real harm in the Court's decision. Allan Bakke did not get rejected from Davis because a minority applicant took "his" spot. The implication of such a suggestion is that the applicants of color to U.C. Davis medical school who were admitted under the racial preference program were less qualified than Allan Bakke. This is the essence of Allan Bakke's allegation that he was unfairly denied admission.

The "affirmative action lowers standards" debate is an extremely frustrating one to enter, not just because it is so misunderstood but because it is so offensive.[80] In fact, this is a major reason some outsiders also offer for opposing affirmative action.[81] Inevitably, the basis of this allegation is that regardless of how "well qualified" the outsider applicant is, there exists an insider applicant who is "better qualified." That an insider applicant

79. Professor Juan Perea suggested this example.
80. *see* STEPHEN CARTER, *supra* note 6 (passim).
81. *Id.*

might be "better" qualified too often implies that the outsider applicant is "unqualified." A major concern that follows from this implication is that many outsider applicants struggle with their own sense of competency and accomplishment.[82]

Let me try to put this into a context by using an example I created for my students to help them understand affirmative action from a perspective that possibly touches them personally. Although my hypothetical example is just that, it also comes very close to reflecting reality for many law school graduates. I ask my students to imagine a world in which only Harvard Law School graduates are hired as associates in Wall Street firms. This policy does not emanate from the government, but is the result of an understanding by the partners of Wall Street firms. They have decided that they want only the "best" lawyers working for them. Of course, in order to attract a sufficient number of Harvard graduates, the partners have agreed to pay the new associates the highest salaries offered anywhere in the United States to new law graduates. As everyone knows, associates who train at Wall Street firms also have the best chances for entering into other law careers, such as teaching, or being chief executive officers of major corporations, or entering national politics, or being national leaders in government service. A student who excels at a non-Harvard law school cannot even get an interview with a Wall Street firm.

I challenge my students. How can they convince the Wall Street partners to interview them? To hire them? I push further. Suppose the demand for legal work increases so that Harvard cannot produce enough Wall Street lawyers to fill the demand. The partners get together and decide that perhaps they should consider interviewing and hiring graduates from other law schools, so long as the applicants are in the top ten percent of their classes. Imagine, I ask my students, that you now have a shot at a Wall Street practice. A firm interviews you. You pass. They hire you. The critical question: Are you an "affirmative action" hire? Even if you were, what does that mean to you? Have these firms lowered their standards by hiring you? Continuing, I ask: What if the partners got together and decided to experiment, just to see what might happen? Suppose they decided that any law graduate could interview for a position, and emphasized that what they were looking for are solid, all-around "good" lawyers – graduates who know law, can write, have good

---

82. STEELE, *supra* note 6 at 117 ("The effect of preferential treatment – the lowering of normal standards to increase black representation – puts blacks at war with an expanded realm of debilitating doubt.") *See also*, CARTER, *supra* note 6. My response to these legitimate concerns is that affirmative action does not mean "lower standards," merely "different" ones.

advocacy skills, are "team players" and so forth. Your classmate, who has a lower grade point average than you do, gets a job and you do not. Have you been unfairly excluded from Wall Street?

This example, perhaps not the best, has been successful in helping my students understand how biases operate to exclude people in unfair and often irrational ways. Specifically, my students begin to see that sometimes policies are set by making assumptions about quality based on characteristics that are not necessarily related to quality. Moreover, they begin to understand how they are subject to being possible victims of bias based on "characteristics" they have that, by and large, are beyond their control.

Returning to the *Bakke* case, even if we concede that Allan Bakke was qualified for medical school,[83] to suggest that he was "more qualified" than minority applicants who were admitted evidences a misunderstanding of the admissions process. Once an initial determination is made about who belongs in the pool of applicants for serious consideration – the "hold" category – it is almost meaningless to talk about one applicant being "more qualified" than others in the pool.[84] Just as two very different exam papers can both earn "A's," it also is possible to have two outstanding applicants who are incomparable in many different ways. Just as an "A" student might be a good research assistant, so might a "B" student who turns out to possess other skills that come to light in interviews. The strength of an admissions or hiring process lies in how much consideration is given to individual applicants' histories, backgrounds, personal accomplishments, and other unique factors that demonstrate an ability to successfully complete a particular program or perform a particular job.[85]

Perhaps Allan Bakke's medical aptitude test scores were higher than the scores of other applicants who were accepted,[86] but surely that alone cannot mean he was more qualified than they. Yet what else could he possibly have been suggesting, and how else could the Court have interpreted this fact? Obviously, many, many factors contribute to decisions

---

83. Allan Bakke did have scores that were higher than applicants who were admitted under the preferential admissions policy. WILKINSON, *supra* note 26 at 254. Nevertheless, he applied to and was rejected from 12 medical schools. *Id.* Obviously, Davis was not the only medical school that preferred other applicants, minority or non-minority, over Allan Bakke.

84. Professor Stephen Carter also makes this point, *see* STEPHEN CARTER, *supra* note 6 at 17.

85. Justice Powell in *Bakke* also saw this as a strength of an admissions process. *Bakke*, 438 U.S. at 317.

86. *Bakke*, 438 U.S. at 276 n.6 and 7. Bakke scored higher on his MCAT (96th percentile) and had about the same GPA (3.46) as the average regular admittees (74th percentile and 3.36 GPA). *Id.* at n.7.

about who gets into school programs, who gets what job, who gets nominated to what court[87] and so forth. In reality, Allan Bakke was not admitted to U.C. Davis medical school because the school did not have room enough for him and many other applicants who failed to persuade admissions officers that their qualifications were more attractive than those of the admitted class members.

A critically attractive quality of some applicants to the U. C. Davis medical school community was their non-whiteness. Moreover, as the late Justice Marshall noted in *Bakke*,[88] equal protection principles could have been interpreted to allow the Court to focus upon the fairness of admitting individual members of minority groups, just as it allowed the Court to focus upon the seeming unfairness to Allan Bakke, a white man, of being denied admission. Either choice relies upon race as the critical factor in the decision,[89] although the Court's ruling suggests that race would have been the persuasive factor only if the Court had upheld the constitutionality of the admissions policy.

Clearly, the court's message after *Bakke* is that it will continue to devalue the color of people of color. Significantly, however, the color-blindness rhetoric does not mean that the Court and other policy makers

---

87. The Clarence Thomas nomination is a prime example of affirmative action, although former President Bush might be the last to admit it. Few would disagree that Judge Thomas was not the "most qualified" for the position, assuming we could even decide what that means. Many, many other people have more legal and judicial experience than does Judge Thomas. Moreover, some people suggested that Judge Thomas was "unqualified," *see, e.g.*, CORNEL WEST, RACE MATTERS 23 (1993) ("The very fact that no black leader could utter publicly that a black appointee for the Supreme Court was *unqualified* shows how captive they are to white racist stereotypes about black intellectual talent.") (emphasis in original), but, again, this suggestion has very little meaning. After all, the Constitution does not specify what qualifications are necessary to be a Supreme Court Justice. Even if some general notion seems to have evolved about what qualifications it takes to be one, the President is free to nominate anyone and if the senate disagrees with the nomination, it can reject the nominee.

Thus, given that Thomas was not the "most qualified," and that he was not unqualified, what other reason could the president have had for nominating him? Obviously, the nominee had to have an ideology similar to the president's. Again, many potential nominees fit that criteria. What is less clear is how many blacks fit within the general notion of a "qualified" candidate with a conservative ideology? Not very many. But that the president would select his nominee from that small pool suggests that, in fact, it was important for him to have a black on the bench. This is the philosophy behind affirmative action.

88. *Bakke*, 438 U.S. at 399 ("There is thus ample support for the conclusion that a university can employ race-conscious measures to remedy past societal discrimination, without the need for a finding that those benefitted were actually victims of that discrimination.") (Marshall, J., dissenting in part, concurring in part). *See also* Ruth Colker, *Anti-Subordination Above All: Sex, Race, and Equal Protection*, 61 N.Y.U.L. REV. 1003 (1986).

89. David Strauss, *The Myth of Colorblindness*, 1986 Sup. Ct. Rev. 99.

want all of us to be colorless – an impossible task in any event.[90] Rather, the effect of the colorblindness rhetoric is to make people of color cope with the world as if they were white. It is remarkable how much less guilty whites can feel when we discriminate against people of color who theoretically are also white.

A devaluation and discoloration theory is particularly damaging to blacks because they continue to suffer the effects of slavery and the acute discrimination that attaches to that history.[91] The historical remnants of slavery, in fact, inform Justice Marshall's opinion that the advancement of people of color *as groups* is legitimate, in and of itself, in light of the history of racial discrimination by whites against blacks.[92] Ironically, the very special appeal of outsiders' cries for racial equality deafened the *Bakke* Court, which ultimately was racist in favor of whites.

IV. Looking to the Future

At least three challenges face proponents of affirmative action who carry the burden of persuading Americans that it is needed. First, I think it is imperative that a more positive definition of affirmative action be fostered. Second, as a society we need to understand that white women and people of color will make up the majority of workers one day. It is important that we begin to invest in the *future* by investing in them *now*. Finally, affirmative action policies are grounded in fundamental democratic principles of equal citizenship and participation. If we fail to achieve this for all Americans, including white women and people of color, the divisiveness among Americans will grow and our commitment to national community will remain fragmented.

90. I read a cartoon recently that shows how much progress is being made to educate younger people about race issues. In "Family Circus," PJ and Dolly are coloring and PJ asks Dolly for the "flesh" crayon. She responds with, "WHICH flesh color?" Bill Keane, "The Family Circus," *The Gainesville Sun*, Jan. 22, 1992, p. 5D, col. l. *See generally*, Neil Gotanda, *supra* note 24 (passim); T. Alexander Aleinikoff, *A Case for Race-Consciousness*, 91 COLUM. L. REV. 1060, 1108 (1991) ("White perceptions of black inferiority cannot be overcome by repressing our implicit recognition of race. Racism can be challenged only when whites *see* blacks as equals.") (emphasis in original).

91. Neil Gotanda, *supra* note 24 at 49 (1991) (arguing that strict scrutiny is an inappropriate standard of review in affirmative action cases; "Judicial review using historical-race *should* be asymmetric because of the fundamentally different histories of whites and Blacks.") (emphasis in original).

92. *Bakke*, 438 U.S. at 386-96. Justice Marshall has consistently espoused this view over the years. *See, e.g., City of Richmond v. J.A. Croson Co.*, 488 U.S. 469, 528 (1989) (Marshall, J., dissenting).

A. Affirmative Action Can Be Affirming

Changing the rhetoric of affirmative action so that it has positive connotations is imperative. Reshaping traditional thinking about affirmative action so that the positive reasons for supporting it are emphasized by the Supreme Court and government officials can reduce hostility and perhaps create more compassion between people of color and whites, and men and women, respectively. Casting affirmative action in a more positive light is also equally important for white women and people of color whose self-esteem suffers from the stigma associated with affirmative action policies that benefit them.

Professor Patricia Williams makes this plea:

> Blacks and women are the objects of a constitutional omission that has been incorporated into a theory of neutrality. . . . It is thus that affirmative action is an affirmation; the affirmative act of hiring – or hearing – blacks is a recognition of individuality that includes blacks as a social presence, that is profoundly linked to the fate of blacks and whites and women and men either as subgroups or as one group. To acknowledge that level of complexity is to require, to seek, and to value a multiplicity of knowledge systems, in pursuit of a more complete sense of the world in which we all live. Affirmative action in this sense is as mystical and beyond-the-self as an initiation ceremony. It is an act of verification and vision, an act of social as well as professional responsibility.[93]

Turning this vision of affirmative action into reality is going to be difficult. It can begin by taking such small steps as not promoting the rhetoric of "reverse discrimination," with all the negative implications of that term. It can continue with refusing to buy into the perception that affirmative action means lowering standards for people of color and white women. Clearly, it does not have to mean that. And, finally, it can focus on the need to educate Americans about the myth of objective standards of measurement. Affirmative action, when seen from this different perspective, can be quite affirming for all Americans.

B. The Social Disutility of Fighting Affirmative Action

A second major challenge lies in convincing Americans, and in particular the decision-makers, of the social disutility of an anti-affirmative action

93. PATRICIA WILLIAMS, *supra* note 38 at 121.

position. In the near future the demographics of our country are going to change dramatically, with the work force consisting of more and more people of color and white women.[94] Preparing this group to become the primary workers of America means taking care now to insure that they are adequately educated and trained for their leadership positions of tomorrow.

In keeping with this goal, programs that promote the entry of educated and trained white women and people of color into the market should be encouraged. Rather than taking away scholarships that are based upon race or sex, efforts should be made to increase their numbers and availability. Within educational institutions, more programs that insure the admission and success of people of color and white women should be developed.

Perhaps the best support for affirmative action would be to convince the Supreme Court that equal protection, as a concept, is less concerned with process and more concerned with results. The "colorblindness" theory imposes unnecessary obstacles to progress. While a "colorblind" process in hiring or admissions might seem fair, in reality, it necessarily works to the disadvantage of people of color by protecting preferences for whites.[95] As Professor Neil Gotanda explains, "Because the technique [of colorblindness] appears purely procedural, its normative, substantive impact is hidden."[96] If our goal is to begin to develop, train, and educate the work force of tomorrow, then colorblind hiring, admissions, and distribution of scholarships – to list a few examples – are socially defeating.

Moreover, this understanding of equal protection and affirmative action principles working together to ensure a trained and educated work force of tomorrow enables the advancement of people of color and white women in other ways as well. For example, within the law school community black students have an opportunity to participate in the national Frederick Douglas Moot Court Competition (which is open only to black students). A state institution considering whether to fund its black students in the competition probably weighs in its consideration the possibility that a white student might sue for denial of equal protection if the school were to fund the event. Current equal protection analysis, an off-shoot of *Bakke*, suggests that everyone must be treated the same, regardless of race.

94. Speech of Mayor Henry Cisneros, AALS Conference, Jan. 1992.

95. *See generally*, PATRICIA WILLIAMS, *supra* note 38 and accompanying text; Kimberle Crenshaw, *Foreword: Toward a Race-Conscious Pedagogy in Legal Education*, 11 NAT'L BLACK L.J. 1 (1989); *see* T. Alexander Aleinikoff, *supra* note 28.

96. Neil Gotanda, *A Critique of "Our Constitution is Color-Blind,"* 44 STAN. L. REV. 1, 17 (1991).

From a different perspective, however, an anti-subordination theory of equal protection analysis could be used to justify a decision to fund the students.[97] Recall that the disadvantages to blacks that inhere in the admissions process also continue within the law school curriculum and grading process. The anti-subordination theory of equal protection acknowledges that students of color have fewer opportunities than white students to excel in law school and in moot court competitions. A moot court competition that promotes and ensures the success of black students enables them to excel in law schools just as whites do in other ways.

Thus, the Fourteenth Amendment's guarantee of equal protection can be achieved by ensuring equal results, rather than equal process. This is a plausible reading of the Fourteenth Amendment. As a theory, it is as sound as many others puts forth,[98] and is entirely consistent with affirmative action goals.

C. Promoting National Community

The challenge of using affirmative action to promote national community is closely related to the first two challenges, and may be even more ambitious. Professor Kenneth Karst reminds us that a fundamental aspect of being an American is the entitlement to equal citizenship and participation in our American community.[99] As Americans, we need to foster among ourselves a greater sense of belonging to America.[100] Equal citizenship and participation often go to the heart of an individual's identity as an American, and when our laws exclude some Americans they also deny the worth of those excluded.[101]

Recent trends to deny equal citizenship and participation in America to people who "differ" from majority standards prevent the goal of

97. Ruth Colker, *supra* note 88.

98. *See also*, Randall Kennedy, *supra* note 22 at 1335 (colorblind theory is only one among many competing theories of equal protection analysis).

99. KENNETH KARST, BELONGING TO AMERICA: EQUAL CITIZENSHIP AND THE CONSTITUTION (1989).

100. *Id.*

101. A sad example of this was brought to my attention by one of my students. Michael Wu, a 25-year-old young man, immigrated to the United States with his parents and siblings several years ago. Because he has Down's Syndrome, passing the naturalization exam has proven too difficult for him. He has failed it six times. Consequently, he has witnessed the rest of his family become American citizens, but is having to appeal to congress for special legislation in order to be included as an American in this country.

229

national community from becoming a reality.[102] Moreover, achievement of this goal seems to be elusive for at least two reasons, both of which relate to the concept of democracy and the role of the judiciary, especially the Supreme Court, in our system of government.

First, most Americans understand democracy to mean "government by the majority." Less obvious to most Americans, at least on the practical if not theoretical level, is an understanding that democracy in this country also means protecting minorities from oppression by the majority. For example, many Americans, including former Presidents Reagan and Bush, still think that prayer in public schools should be allowed, notwithstanding the Supreme Court's ruling that such prayer is prohibited by the First Amendment.[103] A second example is provided by flag burning. When the Supreme Court upheld the right to burn the American flag,[104] most Americans were outraged. In response, former President Bush decried the Court's decision and called for a constitutional amendment.[105] Shortly thereafter, congress actually passed the "Flag Protection Act of 1989" to reverse the Court and outlaw flag burning. Significantly, the Act was ruled unconstitutional by the Court.[106] Consistent with democratic principles, the Court guards the rights of religious minorities to be free from the state's religious influence, guarding as well the individual's right to free speech even when such speech might be offensive to most Americans.

Unfortunately, at times the United States Supreme Court also seems to have lost sight of its critical role in preserving this aspect of democracy.[107] In the area of affirmative action alone, insiders have been quite successful at convincing the Court that favoring women over men, or people of color over whites, is unconstitutional. But the success insiders

102. For an interesting exploration of community, see, R. NISBET, THE QUEST FOR COMMUNITY: A STUDY IN THE ETHICS OF ORDER AND FREEDOM 1953. Mr. Nisbet explores the formation and function of smaller communities in American life, and attributes much of their existence to a sense of alienation from national government. This classic 1953 work has tremendous relevance to the divisiveness among Americans today.

103. *Engel v. Vitale*, 370 U.S. 421 (1962).

104. Texas v. Johnson, 491 U.S. 397 (1989).

105. Quoting former President Bush: "Flag-burning is wrong . . . I have the greatest respect for the Supreme Court, and indeed for the Justices who interpreted the Constitution as they saw fit. But I believe the importance of this issue compels me to call for a constitutional amendment." White House Briefing, June 27, 1989, FEDERAL NEWS SERVICE.

106. United States v. Eichman, 496 U.S. 310 (1990).

107. *See generally* Sharon E. Rush, *Feminist Judging*, 2 U.S.C. REV. OF LAW AND WOMEN'S STUDIES 609 (1993).

have enjoyed at the expense of excluding outsiders extends to other areas as well. For example, equal citizenship and participation in America were lost to gays and lesbians when the Court held that the constitutional right to privacy does not protect homosexuals making love in their bedrooms.[108] Women were told they do not belong to our national community when they lost their right of privacy in the abortion context not long after *Roe*.[109] Native American Indians were excluded when they lost their First Amendment claim to ingest peyote as part of their religious practice.[110] The Court's interpretations of the Fourth Amendment and habeas corpus doctrine have resulted in little substantive protection of criminal defendants in those areas.[111] The insiders keep winning, and the outsiders keep losing. The divide keeps growing.

Admittedly, federal judges and Supreme Court Justices are obligated to shape law and policy according to competing ideals embodied in the Constitution. Although principles of equal citizenship and participation in American society are central democratic principles, the meaning of these terms is unfortunately less than clear for many people, including judges, who not only are not bound to define them according to popular sentiment, but who are entrusted to define them according to democratic ideals that focus upon protecting minorities from majority oppression.[112]

Second, the debate over constitutional interpretation teaches us that the personal views of judges about constitutional interpretation play a significant role in their decision-making.[113] Feminist jurisprudence and other critical theories have demonstrated that "objectivity" is a myth;[114] that normative standards by which "different" people, or outsiders, are judged generally are biased in favor of those who set the standards, the insiders.[115] Thus, even if the debate about constitutional interpretation could be settled, judges would still have to understand how their person-

---

108. *Bowers v. Hardwick*, 478 U.S. 186 (1986).

109. *Harris v. McRae*, 448 U.S. 297 (1980).

110. *Employment Div., Dept. of Human Res. of Oregon v. Smith*, 494 U.S. 872 (1990).

111. Christopher Slobogin, *The World Without A Fourth Amendment*, 39 UCLA L. REV. 1 (1991).

112. JOHN HART ELY, DEMOCRACY AND DISTRUST (1980); Richard Posner, *Democracy and Distrust Revisited*, 77 VA. L. REV. 641 (1991).

113. *see* Anthony Cook, *Book Review: The Temptation and Fall of Original Understanding*, 1990 Duke L.J. 1163 (reviewing THE TEMPTING OF AMERICA: THE POLITICAL SEDUCTION OF THE LAW, by Robert H. Bork (The Free Press, 1989)); *see also* MARK TUSHNET, RED, WHITE AND BLUE (1988) (on inherent indeterminacy in constitutional interpretation).

114. Ann Scales, *The Emergence of Feminist Jurisprudence: supra* note 53.

115. MARTHA MINOW, MAKING ALL THE DIFFERENCE: INCLUSION, EXCLUSION, AND AMERICAN LAW (1990).

al backgrounds and views of the world inform them about what is right, wrong, biased, objective, fair, unfair, just, merciful and so forth.[116] Correspondingly, judges must also begin to understand that the views of those they judge also have merit and value, even though those views also suffer from inherent bias. Unless and until judges understand – and can cross, to the best of their abilities – the divide between insiders and outsiders, they will be unable to perform their job of promoting the essential aspect of democracy that speaks for minorities.

Summary

The next 20 or 30 years are going to be particularly trying times for all Americans. As the gap between rich and poor widens, so will the gap between insiders and outsiders. It is becoming increasingly important, then, that the judiciary and, in particular, the Supreme Court assume its buffer role to minimize the divisiveness between insiders and outsiders and preserve our concept of democracy. The success of the Court's performance during these difficult times will turn on its ability to empathize[117] with outsiders and adopt an outsider's perspective. Focusing upon the effect decision-making has upon outsiders reinforces feminist theory that law is not abstract, but contextual; it emphasizes the connectedness we have with each other.

To the extent outsiders are excluded from equal citizenship and participation in America, they will turn to each other for support. To the extent insiders fail to understand the goals of affirmative action, for example, they will also continue to feel alienated. They will continue to seek solace in groups like the Klan, the white student unions, the groups against diversity. And they will continue to successfully challenge outsider inclusive policies, like affirmative action.

Thus, Americans face a tremendous challenge over the next several decades. Will policy decision-makers come to understand affirmative action, or will they reject it? Will our judges perform their function in our democratic government and hear the outsiders' voices? As Americans, will we recommit ourselves to a democracy that means popular government, but not at the expense of outsiders? Twenty years from now, will we be closer to national community?

116. Professor Katharine Bartlett's article, *Feminist Legal Methods*, 103 HARV. L. REV. 829 (1990) is an excellent source for those who wish to explore the difference between traditional and feminist legal analysis. *See also* Sharon Rush, *Feminist Judging, supra* note 107.
117. Lynne Henderson, *Legality and Empathy*, 85 MICH. L. REV. 1574 (1987).

14
Indefensible Defenses of Affirmative Action

Robert K. Fullinwider

I.

For a broad cross section of Americans – whether workers or students, professionals or laborers, rural or urban, old or young – affirmative action is in bad odor. Extremist politicians like David Duke and Pat Buchanan advance their candidacies by tapping into resentment about "reverse discrimination" and Republican office-holders make political hay by attacking "quotas." College and university campuses divide bitterly over issues of racial representation.

The popular resentment against affirmative action has been building for decades and it is partly the unfortunate harvest of some of affirmative action's own public defenses. What is the problem? Let's illustrate it with two emblematic cases from the history of affirmative action. The first involves the Memphis firefighters and the second involves Allan Bakke.

In the 1970s the Memphis city government began, under an affirmative action plan, finally to integrate its all-white fire department. By the end of the decade, a substantial number of Memphis firefighters were black. But economic hard times came to Tennessee, and the city of Memphis faced revenue shortfalls. Budgets had to be cut and that meant firefighters had to be laid off. Who would go? The recently hired blacks or more senior whites? Would the city breach its seniority agreement with the firefighters union or lose its affirmative action gains? Would it undo the integration it had achieved or would it skip over newly hired blacks to lay off veteran whites? The city faced a dilemma representative of many such conflicts across the country in the 1970s when the interests of individual black and white workers *seemed* pitted against one another, conflicts that often played themselves out in court, as did the Memphis firefighters case.[1]

---

1. The litigation eventually reached the Supreme Court; see *Firefighters Local Union No. 1784 v. Stotts*, 104 S.Ct. 2576 (1984).

Around such dilemmas the public debate in the 1970s took on the polarized shape it has had ever since. One side insisted that equal opportunity requires colorblind procedures and that it is unfair to undo past wrongs at the expense of innocent white workers.[2] The other side insisted that white workers are the possessors of unfair advantages and that no injustice is done them by giving preferences to blacks; white workers are "not innocent".[3]

In her own contribution to this volume, Sharon Rush, who wants to rehabilitate the public perception of affirmative action, dwells at considerable length on Allan Bakke, another emblem of the 1970s. Early in that decade the medical school of the University of California at Davis began setting aside for minority applicants sixteen of the one hundred spots in its entering classes, allowing no whites to compete for them. Bakke applied to the medical school but failed to get into the 1973 and 1974 classes, though his college grades and MCAT scores were better than those of some or all of the applicants admitted to the specially reserved slots.[4] He felt wronged at being excluded simply because of his race from competing for all openings in the medical school, and sued.

Eventually the Supreme Court, in a mixed ruling, granted Bakke admission to the medical school without decisively establishing the propriety or impropriety of racially preferential admissions policies.[5] Justice Powell, who thought the medical school went too far, argued that the school's aim to help victims of "societal discrimination" did not justify disadvantaging Bakke, who had "no responsibility for whatever harm the beneficiaries of the special admissions program" had suffered.[6] Powell further spoke of the "inequity in forcing innocent persons ... to bear the burden of redressing grievances not of their making."[7] Justice Marshall, who thought the medical school's policy was within the law, pointed to

---

2. The principal spokesman for such views during the Reagan years was that administration's Assistant Attorney General for Civil Rights, William Bradford Reynolds. See William Bradford Reynolds, "Individualism v. Group Rights: The Legacy of Brown," *Yale Law Journal* 93 (May 1984), 995-1005; William Bradford Reynolds, "*Stotts*: Equal Opportunity, Not Equal Results," in R. Fullinwider and C. Mills, eds., *The Moral Foundations of Civil Rights* (Totowa, New Jersey: Rowman & Littlefield, 1986), 39-45.

3. For a recent treatment of the unfair advantage theme, see Ronald J. Fiscus, *The Constitutional Logic of Affirmative Action* (Durham, North Carolina: Duke University Press, 1992), pp. 47ff. For the claim that white workers are "not innocent," see the speech by Herbert Hill in St. Louis to the NAACP, June 28, 1977, reported in *The New York Times*, June 29, 1977, p. A14.

4. Joel Dreyfuss and Charles Lawrence III, *The Bakke Case: The Politics of Inequality* (New York: Harcourt Brace Jovanovich, 1979), p. 112.

5. *Regents of the University of California v. Bakke*, 98 S.Ct. 2733 (1978).

6. *Bakke* at 2758.

7. *Bakke* at 2752.

precedents permitting the "remedial use of a racial classification even though it [disadvantages] otherwise 'innocent' individuals." Sharon Rush regrets the court's speaking this way. She protests the idea that Bakke might have been an "innocent victim."[8] For her, defending affirmative action requires our finding Bakke's denial of admission somehow fitting.

"The white Memphis firefighters were not innocent." "Allan Bakke was not innocent." Do we need to accept such claims to defend affirmative action? What useful purpose do they serve?

Go back to the Memphis firefighters. What in justice should the trial court that heard their case have ordered? That the city lay off senior whites and *retain* its affirmative action gains? – or lay off by seniority and *lose* its affirmative action gains?[9]

Surely the best answer is: neither. Consider a third option open to the court: to forbid Memphis to lay off *any* firefighter. The city had a contractual agreement with the firefighters union to lay off by seniority. The court could have enforced that agreement. Furthermore, the city had a duty both legal and moral to overcome its history of racial segregation and integrate its fire department. The court could have found that duty compelling as well. What then would the city have done if it couldn't lay off firefighters and hadn't the money to pay for them all? It would have had to raise taxes to close the gap. That is, it would have had to spread the cost of undoing its past discrimination not among a handful of white firefighters but onto the citizenry of the whole city. And that is where the cost truly belonged. The city had practiced discrimination as a *body incorporated*; its obligation to undo that discrimination was a *corporate obligation*, the obligation of all Memphians in their capacity as citizens, *not* the personal obligation of a few individuals as individuals.

This solution to the firefighters case seems to give some credence to the idea that our country unfairly lets the costs of undoing our national history of discrimination fall on the backs of certain more or less randomly placed individuals. This recognition of a certain unfairness could possibly reach even to cover Allan Bakke – could redeem the idea that he indeed may have been an "innocent victim."

Prominent proponents of affirmative action tenaciously resist this idea because they fear that if we grant it, we must then believe that the "minority applicant who took his [Bakke's] spot in medical school is

8. "Understanding Affirmative Action: One Feminist's Perspective," pp. 206–207, 215–218.

9. The court enjoined the city from laying off recently hired black firefighters and was affirmed on appeal. The Supreme Court reversed. *Stotts* at 2576.

responsible for harming him."[10] Conceding Bakke's victimhood under-cuts the victimhood of the recipient of affirmative action, and it is the recipient's victimhood that must be saved at all costs. It is *his* oppressions we must list; it is *his* deservingness of affirmative action benefits we must insist on.

But this opposition is false and unnecessary. If Allan Bakke was "vic-timized," he was victimized by the State of California, one of whose organs adopted the admissions program in question. And on the other side of the ledger, it is generally irrelevant whether the recipient of affir-mative action is any kind of victim or not. The recipient's personal desert is beside the point. Indeed, consider the very justifications that the University of California offered for its policy of setting aside sixteen slots that Bakke could not compete for. Those justifications pointed toward the socially desirable consequences of creating more black physicians who might then serve the neglected medical needs of black communi-ties, act as role models, and the like. From the point of view of such jus-tifications, it was irrelevant whether the individuals chosen for those racially reserved medical school slots were personally deserving or had been victimized in some way. What mattered was that they were black and that they would succeed as doctors. One of the sixteen special admit-tees in 1973, for example, was a black from Guyana who immigrated to the U.S. as an adult and attended the University of Southern California before applying to medical school.[11] It would take a rather tortuous story to make him out as a victim of U.S. policies and institutions rather than a beneficiary. But the story is not needed. The point in the first place was not to make selections matched to desert but to accomplish a more remote end.

The basic rationale usually offered for affirmative action has the same character as the medical school's justifications. The favoring of people of color helps "make inroads" against the current "hegemonic power struc-ture" that continues to exclude blacks and others.[12] In this rationale what counts are the effects of the favoritism in changing the structure. The desired effects depend only partly upon the personal characteristics of those favored (the favored must be competent and capable) and *not at all on their personal deserts*. The desired effects depend crucially upon the color of skin. The infusion of competent and talented *blacks* into a white structure is what makes the difference. A white who is disfavored by

10. Rush, p. 216.
11. Dreyfuss and Lawrence, pp. 114-15.
12. Rush, p. 197.

affirmative action may be the most deserving human creature in the world – his story may tug at our deepest heartstrings – but adding one more white face to a white structure won't change its whiteness. A black favored by affirmative action may be more advantaged than most of us, but her being black is what changes the white structure; her being advantaged or disadvantaged is of no consequence.

Sharon Rush's contribution to this volume presents a detailed version of this argument.[13] Why, then, does she need to excoriate poor Bakke? Bakke's "innocence" or "guilt" is not what his exclusion from the reserved medical school slots turned on. It turned on his race.

Indeed, a preoccupation with white "desert" is diversionary and destructive of the central defense of affirmative action that Rush adopts. Focusing on the personal deservingness of both the losers and gainers in affirmative action leads to an unedifying and often ugly contest of comparing hardships,[14] for, unless we simply insist without argument that no white can be as disavantaged as any black, affirmative action invariably will throw up situations where some of its black beneficiaries seem personally less deserving than some whites who lose out. Defenders of affirmative action sometimes respond to such instances by proposing the extension of preferences to anyone who has faced great hardship. Such a response plays directly into the hands of conservative opponents like Dinesh D'Souza, who wants to change affirmative action into a preferen-

13. Rush, pp. 197–205.

14. Toni Johnson-Chavis, one of the special admittees to the medical school in 1973, reacted to criticism of the school's policy this way: "Ever since I can remember, all my life, I wanted to be a doctor. My father was an extremely intelligent man, but he had to do demeaning jobs because he came from a poor family and never got a chance for a good education. Through his children, my father felt he had his chance to do something.... I had to do double time to keep up when I went to Stanford [on a scholarship], not knowing even how to use a slide rule, not having basic chemistry, competing with people from top prep schools in the nation. In addition to the educational disadvantages that poor students face when they get to college, I lived with white people burning crosses on my dormitory lawn and putting swastikas on my dormitory door. Nobody did anything special for me. I finished in three years to get the hell out of that kind of environment.... There's a whole public misconception about the Task Force program. The thinking is that somehow the people who came in through the program are different from the rest of the class. They can't understand why we weren't admitted through regular admissions. That's why I'm angry. The people who came through special admissions programs were as qualified or more qualified because, believe me, I feel more qualified than the average person who came in. I have done more." (Dreyfuss and Lawrence, pp. 118-19).

"I have done more," insists Johnson-Chavis, meaning: "How can anyone say I don't deserve this preference?" But can't the essentials of her story be told in any color? For example: White male/father a coal-miner in Harlan County, Kentucky/schools third-rate/works his way through Berea College. Or: white male/parents killed in 1957 Hungarian rebellion/refugee at age ten/teaches himself English/supports himself through high school and college. And so on.

tial system based not on race but on "socioeconomic disadvantage."[15] Keeping the focus on the personal merits of gainers and losers under affirmative action makes it hard to resist such proposals and, what's more, deflects attention from the structural dimension of racial discrimination. Yet by the usual rationale for affirmative action, *that* dimension is the one most important to understand and address.

Perhaps it seems necessary to deny Allan Bakke his "innocence" because of fears that any acknowledged unfairness to Bakke undermines the case for affirmative action. But surely such a conclusion would be mistaken. If racial discrimination is as pervasively and systematically built into society as many think it is, strong measures to overcome it will be justified even if they result in unfairness to some individuals. Not to intervene effectively in the discrimination would itself be to allow persisting unfairness to others. Sometimes the only choices we have are among different courses of unfairness.

II.

Thinking of affirmative action as a reparations system, in which "victims" are compensated for past harm, quite naturally makes us attend to individual desert rather than to system and structure. Affirmative action is *not* a reparations system, although many people misconceive it as being so.[16] Affirmative action is about establishing and securing the conditions to assure there will not be future victims.

The underlying aim of affirmative action policy as expressed in our public law is, ultimately, fairness to individuals. The Civil Rights Act of 1964 and its progeny are directed against a certain kind of unfairness, namely, discrimination. If a factory, school, professional partnership, or other institution has positions to fill or awards to give, the law insists that its procedures not unfairly bias selection against some applicants because

---

15. Dinesh D'Souza, *Liberal Education: The Politics of Race and Sex on Campus* (New York: Free Press, 1991), pp. 251-53. Basing preferences on disadvantage is a sure way to make most affirmative action recipients white, not because whites are comparatively more disadvantaged than blacks but because the number of whites (and thus the number of disadvantaged whites) in the population is so much larger than the number of blacks.

16. This confusion about affirmative action is ubiquitous, even in legal opinions. For example, in their *Bakke* opinion we find Justices Brennan, Marshall, White, and Blackmun referring to the medical school's policy "to integrate its classes by compensating for past discrimination" (at 2792), and straining to prove Bakke's own qualifications "tainted" (at 2786).

of their race.[17] Where an institution fails to comply with the law, it directly wrongs those specific individuals it unfairly selects against, and *those* individuals deserve that the institution make good its injury to them.[18] (To this extent, there is a limited reparative component to nondiscrimination law.) The law thus aims, in the first instance, to secure fairness for individuals *directly*, as institutions comply with anti-discrimination requirements.

But a complication may arise: an institution, because of its history of racial exclusion, may be unable directly to comply successfully. Every facet of its institutional life, from work rules and personnel policy to management culture and physical layout, may so reflect sedimented habits of racial exclusion that neither institutional good will nor deliberate effort at compliance succeeds in overcoming the inertia that continues to bias selection. The solution needed here may be something like an institutional shock: a deliberate inclusion of large numbers of blacks into the institution until the habits that were developed around the reality of no-blacks-present are eroded by the new reality of many-blacks-present. In other words, a resort to outright race-determined selections – quotas.[19] The law provides for these where necessary to create the conditions enabling successful direct compliance.[20] Thus, the law aims in the second instance to secure fairness to individuals *indirectly*, as institutions cleanse their operations of the exclusionary effects built into them by decades of racial segregation.[21]

The kind of institutional change necessary to create conditions of successful direct compliance with the law – necessary to create conditions favorable to direct fairness to all individuals – is not cost-free. The bur-

17. Or because of gender, religion, ethnic origins, disability, or age. See 42 U.S.C. 2000e, 42 U.S.C. 12101, 29 U.S.C. 621.

18. See Reynolds, "*Stotts*," pp. 40, 43-44.

19. In the words of Justice Blackmun, "In order to get beyond racism, we must first take account of race" (*Bakke* at 2807).

20. See the cases cited in notes 13-20, Robert K. Fullinwider, "Achieving Equal Opportunity," in Fullinwider and Mills, *The Moral Foundations of Civil Rights*, p. 133.

21. On a narrow reading of civil rights law, institutions may resort to racial preferences only to overcome their own specific incapacities. On an expansive reading, one that Rush would favor, institutions may, as did the University of California at Davis medical school, resort to racial preferences not to change themselves but to effect change in the larger social system of racial oppression. Quite naturally, people differ about how oppressive our current society is, and about how incapable of direct nondiscrimination different sectors and institutions remain. Indeed, we should expect great variation in the actual abilities of institutions successfully to avoid discriminating. Some institutions do better than others. Some need only modest changes, others need drastic overhaul. The zone of reasonable disagreement about the need for one kind or another of affirmative action will remain large even if everyone agrees on the rationale for affirmative action.

dens must be borne by someone. Unfortunately, when congress in 1964 formulated the Civil Rights Act it had little conception of the broad institutional changes, dislocations, and shocks that would be necessary to achieve genuine compliance with a non-discrimination mandate. Neither then nor later has the United States explicitly and directly confronted the question of how to distribute the costs of necessary institutional change. The courts, in applying and developing federal law, have fitfully considered the problem of trenching on the rights of "innocent" third parties, but have been limited by the absence of any guidance in the legislation and rules they must enforce. Generally, courts and legislative bodies have allowed the costs of institutional change to fall where they may – typically upon white, male applicants or workers denied positions or promotions that might otherwise (in their perceptions, at least) have been theirs.

As the Memphis firefighters case exhibits, letting the costs of change fall upon arbitrarily affected individuals is not a necessary feature of affirmative action. Some situations might permit community-wide cost-sharing. Nevertheless, legal, administrative, and practical barriers often stand in the way of dispersing the costs of affirmative action. Even in the Memphis firefighters case, the court's choosing to force the city to keep all its firefighters and raise taxes to pay for them would have prompted constitutional questions about judicial and legislative separation of powers. Sometimes the costs of social change unavoidably fall arbitrarily.

III.

Professor Rush and those who think as she does deny that the costs fall arbitrarily when they fall on individual white applicants or workers who happen to be in the wrong place at the wrong time. These workers are not innocent. But such thinking is not only irrelevant to the proper defense of affirmative action, it is also confused and meretricious.

It is confused because it puts the matter of social change in *personal* rather than *corporate* terms. Our nation's system of racial segregation and exclusion that affirmative action is meant to overcome was not the outcome of myriad individual discriminations and personal choices coalescing into one uniform effect. It was *official* policy, state, national, and local – policy of our people as a *corporate* body, executed through corporate agencies. The obligation to remedy that system and its effects is similarly a corporate obligation. Individuals have direct obligations to support and bear the costs of that corporate effort, but obligations *in their capacity as cit-*

izens, not in their capacity as white persons simply. The white applicant who loses out in affirmative action owes no more or less *as* a citizen than any other citizen. That the burden of affirmative action falls unevenly on him is unfortunate if unavoidable, and unjust if avoidable.

There are indeed whites – past and present – who bear some personal debt for our system of racial oppression. They favored and actively supported official policy, went out of their way to take advantage of its benefits, impeded change and the like. As a matter of cosmic justice they may personally deserve some loss or penalty. But affirmative action is not in the business of dispensing cosmic justice. It is in the business of institutional change. From that perspective, personal guilt is irrelevant (as is personal deservingness of compensation). What matters is contribution to the desired change. If a particular institution needs to be transformed by a rapid infusion of blacks, then a black who stepped off the boat yesterday from Africa or Europe and who can serve the institution is an appropriate affirmative action beneficiary; and a white Norwegian or Algerian who stepped off the same boat is as liable as any other to losing out to that black. In neither case is the individual's personal desert relevant.

Indeed, insisting here that the white Norwegian or Algerian "is not innocent" and thus deserves to lose out transparently amounts to insisting that he deserves to lose out for no other reason than his whiteness, his skin color. And that is what makes the Bakke-is-not-innocent approach to affirmative action not just confused but meretricious: it reinstates the very racism that affirmative action is meant to destroy. It posits this proposition: guilt travels through skin color. Allan Bakke is white, therefore he is not innocent.

IV.

When the nation is threatened with war, young rather than old men are drafted for service. Does the eighteen-year-old have a greater obligation to his country than the forty-year-old? Is there some moral flaw in his person that gives him a special duty? No one would say so. As a citizen, the eighteen-year-old owes no more than the forty-year-old.

The eighteen-year-old is drafted not because he personally deserves to be burdened while the forty-year-old does not. He is drafted for the impersonal reason that eighteen-year-olds are the best soldiers. It is simply his bad luck to be eighteen rather than forty when the need for a draft materializes.

A just and decent nation tries to compensate for the differential burden it places on the draftee. It creates post-service benefits and privileges to make up for his risks and sacrifices. But such benefits and privileges don't always equalize burdens. The unfortunate draftee may still bear a greater burden than others. Even so, he can reconcile himself to his fate by seeing it as necessary for the defense of communities and institutions he himself cherishes.

We would immediately see the folly of defending a draft by reference to the personal demerits of eighteen-year-olds rather than to the impersonal needs of the moment. We ought by now in this country to have seen the folly of defending affirmative action by reference to the personal demerits of white applicants and workers.

Certainly, no one welcomes material loss and as long as affirmative action imposes (or seems to impose) material loss on some persons, many will dislike it. But whether that dislike mushrooms into virulent resentment depends upon how we defend affirmative action. A defense insisting that affirmative action is never unfair, that every beneficiary of it is personally deserving, and that the Allan Bakkes of the world are never innocent makes affirmative action less rather than more palatable to those adversely affected by it. Many persons are willing, like the draftee, to tolerate asymmetrical burdens on behalf of important principles they themselves accept. A twenty-year veteran white firefighter might grudgingly accept a temporary layoff were he convinced it was impersonally required to advance equal opportunity for everybody. At least he couldn't reject his fate on principle without repudiating a standard he likely publicly endorses. But to make him hate affirmative action *on principle*, you don't need a Pat Buchanan or a David Duke. Just tell him he deserves his fate.

Index

Index